IS THE
REFORMATION
OVER?

IS THE REFORMATION OVER?

AN EVANGELICAL ASSESSMENT OF CONTEMPORARY ROMAN CATHOLICISM

MARK A. NOLL
CAROLYN NYSTROM

Baker Academic
Grand Rapids, Michigan

PATERNOSTER

© 2005 by Mark A. Noll and Carolyn Nystrom

Published by Baker Academic
a division of Baker Publishing Group
P.O. Box 6287, Grand Rapids, MI 49516-6287
www.bakeracademic.com

and

Paternoster
an imprint of Authentic Media
9 Holdom Avenue
Bletchley, Milton Keynes, MK1 1QR, UK
www.paternoster-publishing.com

Printed in the United States of America

Library of Congress Cataloging-in-Publication Data
Noll, Mark A., 1946–
    Is the Reformation over? : an evangelical assessment of contemporary Roman Catholicism / Mark A. Noll and Carolyn Nystrom.
        p.   cm.
    Includes bibliographical references and index.
    ISBN 0-8010-2797-7 (cloth)
    1. Catholic Church—Relations—Evangelicalism. 2. Evangelicalism—Relations—Catholic Church. I. Nystrom, Carolyn. II. Title.
BR1641.C37N65 2005
280′.042—dc22   2004023843

British Library Cataloguing in Publication Data
A catalogue record for this book is available from the British Library.
ISBN 1-84227-387-6

To
J. I. Packer,
discerning pioneer

CONTENTS

ACKNOWLEDGMENTS

This book is a product of its authors' long-standing interests, both historical and personal. But it also exists because of many kinds of help from many others over many years. We are grateful for the inquiry from Robert N. Hosack at Baker Academic that led to the transformation of a conference paper into this book, and to Dennis Okholm and the late Timothy Philips, who requested the paper. For similar invitations in earlier years, we thank Frederick Greenspahn, Charles Colson, and Richard Neuhaus.[1] On many of the book's subjects, a great debt is owed to historian friends at the University of Notre Dame, including Scott Appleby, Jay Dolan, Philip Gleason, Tom Kselman, John McGreevy, George Marsden, Timothy Matovina, Robert Sullivan, and Jim Turner. For indispensable library sleuthing, we thank Maggie Noll. For other kinds of assistance, we are grateful to Ivan Ediger, Jim Gorsh, Nathan and Julie Hatch, James Heft, Phyllis and Andy LePeau, David Livingstone, Robert Moran, Ken Newell, Bill Shea, Peter Steinfels, Donald Sweeting, Jennifer Suvada, David Wells, Ronald Wells, and John Wilson.

Many of the book's insights come from the people mentioned here; all the mistakes are our own.

---

1. Those talks by Mark Noll were eventually published as "The Eclipse of Old Hostilities *between* and the Potential for New Strife *among* Catholics and Protestants since Vatican II," in *Uncivil Religion: Interreligious Hostility in America,* ed. Robert N. Bellah and Frederick E. Greenspahn, 86–109 (New York: Crossroad, 1987); and "The History of an Encounter: Roman Catholics and Protestant Evangelicals," in *Evangelicals and Catholics Together: Toward a Common Mission,* ed. Charles Colson and Richard John Neuhaus, 81–114 (Dallas: Word, 1995). A few sections from these papers, much revised, have made their way into this volume.

INTRODUCTION

In 1873, at the New York meeting of the Evangelical Alliance, a delegate from Canada expressed an opinion that almost all others at that international Protestant gathering would have approved: "The most formidable foe of living Christianity among us is not Deism or Atheism, or any form of infidelity, but the nominally Christian Church of Rome."[1]

Today in Canada, the Catholic-evangelical situation is, to say the least, on a different footing. Canada's best-known mass media evangelical ministry is a television program titled *100 Huntley Street*, which since its start in 1977 has been hosted by founder David Mainse. For more than a decade on this program, Mainse regularly asked a Jesuit priest, Father Bob MacDougall, to preach. According to Mainse, "If you changed the voices, it could have been Billy Graham. Literally tens of thousands of Roman Catholics opened their hearts to Jesus as a result of Father Bob."[2] MacDougall, as it happens, was also instrumental in launching the singing career of one of Canada's leading Christian contemporary musicians, the evangelical Protestant Steve Bell, who now presents about half of his concerts in Catholic churches or to Catholic church groups.[3] Throughout Canada, as in other parts of the world, Christian believers gather annually for a public "March for Jesus." In Winnipeg, where the largest Canadian march occurs, the joint organizers for many years have been Ruth Wall of the evangelical Gateway Christian Community Church and Myrna Kisil of Holy Redeemer Roman Catholic Church. Further

1. Robert Murray, "The British Provinces of North America," in *History, Essays, Orations, and Other Documents of the Sixth General Conference of the Evangelical Alliance* (New York: Harper & Bros., 1874), 130.
2. Quoted in Harold Jantz, "Keeping Company with One Another," *Faith Today* (May/June 1999): 21. Jantz's entire article (20–28, 31) is outstanding.
3. Ibid., 22, as also the material on the "March for Jesus" that follows.

west, another interesting attempt at Catholic-evangelical cooperation has been underway since 1998 at Langley, British Columbia. Under the auspices of the evangelical Trinity Western University, Redeemer Pacific College is the institutional home for a small group of Catholic students studying for degrees offered through Trinity Western. In this cooperative effort with evangelical Trinity Western, Redeemer Pacific is sponsored by the Catholic Archdiocese of Vancouver and advised by Franciscan University of Steubenville, Ohio, which is itself an affiliate member of the evangelical Council for Christian Colleges and Universities.[4]

Also in British Columbia there is Vernon Robertson, a meat cutter in his mid-fifties who works at a Safeway supermarket in Vancouver. In 1978 at a Catholic charismatic prayer meeting, Robertson was struck to the ground and after being helped to his feet received a word from the Lord that led him to say, "I stand there knowing there's something else. God's doing something to me. When this woman spoke, which I would say was charismatically, her words were like nails, physically, into my heart: 'I love you with an everlasting love. . . . I will never leave you nor forsake you.' I had plunged into a love of God."[5] Nearly two decades later, Robertson attended an Alpha course, the video series from Holy Trinity Church, Brompton, England, that has been widely used by evangelicals around the world to explain the basic features of the Christian gospel. Immediately, there was a connection. Robertson sought permission to promote the Alpha course in the Catholic churches of the Vancouver Archdiocese. As of April 2002, he was coordinating Alpha programs in twenty-seven of the archdiocesan churches. According to Monsignor Gregory Smith, chancellor of the archdiocese, "It is quite astonishing. At no point in our history has a lay person without a theology degree given courses in evangelization." Protestants who meet Robertson can be just as astonished. As one youth pastor put it to Robertson, "I never realized Catholics were so in love with the Holy Spirit."[6]

Social science surveys also help put into perspective the distance that has been traveled since the 1873 meeting of the Evangelical Alliance. An extensive Angus Reid poll from 1996, which was constructed in large part to measure the presence of evangelicalism in Canada and the United States, included several questions worded according to the four standard markers of evangelical identity that have been proposed by the British historian David Bebbington.[7] That is, respondents were viewed as evangelical if,

4. Jeremy Lott, "Catholic Redeemer, Protestant Trinity," *Touchstone* (June 2002): 54–55.

5. *Saturday Post* [*Canadian National Post*], April 6, 2002, SP1, 3.

6. Ibid., 4.

7. D. W. Bebbington, *Evangelicalism in Modern Britain* (London: Unwin Hyman, 1989), 2–17. The consultant on the survey's religion questions was the late George Rawlyk of

regarding the *Bible,* they agreed strongly that Scripture "is the inspired word of God" or they agreed to any degree that "the Bible is God's word and is to be taken literally, word for word"; if, regarding *conversion,* they strongly agreed that "I have committed my life to Christ and consider myself to be a converted Christian"; if, regarding *activism,* they agreed or agreed strongly that "it is important to encourage non-Christians to become Christians"; and if, regarding the centrality of the *cross of Christ,* they agreed strongly that "through the life, death and resurrection of Jesus, God provided a way for the forgiveness of my sins." Of the Canadians who responded positively to all four of these evangelical markers, one-fourth were Roman Catholic. Of all Canadian Roman Catholics, 34 percent answered with the "evangelical" response on at least three of the four questions. The same poll found that 11 percent of Canadian Catholics labeled themselves "evangelical" or an equivalent term.[8]

Signs of an altered Canadian landscape for evangelical-Catholic relations extend well beyond polling data. When in 1998 Billy Graham held a preaching campaign in Ottawa, Canada's national capitol, the proportion of Catholic churches among sponsoring congregations was the highest ever in the history of Graham's worldwide ministry. In preparation for these meetings, several thousand Catholics committed themselves to Operation Andrew, a program encouraging Christians to invite their unbelieving friends to Jesus. At the meetings themselves, one-fourth of the inquirers were Catholics. Also important as general encouragement for Graham's campaign was the Ottawa radio station CHRI-FM, which aims its broadcasting deliberately at both Catholics and evangelicals.[9]

Surveying the evidence for this kind of active and vital Christianity within the contemporary Roman Catholic Church and trying to evaluate such evidence with as much discernment as possible are the major goals of this book. It is intended as an evangelical assessment of contemporary Roman Catholicism, with special attention given to the dramatic changes that have taken place since the Second Vatican Council. It deals primarily with conditions in the United States but not to the exclusion of evidence from Canada, Latin America, Europe, and elsewhere in the world. In its pages, we do not propose a final, universal, or dogmatic assessment of Roman Catholicism. Rather, we offer first as much help-

---

Queen's University, Ontario, author of *Is Jesus Your Personal Saviour? In Search of Canadian Evangelicalism in the 1990s* (Montreal: McGill-Queen's University Press, 1996).

8. For details, see Mark A. Noll, *American Evangelical Christianity* (Oxford: Blackwell, 2001), 32–36.

9. Lloyd Mackey, "Capital Gains," *Faith Today* (May/June 1999): 24–25; and Bob Harvey, "Billy Graham's Catholic Crusaders: Support from Area's English Catholics Sets Record," *Ottawa Citizen,* May 5, 1998, sec. A, 1.

ful information as we can in a volume of modest size. Second, we also hope to provide evangelical interpretations, grounded in both classical Christian theology and the broad history of Christianity, of what we see in the contemporary Catholic Church. Longer and more detailed volumes are available for those who want to probe issues between Catholics and evangelicals with the full seriousness they deserve.[10] Our intent is to illuminate a dramatically altered terrain and to offer suggestions as to how to think about the religious landscape as it now exists.

To that end, chapter 1 offers more evidence to support the proposition that both in the Roman Catholic Church and in relations between evangelicals and Catholics things are "not the way they used to be." The next two chapters set the context for the contemporary situation. Chapter 2 sketches the long standoff between Catholics and Protestants that began in the 1520s and seemed almost as firm as ever into the 1950s. Chapter 3 suggests reasons as to why the situation has shifted so rapidly in recent decades.

The next four chapters constitute the most straightforward attempt to inform. They begin with an analysis of many of the official dialogues that have been held between Catholics and other Christian groups since the Second Vatican Council. These dialogues have proven especially useful for highlighting contemporary convergences and divergences between Protestants and Catholics. Then comes an extended examination of the 1994 *Catechism of the Catholic Church,* which provides the most accessible, complete statement of official Roman Catholic teaching that exists today. Our specific intent for chapter 5 is to offer a charitable but also self-consciously evangelical reading of what the *Catechism* reveals about modern Catholicism. This chapter is followed by an analysis in chapter 6 of American-based proposals for new interfaith cooperation that have come from an ad hoc unofficial group known as Evangelicals and Catholics Together (ECT). By outlining what this initiative has tried to achieve, we hope to describe clearly the potential but also the difficulties of ongoing evangelical-Catholic engagement. After these three chapters of reporting on documents, which we have tried to make as fair and objective as possible, we follow with chapter 7, which reports on reactions, specifically the wide spectrum of evangelical attitudes toward the modern Catholic Church and the developments of the past half century. As with the preceding chapters, the primary aim here is to provide objective reporting.

The last two chapters are more evaluative and opinionated. Chapter 8 explores the history of Catholicism in America as a way of gaining perspective on how and why evangelicals and Catholics have understood and

10. See the further reading at the end of the book.

misunderstood each other. It takes advantage of a number of remarkably perceptive books that have recently been published about Catholic history in the United States, including studies concerning why Catholics have always been somewhat ambiguous about, as well as generally supportive of, American notions of liberty, and studies about what the sex scandals in the Catholic Church tell us about contemporary Catholicism in general. The last chapter seeks perspective from the broad history of Christianity to address the question posed by the title of this book: Is the Reformation over? Our answer to that query will not satisfy strong partisans who cluster at the poles of contemporary discussion. But we hope its use of historical analysis may lead to a better grasp of the nature of Christian traditions, including Catholicism and evangelicalism, and that its judgments may stimulate others to make their own assessments of the current character of the Roman Catholic Church.

By asking if the Reformation is over, we mean to use the classic ideals of the Protestant Reformation to measure contemporary Catholic Christianity. *Sola scriptura* (the Bible as supreme authority), *sola fide* (salvation by grace alone through faith alone), and the priesthood of all believers (as a corrective to corruption of the priesthood) were Protestant rallying cries pointing to what has rightly been called a Copernican Revolution in theology.[11] God, instead of humanity, the Reformers asserted, needed to be recognized as the center of the spiritual universe. This book is an assessment of the contemporary Catholic Church based on these same Reformation criteria. The question appears straightforward, but, as the last chapter suggests, it is not by any means a question to be answered simply.

Part of the reason the question cannot be answered simply has, of course, to do with evangelicals like ourselves who are doing the asking. Thus, and not incidentally, we hope that our examination of contemporary Roman Catholicism will enable evangelical Protestants to understand themselves more clearly and therefore will help them to grasp, internalize, and proclaim the essential principles of the Christian gospel that were at issue in the Reformation itself.

To make such assessments, however, it is necessary to go farther and to indicate in greater detail why the question in this book's title has become so interesting and so important.

---

11. For expansion on the theological Copernican Revolution of the Reformation, see Philip S. Watson, *Let God Be God: An Interpretation of the Theology of Martin Luther* (London: Epworth, 1947).

1

THINGS ARE NOT THE WAY THEY USED TO BE

Evidence of Change

The career of America's best-known public evangelical, Billy Graham, spotlights as well as anything the rapidly shifting terrain in relations between evangelicals and Catholics. Graham, of southern fundamentalist extraction and nativist evangelical education, enjoyed less than cordial relations with Roman Catholics early in his evangelistic career. During the 1950s, Catholic officials in South America and the Philippines forbade their co-religionists to attend his meetings; during the same years, local priests and bishops in the United States also often discouraged attendance at Graham crusades. Graham was equally antagonistic toward Catholics. In the presidential election of 1960, Graham only just succeeded in muting his enthusiasm for Richard Nixon and hiding his apprehensions about a Democratic regime that would include not only John F. Kennedy as the nation's first Catholic president but also a Catholic majority leader in the Senate (Mike Mansfield) and a Catholic Speaker of the House (John McCormack).[1]

1. William Martin, *A Prophet with Honor: The Billy Graham Story* (New York: Morrow, 1991), 278–80.

An About-face

Graham, however, was undergoing a personal transition that mirrored and then led developments in the larger world of evangelical-Catholic relations. In 1950, when Robert Ketcham of the General Association of Regular Baptists asked whether Billy Graham might be getting soft toward Catholics, Graham's executive secretary Jerry Beaven replied, "You asked if Billy Graham had invited Roman Catholics and Jews to cooperate in the evangelistic meetings. Such a thought . . . seems ridiculous to me. . . . Mr. Graham would [never] turn over any decision card to the Roman Catholic Church."[2] As late as 1962, Graham associate Robert Ferm wrote to a minister in Kansas, "Certainly Catholic priests do not attend [crusade services]. [They] have not been invited to participate in any way. Nor would they do so if they were invited."[3] Yet years later Billy Graham wrote in his autobiography, *Just as I Am*, that he had experienced internal convictions toward ecumenism as early as the late 1940s. It appears that Catholics took the first step, nudging Graham to make those convictions public. In 1964, Richard Cardinal Cushing welcomed Graham to New England with "the prayer of Catholics in the Boston area that God will bless his preaching and crusade, and will lead many to the knowledge of our Lord." Graham replied that he felt "much closer to Roman Catholic tradition than to some of the more liberal Protestants."[4] Though startled at first, many other evangelical leaders soon came to similar conclusions. By the 1980s, Catholic leaders appeared on crusade planning committees, crusade platforms, and counselor training classes—with growing mutual respect from both sides. And, yes, Graham did indeed begin to send decision cards of professed Catholics to the local Catholic archdiocese.[5]

Tangible evidence of Graham's transcendence of interconfessional antagonism multiplied rapidly after the late 1960s. In 1977, he was granted permission to hold a crusade in one of American Catholicism's most hallowed locations, the football stadium at the University of Notre Dame. In 1978, he became the first Protestant leader to be entertained by the abbot of the shrine of the Black Madonna in Czestochowa, Poland. In 1981, he sought and was granted an audience at the Vatican by Pope John Paul II, who when he was Cardinal Karol Wojtyla in Krakow,

2. John Ashbrook, *New Neutralism II* (1992), quoted in Donald W. Sweeting, "From Conflict to Cooperation? Changing American Attitudes towards Roman Catholics: 1960–1998" (Ph.D. diss., Trinity Evangelical Divinity School, 1998), 114–15.

3. Ferm to E. Loren Pugsley, Newton, Kansas, 31 July 1962, CN 19 (Ferm papers), box 4, folder 21 (general correspondence), Billy Graham Center Archives, as quoted in Sweeting, "From Conflict to Cooperation?" 115.

4. Martin, *Prophet with Honor*, 309–10.

5. Sweeting, "From Conflict to Cooperation?" 132.

Poland, had made it possible for Graham to preach in Catholic churches during an evangelistic tour of that country.[6] In the 1990s and early twenty-first century, Catholics have made up a considerable portion of the people who attend his meetings, record decisions for Christ, and watch the crusades on television.

In the year 2000, the more than ten thousand participants who gathered in Amsterdam from around the world for a Graham-sponsored conference on the theology and practice of evangelism included a group of fifteen Catholic delegates officially sanctioned by the Vatican. Bishop Michael Warfel, chairman of the United States Bishops' Committee on Evangelization, soon thereafter wrote of his experience at Amsterdam:

> The zeal of the participants was quite genuine and their spiritual energy contagious. While many did not appreciate the same need for sacramental celebration as the attending Catholics and Orthodox (concentrating mostly on the biblical text and their experience of the Spirit in their lives) they did manifest an exceptional commitment to their Christian faith and a desire to share it with the world. Christ was their reason for being. He was their life. As I shared with one evangelical, "I wish I could get more Catholics to have such enthusiasm for their faith in Christ!"[7]

More Reversals

Many other venues have witnessed the same trajectory of improving relations between Catholics and evangelicals as seen in Billy Graham's career. In 1960, several prominent leaders of the United States' neo-evangelical movement mobilized against what was for them the bleak prospect of electing the Catholic Kennedy as the nation's chief executive. Evangelical leaders, including Harold John Ockenga of Boston's Park Street Church, Daniel Polling of the *Christian Herald*, L. Nelson Bell of *Christianity Today*, and Clyde W. Taylor of the National Association of Evangelicals, joined 150 other prominent Protestants, including Norman Vincent Peale and Charles Clayton Morrison of the *Christian Century*, in declaring, "It is inconceivable that a Roman Catholic President would

6. Martin, *Prophet with Honor*, 278–80, 488–91; Marshall Frady, *Billy Graham: A Parable of American Righteousness* (Boston: Little, Brown, 1979), 326, 441–46; John Pollock, *Billy Graham: The Authorized Biography* (New York: McGraw-Hill, 1966), 129–30, 218–20, 290–91, 307–10; and Richard V. Pierard, "From Evangelical Exclusivism to Ecumenical Openness: Billy Graham and Sociopolitical Issues," *Journal of Ecumenical Studies* 20 (1983): 428.

7. ExPRESS (National Conference of Catholic Bishops Committee on Evangelization), September 2000, www.nccbuscc.org/evangelization/newsletter/092000.htm (accessed September 23, 2000).

not be under extreme pressure by the hierarchy of his church to accede to its policies with respect to foreign relations," and then in asking, "Is it reasonable to assume that a Roman Catholic President would be able to withstand altogether the determined efforts of the hierarchy of his church to gain further funds and favors for its schools and institutions, and otherwise breach the wall of separation of church and state?" At the news conference in early September where their manifesto was promulgated, Ockenga, according to the *New York Times,* claimed that Kennedy's statements upholding the separation of church and state should be viewed in the same light as statements by Nikita Khrushchev of the Soviet Union in support of world peace. According to Ockenga, "Mr. Khrushchev's meaning of the word 'peace' equaled the world-wide victory of Marxism."[8]

Half a century later, cooperation in the United States between Catholics and evangelicals on issues of social action, civic freedom, and public moral responsibility has advanced far beyond the suspicion expressed by Harold John Ockenga. For at least two decades, Catholics and evangelicals have been working hard with each other to subvert the very concept of "the wall of separation of church and state" that the anti-Kennedy coalition of evangelicals and liberals had used as a tool of public rhetoric in 1960. Especially on pro-life and pro-family questions, the difficult thing to imagine now is how evangelicals and Catholics could ever have been at odds. In the run-up to the 2004 presidential election, Gary Bauer, head of a conservative advocacy group, spoke for a growing number of his fellow evangelicals when he stated, "When John F. Kennedy made his famous speech that the Vatican would not tell him what to do, evangelicals and Southern Baptists breathed a sigh of relief. But today evangelicals and Southern Baptists are hoping that the Vatican *will* tell Catholic politicians what to do."[9]

Evangelicals at the Vatican

Signs of change between Catholics and evangelicals have multiplied on every side. On December 3, 2003, Pope John Paul II held an audience in the Vatican that revealed much not only about contemporary Catholic-evangelical relations but also about significant currents within evangelicalism. Present at this audience were Thomas Oden and several of his coeditors who are publishing the Ancient Christian Commentary series with InterVarsity Press. This ambitious series

8. *New York Times,* September 8, 1960, 1, 25. Our thanks to Peter Swarr for digging up this reference and for much other research help.

9. Quoted in Susan Page, "Churchgoing Closely Tied to Voting Patterns," *USA Today,* June 3, 2004, 2A.

(with fourteen of twenty-eight projected volumes already out by the end of 2003) collects and reprints scriptural commentary from the early church fathers. Oden, a Methodist who began his theological career as a liberal Protestant, was himself won back to orthodox and evangelical faith through study of the early Christian fathers. The commentary series represents a noteworthy effort to encourage the growth in faith that Oden and other evangelicals like him experienced as they followed early Christian leaders in their meditations on biblical passages.

InterVarsity Press (IVP) is the publishing arm of the American InterVarsity Christian Fellowship and has long been a producer of thoughtful evangelical books from authors such as Francis Schaeffer, Rebecca Pippert, J. I. Packer, John R. W. Stott, Donald Bloesch, Phillip Johnson, and others on the theology and practices of Christian life. With Oden, IVP has recruited a team of scholarly experts to edit the individual volumes of the series. Some of those editors are evangelical Protestant, while others are Roman Catholic or Eastern Orthodox. Interest in the series has exceeded IVP's early expectations, with initial volumes each selling more than twenty thousand copies as of early 2004 (20 percent of sales are to Catholics). The purpose of the Vatican invitation to these evangelical scholars was for the pope to pronounce his blessing on the translation of the first volumes of the commentary series into Spanish and Italian and to commend personally its evangelical editors.[10]

This kind of Vatican reception for an evangelical enterprise was, in fact, becoming routine. Only a few months before the InterVarsity Press editors arrived, leaders of the Alpha course had also been hosted by the Vatican. In a five-day series of meetings in Rome, Alpha keynoter Nicky Gumbel and some of his associates met with the Congregation on the Doctrine of the Faith, the Pontifical Council for Promoting Christian Unity, and several other official Catholic organizations. The personal meeting between Gumbel and the pope had been arranged by Father Raniero Cantalamessa, preacher to the papal household, who had known Gumbel for several years. Their meeting also included Kitty Arbuthnott, who is the head of Alpha for Catholics. The Alpha course news release that provided details on this meeting quoted four Catholic cardinals who made public comments recommending this evangelical program to their own Catholic faithful.[11]

10. Personal communications from participant and series translation coordinator Joel Scandrett.
11. See uk.alphacourse.org/runningacourse/news/2004/03/papalaudience.htm (accessed April 28, 2004).

Shared Resources

Breakthroughs in relations between Catholics and evangelicals occur even more often at local levels than in lofty places like the Vatican. In Madison, Wisconsin, Tim Kruse has for several years run a nonprofit charitable organization called the Evangelical Catholic. Its purpose is to promote "an Evangelical Catholic Life" marked by "interior conversion, costly discipleship, devotion to the Scriptures, and a prayerful life," as well as "obedience to the Church." It publishes its own books and booklets (such as *Studies in Evangelical Catholic Life*), runs a well-attended Alpha-Omega program for University of Wisconsin students at St. Paul's University Catholic Center, and promotes Bible study aids from the Navigators. In April 2004, the St. Paul's Institute of Evangelical Catholic Ministry featured workshops on generically Christian subjects such as "Costly Christian Discipleship" and "Protestants and Catholics Laboring Together in Evangelical Ministry," as well as workshops with a stronger Catholic flavor such as "Explaining Catholic Distinctives" and "How to Be Evangelically Catholic without Being Fundamentalist."[12]

Recently, the Baltimore Archdiocese issued a pamphlet concerning the Alpha course. It begins with quotations from Pope Paul VI and Pope John Paul II on the need for evangelization and then specifies where Alpha falls short—by neglecting the role of the church in salvation and particularly the role of the sacraments. But the main purpose of the pamphlet is to offer an endorsement: "The basic thrust of Alpha is to communicate the essentials of the Christian faith, with its understanding of God the Father, of Jesus Christ—his incarnation, death, and resurrection—and the gifts of the Holy Spirit. It is the historic faith expressed in ancient creeds. Alpha is, therefore, compatible with Catholic teaching."[13]

In yet another indication of the distance moved on questions of evangelism, the staunchly evangelical American Tract Society issued a tract in 2003 titled "The Road to Heaven: According to Catholic Sources." It employed quotations only from the New American Bible, which was prepared especially for Catholic use, and the *Catechism of the Catholic Church* to present its traditional evangelical message: "Recognize that God is holy. . . . Acknowledge that man is sinful. . . . Believe that Christ alone paid for your sin. . . . Repent and trust in Christ alone for your salvation. . . . Live your faith by good works."[14]

12. Various newsletters and promotional material.
13. Pamphlet of Baltimore Archdiocese on Alpha (n.d.), 6. We thank Paul Heidebrecht for bringing this document to our attention.
14. American Tract Society, "The Road to Heaven: According to Catholic Sources" (Garland, TX: American Tract Society, n.d.).

Hymns, worship songs, and other types of Christian music have built an especially sturdy bridge for spiritual traffic between the once isolated camps of Catholics and evangelicals. John Michael Talbot, who is discussed more fully in chapter 7, is among the best known of several Catholic troubadours whose performances, CDs, books, and website are avidly patronized by evangelicals. For such audiences, Talbot's evocative expression of New Testament themes such as the kingdom of God—as well as his use of language that is, in Stephen Marini's phrase, "steeped in the rhetoric of evangelical Protestants"—is much more important than his status as a Third Order Franciscan and loyal Roman Catholic.[15]

Bridges built of song now extend deep into the congregational life of both evangelical and Catholic churches. Music from Catholic publishers, especially composed since the 1960s, is frequently heard among evangelicals (e.g., "The King of Glory," "I Am the Bread of Life," and "You Satisfy the Hungry Heart" from publishers such as G. I. A. Publications and North American Liturgy Resources). Catholic hymnbooks published since the late 1950s have returned the favor by including many hymns of purest Protestant lineage. In an extensive recent study, Felicia Piscitelli found that the thirty hymns most often reprinted in sixty-seven Catholic hymnals included two by Charles Wesley ("Jesus Christ Is Risen Today" and "Hark! The Herald Angels Sing"), as well as Isaac Watts's "O God, Our Help in Ages Past," Edward Peronnet's "All Hail the Power of Jesus' Name," John Newton's "Amazing Grace," and Martin Luther's "A Mighty Fortress Is Our God."[16]

Polling data in the United States, as in Canada, add intriguing dimensions to the new state of affairs. In the same 1996 Angus Reid poll that showed a strong evangelical presence in Canadian Catholicism, a remarkable 50 percent of American Catholics provided the "evangelical" response to at least three of the four indicators; 13 percent of the Americans who affirmed all four evangelical markers were Roman Catholic. The same poll indicated that 12 percent of American Catholics refer to themselves as "evangelical" or an equivalent term.[17]

Public taste in literature shows the same inattention to the great divide of the sixteenth century, with evangelicals buying vast quantities

15. See Michael G. Smith, "Troubador of the Kingdom," *Christianity Today*, February 1, 1985, 88; and Stephen A. Marini, *Sacred Song in America* (Urbana: University of Illinois Press, 2003), 244.

16. Felicia Piscitelli, "Appendix III: Hymns in Roman Catholic Hymnals," in *Wonderful Words of Life: Hymns in American Protestant History and Theology*, ed. Richard J. Mouw and Mark A. Noll, 269–72 (Grand Rapids: Eerdmans, 2004).

17. Mark A. Noll, *American Evangelical Christianity* (Oxford: Blackwell, 2001), 34–36.

of popular books written by Catholics Thomas Merton, Henri Nouwen, and J. R. R. Tolkien. Likewise, Catholics regularly read evangelicals Richard Foster, Richard Lovelace, and Max Lucado. American Christians of all sorts devour the books of Britain's C. S. Lewis and G. K. Chesterton without caring a great deal that the former grew up in an evangelical ethos *before* finding "mere Christianity," while the latter moved from Anglicanism to Catholicism without ever embracing evangelicalism. American publishers have encouraged the growing traffic between the traditions by bringing out numerous books that treat interconfessional differences far more relatively than authors in the 1950s could have imagined. Samples from the last few decades include popular titles such as Albert Boudreau's *Born-Again Catholic* and a report from the Jesuit Thomas Rausch on "The Los Angeles Catholic/Evangelical Dialogue."[18] Similar studies from the academic realm include George H. Tavard's *Justification* (1983) from Paulist Press, which argues that Luther's construction of this key doctrine is compatible with the theology of the Council of Trent; *The Condemnations of the Reformation Era, Do They Still Divide?* a translation from the German published by Fortress in 1990; and *Reformations: A Radical Interpretation of Christianity and the World, 1500–2000* from Scribner (1997), in which the Catholic Felipe Fernández-Armesto and the evangelical Derek Wilson offer a striking reinterpretation of what the Reformation means today.[19] More recent signs of flourishing interconfessional exchange include titles featuring direct, friendly, and honest debate (such as a book on how Catholics and evangelicals regard Mary),[20] books offering challenges in a constructive way across the confessional divide,[21] and others in which evangelical authors use Catholic resources to make their points for evangelical audiences.[22] In sum, while it is still possible to identify an "evangelical press" and a "Catholic press," the crossover lines are much more common and much more heavily traveled than only scant decades ago.

18. Albert Boudreau, *The Born-Again Catholic* (Locust Valley, NY: Living Flame Press, 1980); and Thomas Rausch, "The Los Angeles Catholic/Evangelical Dialogue," *Ecumenical Trends* 26 (1997): 93–95.

19. An important early example of such academic literature from the Protestant side was T. F. Torrance, *Theology in Reconciliation: Essays towards Evangelical-Catholic Unity in East and West* (Grand Rapids: Eerdmans, 1976).

20. Dwight Longenecker and David Gustafson, *Mary: A Catholic-Evangelical Dialogue* (Grand Rapids: Brazos, 2003).

21. For example, Carl E. Olson, *Will Catholics Be "Left Behind"? A Catholic Critique of the Rapture and Today's Prophecy Preachers* (San Francisco: Ignatius, 2003).

22. For example, Daniel H. Williams, *Retrieving the Tradition and Renewing Evangelicalism* (Grand Rapids: Eerdmans, 1999); and J. Daryl Charles, *The Unformed Conscience of Evangelicalism* (Downers Grove, IL: InterVarsity, 2002).

New Perspectives on Old Battles

Even on matters concerning the Bible, always a sensitive barometer of public sentiment in America, recent decades have witnessed a series of marvels. From rioting over Catholic desires to read the Douay-Rheims Bible in public school during the nineteenth century to the creation of mutually exclusive networks of professional Bible scholars in the first half of the twentieth, the study and reading of Scripture have now become venues of nonsectarian cooperation.[23] Catholics currently may read the Living Bible and the Good News Bible, both produced under Protestant auspices, with the *imprimatur* and *nihil obstat*. So unpredictable have the times become that a Catholic group set records in the distribution of Scripture, with the Sacred Heart League placing record orders from the American Bible Society for 775,000 New Testaments in 1979 and 800,000 in 1983.[24] In 2003, the American Bible Society's Bible sales and distribution to Catholic audiences reached more than 912,000.[25]

Another indication of rapidly changing opinions is the stunning Catholic *volte-face* on Martin Luther. Although the antagonisms of centuries had cooled somewhat by the 1950s, Luther was still treated harshly or ignored entirely by the Catholic populace at large. Only two out of thirty American Catholic periodicals in one survey provided reviews of Roland Bainton's life of Luther, the most compelling modern study, when it appeared in 1950.[26] Catholic reaction to the black-and-white Martin Luther movie of 1953 was also decidedly unfavorable. One commentator in the *Priest* summed up his judgment by calling Luther "a lewd satyr whose glandular demands were the ultimate cause of his break with the Christian Church."[27]

In the wake of the Second Vatican Council, however, an altogether different attitude rapidly filtered down to popular levels. By 1965, the pages of the *Priest* reflected a different picture. According to one writer, "We'd feel quite silly today declaiming against Luther in the intemperate words of yesterday."[28] Scholarly and popular reassessment of Luther went on apace until 1980 when a series of meetings to celebrate the 450th anniversary of the Lutherans' Augsburg Confession heard from

23. For background, see Nathan O. Hatch and Mark A. Noll, eds., *The Bible in America* (New York: Oxford University Press, 1982), 4, 8, 16n36, 17n43, 165–66.

24. As reported in the *Presbyterian Journal*, July 6, 1983, 3.

25. John Greco, director of operations for the American Bible Society, via email to Carolyn Nystrom, June 3, 2004.

26. Survey conducted by Cy Hulse, "Luther's Changing Image among Catholics," prepared for a course at Trinity Evangelical Divinity School, c. 1978. This fine paper is also the source for the quotations from the *Priest* below.

27. "Should We Speak or Hold Our Tongue?" *Priest* 12 (February 1956): 134.

28. Perplexus (pseud.), "The Charm of Melody," *Priest* 21 (July 1965): 585.

many Catholics about the usefulness of that confession for their own tradition.[29] The reevaluation reached a new level of visibility in 1983 during the celebrations marking the five-hundredth anniversary of Luther's birth. Local Catholic officials, anticipating the pope's own appearance in Rome's Evangelical-Lutheran Christ Church on December 11, 1983, accepted invitations to preach in Protestant services.[30] In that year, conciliatory Protestant titles such as *Martin Luther: Prophet to the Catholic Church* were echoed by Catholic books of similar spirit such as *Luther: A Reformer for the Churches.*[31] Two events reflect the startling changes wrought by the passage of only a few years. In the mid-1950s, Chicago Catholics fought to keep the Luther film off local television, while in 1983, the Notre Dame alumni magazine devoted much of one issue, including an attractive cover portrait, to a discussion of "What Martin Luther Means to Us."[32] Only two years before, a similar chorus of Protestant and Catholic voices had marked the eight-hundredth anniversary of the birth of St. Francis. But the dramatically altered position of Martin Luther in Catholic-Protestant relations especially testified eloquently to an unprecedented improvement in interconfessional attitudes.

It is thus no surprise that Catholic response to the Martin Luther movie in 2003 (by Eric Till) was moderate and nuanced. The review on the website of the U.S. Conference of Catholic Bishops did criticize the film for distorting the character of early sixteenth-century Catholicism and for shying away from defects in Luther's character. But the balanced tone of its concluding recommendation could hardly have been imagined fifty years earlier:

> While shaded by a suspect reading of the issues involved, the historical importance of the subject matter and its central character offers much in the way of thoughtful discussion. And while its oversimplifications and revisionist tendencies warrant caution when viewing the film with adolescents, "Luther" imbues the personalities involved with an appealing humanity, breathing new vitality into events and ideas which, though fossilized by centuries of academic debate, still affect us as Christians today. For that reason alone, "Luther" is worth seeing.[33]

29. For a review of this discussion, see Avery Dulles, S.J., "The Catholicity of the Augsburg Confession," *Journal of Religion* 63 (October 1983): 337–54.

30. *New York Times*, December 12, 1983, 1, 4.

31. James Atkinson, *Martin Luther: Prophet to the Catholic Church* (Grand Rapids: Eerdmans, 1983); and Mark Edwards and George H. Tavard, *Luther: A Reformer for the Churches* (New York: Paulist Press, 1983).

32. Jaroslav Pelikan, *The Riddle of Roman Catholicism* (New York: Abingdon, 1959), 219; and Kenneth L. Woodward, "Luther in Excelsis," *Notre Dame Magazine*, October 1983, 11–15.

33. See www.usccb.org/movies/1/luther.htm (accessed January 14, 2004).

Nor is it any surprise that a recent review by a Catholic of Martin Marty's new biography of Luther would conclude that Luther "could not, of course, have foreseen that the Church of Rome would some four centuries later, at Vatican Council II, adopt many of the reforms that he championed."[34]

Beyond North America

Outside North America, relationships between evangelicals and Catholics vary widely. In some places, harmonious cooperation between Catholics and evangelicals flourishes even more obviously than in the United States. In other regions, age-old antagonisms retain great vigor. Especially in Latin America and southern Europe, the places where Roman Catholicism was most strongly institutionalized, where it has tried hardest to maintain its traditional monopoly over religious life, and where the greatest syncretism has occurred between Catholic ritual and pre-Christian pagan practice, evangelical rejection of anything Catholic is still prominent.[35]

Given the long-standing struggles of Protestants in Spain, Portugal, Italy, and Latin America to secure legal and cultural freedom for themselves, it is no surprise that evangelicals in these regions are much more skeptical about supposed evangelical-Catholic breakthroughs than in North America or other parts of Europe. Incidents of cultural strife, including forced migrations and even murder, keep the older mutual suspicions alive in at least some parts of the world.[36]

Yet even in these parts of the globe, there are signs of change. In 1997, for instance, the Catholic bishops of Italy issued an official apology to the Waldensians and other Protestants of their country for the "suffering and injury" they had inflicted.[37] American Catholics involved in the Evangelicals and Catholics Together initiative have written forceful letters to their counterparts in Latin America, urging full religious freedom for all citizens, whether Catholic, older Protestant, newer Pentecostal, or secular.[38]

34. Kenneth L. Woodward, "Martin Marty's Martin Luther," *Books & Culture* (May/ June 2004): 7.

35. See below for further consideration. For general orientation, useful perspectives are provided by M. Daniel Carroll R., "The Evangelical-Roman Catholic Dialogue: Issues Revolving around Evangelization: An Evangelical View from Latin America," *Trinity Journal* 21 (2000): 189–207; and Joe Couto, "The Latin Experience," *Faith Today* (May/June 1999): 29–31.

36. See, for example, "In a Warring Mexican Town, God's Will Is the Issue," *New York Times*, August 14, 2000.

37. "Italian Bishops Ask for Protestants' Forgiveness," *Christian Century*, April 23–30, 1997, 406.

38. Copies of correspondence in personal possession of Mark Noll.

If uncertainty remains for evangelicals about Catholic domination in some parts of the world, the activities of John Paul II, pope since 1978, have offered Protestants throughout the world much food for thought. The pope's pontificate is far too complex to treat succinctly (though it very much deserves book-length considerations from evangelical authors). Two publications from 1995 suggest why, from an evangelical angle, this pope is so intriguing. In that year, the Vatican issued the pope's encyclical *Ut Unum Sint,* a plea for the unity of the church that set aside a great deal of the Catholic Church's historic triumphalism. This encyclical specified in particular that distinctly Catholic doctrines such as the supremacy of the pope should be debated openly in future dialogue between Catholics and other Christians.[39] That same year John Paul II also published *Crossing the Threshold of Hope,* which immediately became an international best-seller. Besides a fair bit of prose that sounded odd to a Protestant ear and a few bits that seemed simply wrong, many passages expressed what an evangelical could only regard as the purest gospel. For example, "God does not cease to be at work. *His essential work will always remain the Cross and the Resurrection of Christ.* This is the ultimate word of truth and love."[40] It is certainly a sign of changing times that in early 2004 a survey of American evangelicals revealed a higher favorability rating for John Paul II (59 percent) than for either Jerry Falwell (44 percent) or Pat Robertson (54 percent).[41]

Signs of embracing what to an evangelical looks an awful lot like evangelical Christianity have showed up with some regularity in the wake of the pope's many travels. For instance, on the night of August 19, 2000, at the Roman Catholic World Youth Day in Rome, the pope presented an address to the over one million young people from many countries who had gathered for this annual Catholic event. After the speech was over, a coordinated set of projection equipment broadcast the *Jesus* film to the assembled youth. The film, to be sure, was shown late at night and after an exhausting day of activity, but it was still striking for this film to show up in that place. It had been first produced in 1979 and then aggressively distributed around the world by Campus Crusade for Christ International. Mother Teresa had asked that it be shown in all her houses for the dying in Calcutta, India. The most active promoters of the film, however, have been the mission boards of two

39. The reason why a book-length treatment would be necessary for a full evangelical assessment of this pope's activities is that other official Catholic statements, such as *Dominus Iesus* (2000), seem to present a more traditional picture of Catholic insistence on historic Catholic teachings, such as the supremacy of the pope.

40. John Paul II, *Crossing the Threshold of Hope* (New York: Knopf, 1995), 134.

41. Laurie Goodstein, "How the Evangelicals and Catholics Joined Forces," *New York Times,* May 30, 2004, Week in Review, 4.

American evangelical denominations (Southern Baptist Convention and Church of the Nazarene), two American interdenominational agencies (World Vision and Operation Mobilization), and the Roman Catholic Church.[42] Those who have seen the movie know that it concludes with a direct appeal for viewers to recognize that Jesus, "the Son of God, the Savior, . . . wants to come into your life," and offers a model prayer that includes the statement, "I open the door of my life and receive you as Savior and Lord."[43]

In Poland, before he became pope, Karol Wojtyla, as bishop of Krakow, had been one of the key Catholic leaders easing the way for a striking effort at ecumenical youth evangelism. This initiative involved a Polish Catholic renewal movement called Light-Life, led by Father Franciszek Blachnicki, and Joe Losiak, a Polish-American Catholic from Chicago and staffworker with Campus Crusade for Christ. After a series of meetings in the early 1970s, Losiak was invited to Poland to use Campus Crusade materials at youth rallies and summer camps organized by an arm of the Polish Catholic Church. For seven years, until Father Franciszek was caught outside Poland in December 1981, when the communist regime imposed martial law, Losiak was given a free hand to show Campus Crusade's *Jesus* film and to use the lessons he had learned at Awana clubs and with Campus Crusade in evangelizing and discipling Polish youth.[44]

A few years after this experiment came to an end, a personal friendship in Italy led to another noteworthy breakthrough in Catholic-evangelical relations. Here the medium of exchange was the charismatic movement, which brought together the Catholic layman Matteo Calisi of Bari and the Pentecostal pastor Giovanni Traettino of Caserta. Annually, since 1992, these two have convened an evangelical-Catholic conference where both Catholics and Pentecostals are recruited as speakers.[45] The work of these two pioneers in Italy reflects much broader evangelical-Protestant contacts mediated by the worldwide charismatic renewal.[46]

In France, where ever-advancing secularism has become a far greater problem for Christian witness of all kinds than traditional strife between

42. Paul A. Eshleman, "The 'Jesus' Film: A Contribution to World Evangelism," *International Bulletin of Missionary Research* 26 (April 2002): 68–72.

43. *Jesus* (Inspirational Films/The Genesis Project, 1979; distributed by Campus Crusade for Christ, Liguna Niguel, CA).

44. The story is told in David Hill Scott, "Evangelicals and Catholics Really Together in Poland, 1975–1982," *Fides et Historia* 34, no. 1 (Winter/Spring 2002): 89–109.

45. Peter Hocken, *The Spirit of Unity: How Renewal Is Breaking Down Barriers between Evangelicals and Roman Catholics* (Cambridge, Eng.: Grove Books, 2001), 5.

46. For documentation, see the website of the International Catholic Charismatic Renewal Services, www.iccrs.org.

the Christian traditions, the story of David Bjork (told more fully in chap. 7) offers another instance of the kind of cooperation that was simply unimaginable short decades ago. Bjork went to Normandy in 1979 as an evangelical church planter, but within a decade, he was working closely with local Catholic priests as evangelist, Bible study leader, and discipler.[47]

At least in the developed world, where documentation is more easily available, Ireland has been the scene of the most advanced movement of evangelicalism within the Catholic Church. In November 1990, a group of more than forty Irish Catholics, mostly priests or religious, was joined by a handful of other Catholics from outside Ireland in publishing a pamphlet "with official church permission" titled "What Is an Evangelical Catholic?" The pamphlet began with this paragraph:

> Millions of Roman Catholics throughout the world have a personal rela-
> tionship with Jesus, many of them through the various Renewal Move-
> ments in the Catholic Church. They are evangelical in the strictest sense
> of the term in that they have received the basic gospel, accepted Jesus
> as personal Lord and Saviour and are manifesting the fruit of the Holy
> Spirit in their daily lives.[48]

A few years later, in 1998, leading figures behind the earlier statement were instrumental in producing a longer document called "Evangelicals and Catholics in Ireland," with an extended subtitle: "A call to Christians in Ireland—Protestant, Roman Catholic, Pentecostal, and New Church—to build relationships as disciples of Jesus Christ, that we may more clearly witness to Him, our only Saviour and Lord." Arising out of Ireland's own history of sectarian conflict between Protestants and Catholics but also drawing strength from numerous personal bonds that had been forged among priests and pastors, Protestant laity and Catholic laity, this document offered a particular eloquent statement of shared Christian concerns:

> Salvation is by grace, received by faith, with no help needed from good
> works or religious observances done to improve our chances of being
> saved. . . . Through prayer and study of Holy Scripture, and aided by the
> Church's reflection on the sacred text from earliest times, we have found

47. David E. Bjork, *Unfamiliar Paths* (Pasadena: William Carey, 1997); and idem, "When Obedience Leads Us into the Unknown," in *Catholics and Evangelicals: Do They Share a Common Future?* ed. Thomas P. Rausch, 149–70 (Downers Grove, IL: InterVarsity, 2000).

48. "What Is an Evangelical Catholic?" issued from Dublin, Ireland, and Rostrevor, Northern Ireland, June 1992.

that, notwithstanding some persistent and serious differences, we can together bear witness to the gift of salvation in Jesus Christ.[49]

Polling efforts aimed at the entire world are fraught with difficulty when they venture into sensitive issues of religious belief and practice. But with all due caution being exercised, it is still noteworthy to see what such surveys reveal. The Angus Reid World Survey of 1997, like the 1996 Angus Reid cross-border poll of the United States and Canada, included an unusually full set of questions about religion. Using the evangelical markers defined by David Bebbington and guided by the advice of George Rawlyk, the poll asked respondents to agree or disagree with this statement: "I have committed my life to Christ and consider myself to be a converted Christian." Granting difficulties in translation and realizing that sample size was fairly small (five hundred telephone respondents in each of thirty-three countries), the results are still worth pondering. As might be expected, the survey found significant numbers of self-identified Protestants who agreed with the statement about conversion and who also attended church once a week or more, prayed daily or more, and considered religion to be very important (28 percent of the population in the United States, 28 percent in South Africa, 10 percent in each of the Philippines, South Korea, and Brazil). Less expected, at least in light of how the question about conversion was phrased, was the fact that significant numbers of self-identified Roman Catholics also responded in exactly the same way to the four queries—28 percent of the population in the Philippines, 26 percent in Italy, 22 percent in Poland, 17 percent in Spain, 16 percent in South Korea, 15 percent in Brazil, and 14 percent in Mexico. Even if the survey results were only approximate, the data still meant that many Roman Catholics were willing to respond to the pollsters with answers that seemed quite evangelical.[50]

Voices from Europe

If the historic shift recorded in this book—from all-out Catholic-evangelical antagonism to modest Catholic-evangelical engagement—marks a genuine moment of grace in the long history of the church, the way to exploit that grace will certainly not be simply to ignore the past but to find a middle way of hope. In recent years, a number of significant voices have shown what that middle way of realistic, historically informed

49. "Evangelicals and Catholics in Ireland" (1998). We thank Ken Newell and David Livingstone for help in obtaining and understanding these documents.
50. For further attention to this poll, see Noll, *American Evangelical Christianity*, 38–41.

hope might look like. These voices usually come from those who know the past history well but who think that the impasses of history are the result of human rather than divine purpose.

From the Catholic side, such a message was voiced by Pope John Paul II when he spoke to the Lutherans in Rome at the observation of Martin Luther's five-hundredth birthday.

> So we see ourselves in the midst of all the evident separations that still exist in teaching and life deeply linked in the solidarity of all the Christians of Advent. . . . We believe, in the year of remembrance of the birthday of Martin Luther five centuries ago, that we see as if in a distance the dawning of the advent of a reconstruction of our unity and community. This unity is a fruit of the daily renewal, conversion, and penitence of all Christians in the light of the eternal word of God. It is at the same time the best preparation for the coming of God in our world.
>
> Let us follow the great figure of the time of Advent, let us follow the example of John the Baptist, the voice of the caller in the desert: "Make straight the way of the Lord" (John 1:23). Let us follow the invitation to reconciliation with God and among ourselves. Christ, the ruler of all, is not only above us but also in our midst as the Lord who was, who is, and who will be in eternity.[51]

A similar voice of realistic hope came as the result of a significant series of modern discussions in Europe. The book summarizing those discussions is titled *The Condemnations of the Reformation Era: Do They Still Divide?* The answer was measured but hopeful:

> Today it is possible to say the following: Far-reaching agreement in the interpretation of Holy Scripture, clearer insights about the historical contingency of traditional doctrinal formulations, and the new spirit of ecumenical dialogue, in awareness of the ties linking Christians of different denominational traditions through their faith in the one Lord, have all contributed essentially to the achievement of a large measure of mutual understanding. This understanding is not confined to the fundamental acknowledgment of the one Lord Jesus Christ. It applies also to central themes of Christian doctrine.[52]

The European Catholics and Protestants who published this book on the condemnations of the Reformation era concluded that these condemnations did not need to be maintained. Because the condemnations

---

51. "Text of John Paul's Sermon at a Lutheran Church," *New York Times*, December 12, 1983, 4.

52. Karl Lehmann and Wolfhart Pannenberg, *The Condemnations of the Reformation Era: Do They Still Divide?* trans. Margaret Kohl (Minneapolis: Fortress, 1990), 27.

were based only partly on the way things really were—but also on misconceptions based on taking extreme statements of the other position
as normative, eternally unchanging points of view—there was no need
to apply them to situations in the late twentieth century. The authors of
this volume concluded that, while genuine differences remained, those
differences were not as universal, categorical, or all-encompassing as
they once seemed.

Of most relevance to American evangelicals were words written by
George Carey when he was principal of Trinity Theological College in
England. After he wrote them, Carey became the archbishop of Canterbury, where, in one of the unlikeliest surprises of recent history, he used
that ancient Anglican office to promote a program at once evangelical
and catholic. Before going to Canterbury, Carey outlined his hope for
the evangelical–Roman Catholic future:

> How can Protestants with their faith anchored in the New Testament
> have unity with Catholics, whose official teachings include doctrines they
> cannot accept? The question is reciprocated from the Catholic side. How
> can the historical faith of the church be reconciled with the somewhat
> reduced faith of the Protestants? . . . There is, I believe, a way through this
> dilemma. The Second Vatican Council, in fact, opened new possibilities
> through a statement in the Decree on Ecumenism. The decree suggested
> that closer agreement among Christians is possible if we think in terms
> of a hierarchy of truths. What the decree is getting at is this: unity is often
> barred by the attention given to our differences, but not all doctrines have
> the same importance for faith. Could we arrive at an understanding of the
> common core of the faith we share while allowing freedom with respect
> to other teachings less essential? This looks like a promising way forward.
> It is biblically true that not all the doctrines of the Christian faith have
> the same value for *saving faith* even if they are regarded as important in
> their own right.[53]

The voices of John Paul II, of the European Catholics and Protestants
who set aside the anathemas of the sixteenth century, and of Archbishop
Carey do not speak with American accents. Since they do not, for example, reflect the American way of intermingling religion and public
life, they do not address the historic role that political values have played
in American interconfessional attitudes. In the end, the exhortations
of outsiders require American confirmation. It remains for Americans,
both evangelicals and Roman Catholics—and, even more, for divine

53. George Carey, *A Tale of Two Churches: Can Protestants and Catholics Get Together?*
(Downers Grove, IL: InterVarsity, 1985), 160, with Carey's own list of six "central points"
that he regards as essential to Christian communion on 161–62.

grace—to determine whether they too can find a middle way of historical realism and hope for the future.

Taking Stock

As this parade of incidents, and many others that could be cited, indicates, so many unexpected developments have taken place in recent
decades within the Catholic Church and between Catholics and other
Christians that fresh evangelical assessment cannot be avoided. Already
in the 1960s, the dam that restrained positive evangelical assessment of
Roman Catholicism was beginning to crack. When the fundamentalist
leader and arch anticommunist Carl McIntyre claimed in 1945 that he
would rather be ruled by communists than by Catholics, he was making
an extreme statement but one that spoke for many other evangelicals.
By 1969, McIntyre's message had changed at least a little: "I'm much
closer to the Catholics in my belief in the Virgin Birth than I am to
liberal Protestants who deny it."[54]

Other Protestants who started out more flexible than McIntyre have
moved a proportionately greater distance. One important testimony to
that distance was provided in late 1983 by the conservative Anglican
theologian J. I. Packer, who began a book review with a revealing bit
of autobiography. Packer had been nurtured in his faith by the robust
evangelicalism of the English Puritans; his published writings had gained
him renown in Britain, Canada, and the United States as one of the most
articulate modern advocates of thoughtful Reformed evangelicalism.[55]
Packer's remarks about the book *The Born-Again Catholic* spoke of a
momentous alteration in a long-standing religious quarrel:

> If when I was a student you had told me that before old age struck I should
> be reviewing a popular Roman Catholic book on the new birth which used
> Campus Crusade material, carried an official *nihil obstat* and *imprimatur*,
> and was already in its fourth printing in three years, I doubt whether I
> would have believed you. But that is what I am doing now. Again, if at that
> time you had predicted that one day an Anglican bishop would tell me
> how the last Roman Catholic priest to whom he talked quizzed him hard
> as to whether Anglicans really preached the new birth as they should, I

54. Quoted in James Morris, *The Preachers* (New York: St. Martin's, 1973), 200.
55. On Packer's own influential career as an evangelical spokesman, see Mark A. Noll,
"J. I. Packer and the Shaping of American Evangelicalism," in *Doing Theology for the People
of God: Studies in Honor of J. I. Packer,* ed. Donald Lewis and Alister McGrath, 191–206
(Downers Grove, IL: InterVarsity, 1996).

would probably have laughed in your face. But this month it happened. Things are not as they were![56]

Mutual antagonism between Roman Catholics and Protestant evangelicals was once an apparently permanent fixture. But that was then. Since 1960 a new age has dawned.

56. J. I. Packer, review of *The Born-Again Catholic,* by Albert Boudreau, *Eternity* (December 1983): 92.

2

HISTORIC STANDOFF

Once upon a time, within the memory of many people still very much alive, Catholics and evangelical Protestants regarded each other with the gravest suspicion—consistently, persistently, and insistently. That suspicion reflected a climate of religious strife dramatically different from what has developed since the early 1960s. While Roman Catholics and evangelicals still debate many matters of difference, the possibilities that now exist for communication, theological and social cooperation, and mutual encouragement are so much greater than even a generation ago as to constitute a minor revolution. To illustrate how long the age of combat existed between Catholics and Protestants, it is necessary only to observe that the ancient animosity remained substantially in place during the years immediately following World War II. The standoff appeared fixed, seemingly in place forever.

Hardened Attitudes at Mid-century

By the mid-twentieth century, grosser forms of religious hostility that had prevailed widely throughout much of American history were mostly dying down, but the change was a matter of degree, not kind.[1]

1. In the literature on Catholic-Protestant hostility, one of the earliest books is still among the best: Ray Allen Billington, *The Protestant Crusade, 1800–1860* (New York:

Two comments, two events, and two books reveal the extent of Protestant-Catholic disengagement that existed in the postwar world.

The first of the comments was that of Carl McIntyre excerpted in chapter 1. It is worth quoting at greater length here since in 1945, when these words were spoken, this Presbyterian fundamentalist was more centrally located on the religious spectrum than he later became. His assessment of the world situation was shared by many other evangelicals of his day:

> As we enter the post-war world, without any doubt the greatest enemy of freedom and liberty that the world has to face today is the Roman Catholic system. Yes, we have Communism in Russia and all that is involved there, but if one had to choose between the two . . . one would be much better off in a communistic society than in a Roman Catholic Fascist set-up. . . . America has to face the Roman Catholic terror. The sooner the Christian people of America wake up to the danger the safer will be our land.[2]

Three years later, the Protestant church historian Wilhelm Pauck, who moved in much more liberal circles than McIntyre, took stock of the interreligious situation and concluded that "the difference between Protestantism and Roman Catholicism is so profound that it seems almost impossible to recognize them as two forms of one Christianity."[3]

Macmillan, 1938). Other helpful discussions are found in John J. Kane, *Catholic-Protestant Conflicts in America* (Chicago: Regnery, 1955); David Brion Davis, "Some Themes of Countersubversion: An Analysis of Anti-Masonic, Anti-Catholic, and Anti-Mormon Literature," *Mississippi Valley Historical Review* 47 (1960): 205–24; John Higham, *Strangers in the Land: Patterns of American Nativism, 1860–1925* (Westport, CT: Greenwood, 1980); Richard Hofstadter, *The Paranoid Style in American Politics* (New York: Knopf, 1965); James H. Smylie, "Phases in Protestant Anti-Roman Catholic Relations in the United States: Monologue, Debate, and Dialogue," *Religion in Life* 34 (Spring 1965): 258–69; Jay P. Dolan, "Catholic Attitudes toward Protestants," in *Uncivil Religion: Interreligious Hostility in America,* ed. Robert N. Bellah and Frederick E. Greenspahn, 72–85 (New York: Crossroad, 1987); Barbara Welter, "From Maria Monk to Paul Blanshard: A Century of Protestant Anti-Catholicism," in *Uncivil Religion,* 43–71; Philip Jenkins, *The New Anti-Catholicism: The Last Acceptable Prejudice* (New York: Oxford University Press, 2003); and Mark S. Massa, S.J., *Anti-Catholicism in America: The Last Acceptable Prejudice* (New York: Crossroad, 2003). For a trans-Atlantic perspective, see John Wolffe, *The Protestant Crusade in Great Britain, 1829–1860* (Oxford: Clarendon Press, 1991); and idem, "Anti-Catholicism and Evangelical Identity in Britain and the United States, 1830–1860," in *Evangelicalism: Comparative Studies of Popular Protestantism in North America, the British Isles, and Beyond, 1770–1990,* ed. Mark A. Noll, David W. Bebbington, and George A. Rawlyk, 179–97 (New York: Oxford University Press, 1994).

2. Quoted in James Morris, *The Preachers* (New York: St. Martin's, 1973), 199.

3. Wilhelm Pauck, "The Roman Catholic Critique of Protestantism," originally published in *Theology Today* (1948), in Wilhelm Pauck, *The Heritage of the Reformation* (New York: Oxford University Press, 1968), 231.

These evaluations reflected a general climate of mutual suspicion suggested by two incidents. In 1946, President Truman's appointment of a formal representative to the Vatican was greeted with a frightening din from all along the Protestant spectrum. G. Bromley Oxnam, bishop of the Methodist Church in New York and president of the Federal Council of Churches, criticized the move as "encouraging the un-American policy of a union of church and state," which the Catholic Church pursued.[4] Nor was suspicion all on one side. When the second General Assembly of the World Council of Churches met at Evanston in 1954, Chicago's Samuel Cardinal Strich issued a pastoral letter forbidding priests to attend even as reporters and urging Catholics in general to stay away.[5]

Even authors who attempted to write sympathetically about Catholic-Protestant differences could at best describe a barely contained antagonism. Two books serve as examples. When Jaroslav Pelikan published *The Riddle of Roman Catholicism* from a Lutheran perspective in 1959, he admitted "that the prejudices and clichés of past generations continue to dominate the image of the Roman church current in America." His book, by contrast, was a charitable effort to dispel prejudice. Yet when Pelikan described the current situation, he turned instinctively to metaphors of conflict—"unconditional surrender," "the great divide," "theological alienation." Neither did he hold out high hopes for an improvement in "what we have now . . . , on both sides, a picture of the other side that is part photograph, part old daguerreotype, and part caricature."[6] For Catholics, Newman Press translated Louis Bouyer's *Spirit and Forms of Protestantism* for American readers in 1956, the year of its original French publication. Like Pelikan, Bouyer was eager to replace prejudice with sympathy, and he was willing to concede a great deal to various Protestant insights. But also like Pelikan, he soon reached a point where the language of antithesis took over. Bouyer's conclusion was that while the religion of Luther, Calvin, and their theological descendants contained insights which the Catholic Church needed, it was "compromised . . . irremediably" by its fatal attachment to the philosophical and theological nominalism of the sixteenth century.[7] In sum, on the very eve of Pope John XXIII's pontificate, which

4. Quotation from "Controversies Aroused in U.S. by Taylor Mission to Vatican," *U.S. News & World Report*, June 28, 1946, 21.

5. John B. Sheerin, C.S.P., "American Catholics and Ecumenism," in *Contemporary Catholicism in the United States*, ed. Philip Gleason (Notre Dame: University of Notre Dame Press, 1969), 75.

6. Jaroslav Pelikan, *The Riddle of Roman Catholicism* (New York: Abingdon, 1959), 12, 176, 189, 201, 219.

7. Louis Bouyer, *The Spirit and Forms of Protestantism*, trans. A. V. Littledale (Westminster, MD: Newman, 1956), 223.

began in 1958, and the American presidential election in 1960, there seemed to be no particular reason to expect a quantum leap forward in Protestant-Catholic goodwill.

A Long History of Evangelical-Catholic Polemic

It is important to stress that evangelicals were every bit as vigorous as other Protestants in their denunciation of Rome. After the Second World War, evangelical publishing maintained a steady drumbeat of anti-Catholic polemic. New books appeared with titles such as *A Priest Speaks His Mind: Why He Returned to the Protestant Faith of His Fathers* and *Catholicism under the Searchlight of the Scriptures,* even as evangelical publishers reissued classic anti-Catholic works from the previous century such as Charles Chiniquy's *Fifty Years in the Church of Rome.*[8] In 1962, the conservative Presbyterian Loraine Boettner published his lengthy study *Roman Catholicism,* which came to be regarded by many evangelicals as a definitive exposition and rebuttal of the Catholic faith. Boettner's conclusions summarized a long history of evangelical complaint:

> That the Roman Church has within it much of truth is not to be denied. It teaches the inspiration of the Scriptures, the deity of Christ, the virgin birth, the miracles, the resurrection of the body, a future judgment, heaven and hell, and many other Scripture truths. In every instance, however, it nullifies these truths to a considerable extent by adding to or subtracting from what the Bible teaches. . . . The Roman Church thus has such serious inherent defects that over the broad course of history it cannot possibly emerge successful. Clearly it has lost its power to evangelize the world, and instead has become so confirmed in its present course that it cannot be reformed either from within or from without. In the main it is as antagonistic and as much an obstacle to evangelical Christianity as are the pagan religions. . . . Its interpretation of the Scriptures is so erroneous and its principles are so persistently unchristian that over the long period of time its influence for good is outweighed by its influence for evil. *It must, therefore, as a system, be judged to be a false church.*[9]

8. W. E. R. O'Gorman, *A Priest Speaks His Mind: Why He Returned to the Protestant Faith of His Fathers* (Glendale, CA: n.p., 1954); John Carrara, *Catholicism under the Searchlight of the Scriptures* (Grand Rapids: Zondervan, 1943); and Charles Chiniquy, *Fifty Years in the Church of Rome* (1886; repr., Grand Rapids: Baker, 1958).

9. Loraine Boettner, *Roman Catholicism* (Philadelphia: Presbyterian & Reformed, 1962), 455, 459 (emphasis in original).

Attitudes toward Catholicism that evangelicals maintained with something close to unanimity into the 1960s had been around for a long time. In fact, they were set firmly in place soon after the Reformation began, at least since the middle decades of the sixteenth century. A combination of attacks on church abuses and fresh articulations of biblical truths—which constituted the negative and positive poles of the Protestant Reformation—long dominated evangelical attitudes toward Catholicism. Slightly different points that mark the hardening of religious division can be specified. In 1541, a blue ribbon panel of Catholic and Protestant theologians gathered at Regensburg (or Ratisbon) in Germany in an effort to iron out differences. Although this group did make initial progress in its discussions, the effort at reconciliation soon collapsed over disagreements concerning church authority, biblical hermeneutics, and the nature of the Eucharist.[10] Shortly thereafter, in 1546, Pope Paul III convened the first session of the Council of Trent, which would meet intermittently until 1563. Its definitive statement of Catholic teaching seemed to offer nothing but rebuke to Protestant efforts at reform. Substantial rebuttals from major Protestant leaders such as John Calvin and the Lutheran Martin Chemnitz were almost as welcomed by Catholics, who saw them as proof-positive of Protestant malfeasance, as they were by Protestants, who read them as defining the worst mistakes of Rome.[11]

Exact dating of the onset of hardened attitudes between Protestants and Catholics is, however, immaterial, for Catholic-Protestant antagonism rapidly became a fixed planet in the western religious sky. Already by the second half of the sixteenth century, efforts to speak sympathetically about Protestant-Catholic similarities were met with stern opposition from both sides. Church historians of the era who tried to write with some appreciation for the opposition—such as the Lutheran John Sleidan or the Huguenot Lancelot du Voisin, sieur de la Popelinière—were blasted by both Catholics and Protestants.[12]

The Protestant brief against Catholicism was expressed in a Niagara of books, pamphlets, and sermons so voluminous that no one person could possibly take the measure of it all. But the main points of that brief can be summarized quite easily. Catholics, in Protestant view,

10. See Peter Matheson, *Cardinal Contarini at Regensburg* (New York: Oxford University Press, 1972).

11. John Calvin, *Antidote to the Council of Trent (1547)*, in John Calvin, *Tracts Relating to the Reformation*, 3 vols. (Edinburgh: Calvin Translation Society, 1844–51), vol. 2; and Martin Chemnitz, *Examination of the Decrees of the Council of Trent*, trans. Fred Kramer (St. Louis: Concordia, 1971).

12. A. G. Dickens and John M. Tonkin, *The Reformation in Historical Thought* (Cambridge: Harvard University Press, 1985), 16, 84.

- taught that people earned their salvation by doing good deeds;
- prevented common people from reading the Bible and from taking their guidance for life from Scripture;
- manufactured extrabiblical saints, festivals, and rites that substituted human imagination for biblical patterns of worship;
- took away glory from Christ by making Mary a coauthor of salvation;
- wantonly corrupted Scripture by forcing new doctrines onto the people merely at the whim of popes and councils whose supposed authority was no more than the imperialistic expression of their own selfish ambition; and
- promoted a corrupting, despotic hierarchy that stripped the faithful of their proper status as priests before God.

In their turn, Catholics gave as good as they got. Wherever Catholic communities were placed in physical or intellectual connection with Protestants, a literature sprouted that reversed the charges. Rather than rescuing Christianity from corruption, Protestantism was hastening it toward decay. According to the Catholic view, Protestants

- offered a "salvation" by faith that denied the need for holiness before God;
- abandoned the Bible to the interpretation of every Tom, Dick, and Mary (no matter how bizarre those interpretations might be) and, by so doing, effectively stripped the Bible of normative, authoritative meaning;
- denied the ability of the Holy Spirit to work through ongoing teaching officers in the church as the Spirit had earlier worked to bring the church into existence;
- scandalously neglected God's gracious help provided to humanity in the person of the blessed Virgin Mary and the exemplary saints;
- rejected the apostolic authority of bishops, councils, and popes and so abetted the rising Western tide of rationalism, secularism, and moral anarchy;
- foolishly neglected the seven sacraments that brought God's grace to every crucial point in a person's life; and
- forsook genuine ecclesiastical leadership of the God-given community of faith in favor of a political free-for-all in which authority was reduced to individualism as a principle and individualistic manipulation as a practice.

Hardened Attitudes in Early America

These polemics, which have echoed around the world since the mid-sixteenth century, also arrived early in the North American regions that eventually became the United States. Although the number of Catholics in the thirteen colonies was small (only twenty-five thousand by 1790), Protestant anti-Romanism was a staple of the American theological world. It was fueled first by the background of Catholic-Protestant strife dating from the English Reformation but was also given fresh impetus in the eighteenth century by warfare between Protestant Britain and Catholic France.

The antagonism was enshrined for generations of English-speaking Protestants in the pages of John Foxe's *Book of Martyrs* (first English edition, 1563), which added persecutions by Catholics to a long line of sufferings endured by true (Protestant) servants of Christ. Merely one instance of the antagonism as it came to America is the language used when the Massachusetts judge Paul Dudley in 1750 left a legacy to Harvard College for the purpose of establishing a series of theological lectures. The third of the lectures in a rotating cycle was to be devoted to "detecting and convicting and exposing the Idolatry of the Romish Church, Their Tyranny, Usurpations, damnable Heresies, fatal Errors, abominable Superstitions, and other crying Wickednesses in their high Places; and Finally that the Church of Rome is that mystical Babylon, That Man of Sin, That apostate Church spoken of, in the New-Testament."[13] By the time Catholic immigration began on a major scale in the nineteenth century, anti-Catholic literature was a well-entrenched theological genre. Ray Allen Billington's study of the six antebellum decades included a bibliography of nearly forty pages devoted exclusively to anti-Catholic periodicals, books, and pamphlets.[14]

An incident from the mid-1840s illustrates how difficult it had become to maintain even the most vestigial respect across the Catholic-evangelical divide. With the growing numbers of Catholics in the country and the conversion of some of them to Protestantism, evangelical denominations that practiced the baptism of infants were faced with the question of how to regard the status of Catholic baptism. It offered a poignant sign of the current state of affairs when the conservative Presbyterian theologian Charles Hodge called down great wrath on his own head by defending the validity of Catholic baptism, even though that defense fully maintained Protestant arguments about the mistakes of Rome.

13. Quoted in Sister Mary Augustina (Ray), B.V.M., *American Opinion of Roman Catholicism in the Eighteenth Century* (New York: Columbia University Press, 1936), 128.
14. Billington, *Protestant Crusade*, 445–82.

Hodge was far from a crypto Catholic, since throughout his long career he regularly chastised Catholicism for what he thought were its manifest theological errors. At the same time, however, Hodge held that proper discriminations had to be made. His reasoning against the action of the Old School General Assembly in 1845, which denied the validity of Catholic baptism, is worth quoting at length, both to show the normal terms that evangelicals used in talking about Catholics and to indicate how difficult it was for even a well-respected evangelical leader to gain a hearing for even the most modest gesture of respect toward Rome:

> Baptism therefore, not being an ordinance of any particular church, but of the church catholic, and every man who professes saving truth being a member of that church, Romish baptism if administered by a man professing such truth, is Christian baptism. . . . We maintain therefore Romish baptism to be valid; that is, that it avails to make the recipient a member of the church catholic, because it is a washing with water, in the name of the Trinity, with the design to signify, seal and apply the benefits of the covenant of grace. . . . If the church of Rome is antichrist, a syna-gogue of Satan, how can its ordinances be Christian sacraments? This we doubt not is the difficulty which weighs most with those who reject Romish baptisms as invalid. We would ask such persons, whether they admit that a Roman Catholic can be a child of God? If he can, how can a man be a member of the synagogue of Satan and of the body of Christ at the same time? Is there no inconsistency here? If not, then there is no inconsistency in declaring that the Romish system, so far as it is distin-guished from that of evangelical churches, is antichristian, and yet that those who are groaning under that system are in the visible church. The terms antichrist, synagogue of Satan, etc., refer not to the mass of the people, nor to the presbyters of that communion, nor the word of God, nor the saving truths which they profess, but to the Popish hierarchy and its corruptions. That hierarchy with its usurpations and errors, is the mystery of iniquity, the man of sin, which in the church catholic, the temple of God, exalts itself above all that is called God or that is worshipped. If Roman Catholics are no part of the visible church, then the Romish hierarchy is not "the man of sin" spoken of by the apostle, for he was to rise and rule in the church. It is, therefore, one thing to denounce the Roman system, and another to say that Romanists are no part of the church catholic. And if they are in the church, their baptism being a washing with water in the name of the Trinity, is Christian baptism; just as the word of God, when read or preached by them, is still his word, and is to be received and obeyed as such.[15]

15. Charles Hodge, "The General Assembly," *Princeton Review* 17 (July 1845): 469–71. For a full statement, see Charles Hodge, "Is the Church of Rome a Part of the Visible Church?" *Princeton Review* 18 (April 1846): 320–44. More on Hodge's position and also related material for Calvin and other Reformed theologians, which was occasioned by a

The attitudes that Hodge both reflected and combated remained particularly strong among evangelicals. Even after the momentous shifts of recent decades had begun, observers noted that conservative Protestant positions were highly resistant to change. In 1978, the ethicist James Gustafson wrote that a wide range of Protestant-Catholic dialogue was under way in the United States, with the exception that "the most conservative Catholic and Protestant theologians do not relate to each other at all."[16] Gustafson may have been overstating things a little, but he was correct in concluding that many among the firmer sort of Protestants still retained much of the hereditary anti-Catholicism of traditional evangelicalism.

Religious Standoff, Civil Mistrust

As steadily as American Protestants maintained anti-Catholicism for strictly theological reasons, almost from the start of European settlement in the New World, they were just as concerned about Catholicism's civil tendencies. The reputation of Catholicism as a promoter of tyranny contributed to the first stages of the American love affair with liberty that began in earnest with the eighteenth-century colonial wars.[17] When military strife between France and England swept over the colonies, colonial Protestants immediately made fateful rhetorical connections. As propounded from countless colonial pulpits during the mid-eighteenth century, Protestants proclaimed that they were fighting for the glories of Britain against the depredations of France, the truth of Protestantism against the lies of Catholicism, and the blessings of freedom against the perils of tyranny.

Two citations, from hundreds that could be quoted, show how, even before there was a United States, American commitments to republican principles functioned as an ally of Protestantism and an enemy of Catholicism. George Whitefield, the great evangelist, was in Philadelphia in August 1746 when news arrived that Bonnie Prince Charles, the Jacobite (and Catholic) pretender to the British throne, had been decisively defeated at the battle of Culloden. Whitefield immediately preached a sermon thanking God for rescuing the British from the multiplied woes

---

fresh outbreak of anti-Catholic polemic in contemporary Scotland, is contained in John Tallach, *A Plea against Extremism: The Views of Calvin, Hodge, and Others on Some Aspects of the Roman Catholic Church* (Tain, Ross-shire: Christian Focus, 1989).

16. James M. Gustafson, *Protestant and Roman Catholic Ethics: Prospects for Rapprochement* (Chicago: University of Chicago Press, 1978), 30.

17. For an outstanding treatment of this theme, see John T. McGreevy, *Catholicism and American Freedom: A History* (New York: Norton, 2003).

of a Catholic monarchy: "How soon would our pulpits every where have been filled with these old antichristian doctrines, free-will, meriting by works, transubstantiation, purgatory, works of supererogation, passive-obedience, non-resistance, and all the other abominations of the whore of Babylon?"[18]

Ten years later, the president of the College of New Jersey at Princeton, Aaron Burr Sr., rallied his evangelical audience at the start of the French and Indian Wars with a frightful vision of France's Catholic religion:

> We have heard of the Policy and Perfidy of France, of her arbitrary Power, Popish tyranny and Bigotry. . . . If we view our Enemies, in a religious as well as political Light, we shall see the Necessity of guarding against them with all possible care. Their established religion is Popery; which, beside all its other Corruptions, disposes them from Principle, to be cruel to Protestants.[19]

Only two decades later, American colonists found proof positive that Britain was acting tyrannically when it extended civil rights and historic privileges to the Catholic Church in Quebec. Until their own self-interest became involved, New England ministers saw the act not as an overdue recognition of human rights but as an effort "to cut off all the liberties of the colonies."[20]

After the American War for Independence—and the social revolution arising from the Revolution that made liberty the heart of American ideology—evangelical anti-Romanism was given new life by the rising current of Catholic immigration into the United States. Protestant writing against Catholicism retained a vigorous theological critique, but it was almost always a political expression as well.

In fact, one of the main engines of the reform movements that galvanized American Protestants in the antebellum period was anti-Catholicism, sometimes of the rabid variety. Lyman Beecher, the whirlwind Congregationalist and Presbyterian who, in a long career, spearheaded Protestant outreach in rural Connecticut, urban Boston, and frontier

18. George Whitefield, "Britain's Mercies, and Britain's Duty, preached at Philadelphia, on Sunday, August 24, 1746, and occasioned by the suppression of the late unnatural rebellion," in George Whitefield, *Sermons on Important Subjects* (London: William Baynes, 1825), 56.

19. Aaron Burr, *A Discourse delivered at New-Ark, in New Jersey, January 1, 1755. Being a Day set apart for solemn Fasting and Prayer, on Account of the late Encroachments of the French, and their Designs against the British Colonies in America* (New York: Hugh Gaine, 1755), 16, 19.

20. John Lathrop, *A Discourse Preached December 15, 1774* (Boston), 28, quoted in Nathan O. Hatch, *The Sacred Cause of Liberty: Republican Thought and the Millennium in Revolutionary New England* (New Haven: Yale University Press, 1977), 75.

Cincinnati, often warned Americans about the threat from the Catholic Church. Historian Sydney Ahlstrom once summarized a major section of one of Beecher's most influential books, his *Plea for the West* (1834), as "a 140-page tirade which depicts the pope and Europe's reactionary kings, with the Austrian emperor at their head and Catholic immigrants for agents, as engaged in an organized conspiracy to take over the Mississippi Valley."[21]

When ideological controversy increased between North and South over the issue of slavery, northern Protestants knew how to put to use their long habit of linking Rome to tyranny. In the mid-1850s, a broadside from the American (or Know Nothing) Party tried to enlist anti-Catholic sentiment in the struggle against slavery:

> Whereas, Roman Catholicism and slavery being alike founded and supported on the basis of ignorance and tyranny; and being, therefore, natural allies in every warfare against liberty and enlightenment; therefore, be it Resolved, That there can exist no real hostility to Roman Catholicism which does not embrace slavery, its natural co-worker in opposition to freedom and republican institutions.[22]

In the two decades before the Civil War, anti-Catholicism was a political staple in shaping the political actions of many Protestants in the North as well as some in the South.[23]

In the post–Civil War period of renewed Protestant enthusiasm for the future of the reunified country, Protestants were again quick to paint Catholics as antidemocratic and antirepublican. One of the most popular works of this type, which described both the day's moral crisis as well as hope for the future, was written by the midwestern Congregationalist Josiah Strong. The fifth chapter of Strong's *Our Country* from 1885 was titled "Conflict of Romanism with the Fundamental Principle of Our Government."[24]

A sampling of Protestant book titles shows how the civic qualities of Catholicism were seen as cause for complaint in evangelical polemics. Only a few examples include N. L. Rice, *Romanism Not Christianity: A Series of Lectures in Which Popery and Protestantism Are Contrasted, Showing the Incompatibility of the Former with Freedom and Free Institu-*

21. Sydney E. Ahlstrom, *A Religious History of the American People* (New Haven: Yale University Press, 1972), 561.

22. Quoted in Billington, *Protestant Crusade*, 425.

23. See especially Richard J. Carwardine, *Evangelicals and Politics in Antebellum America* (New Haven: Yale University Press, 1993), 80–84, 199–203.

24. Josiah Strong, *Our Country: Its Possible Future and Its Present Crisis* (New York: American Home Missionary Society, 1885).

tions (Cincinnati, 1847); Thomas Bayne, *Popery Subversive of American Institutions* (Pittsburgh, 1856); Joseph Smith Van Dyke, *Popery: The Foe of the Church and of the Republic* (Philadelphia, 1871); and Jeremiah J. Crowley, *Romanism: A Menace to the Nation; Together with My Former Book, The Parochial School, a Curse to the Church, a Menace to the Nation* (Wheaton, 1912). This last volume, in a typically Protestant conjunction of values, was dedicated to "the lovers of liberty, enlightenment and progress throughout the world."

Almost universally, evangelical Protestants felt that Catholics threatened the biblically based character of American civilization. Thus, active anti-Catholicism in the nineteenth century was sparked especially by the belief that the Catholic hierarchy discouraged, or even prohibited, the use of Scripture among the laity. This belief, in turn, led to the conclusion that Catholicism was inimical to the American way of life, a conclusion set out with disarming frankness by an attorney arguing in 1887 to preserve the right of a Wisconsin school board to continue daily readings from the King James Version: "The decrees of the councils, the encyclicals of the Popes, the pastoral and other letters of the Archbishops and Bishops, and the writings of learned Catholics furnish abundant evidence that the Catholic Church is opposed to popular government, that it is opposed to liberty of conscience, and of worship, and that it is opposed to our public school system."[25] (In point of fact, Catholic objections to reading the Bible in public school usually concerned the text being used—the Protestants' King James Version—rather than the act of Bible reading itself.)

It only added fuel to Protestant fires when a few well-known figures raised as Protestants actually joined the Catholic Church. Outrage at such actions was mitigated by the observation that some of the converts—like Mrs. Sophia Ripley and Orestes Brownson—had already been tainted by earlier associations with the suspect Transcendentalist movement.[26]

In the twentieth century, evangelicals eagerly joined the general Protestant chorus, maintaining the charge that Catholicism entailed a direct threat to American freedoms. *The Fundamentals* of 1910–15, which represented mostly moderate rather than extreme forms of conservative

25. Quoted in John O. Geiger, "The Edgerton Bible Case: Humphrey Desmond's Political Education of Wisconsin Catholics," *Journal of Church and State* 20 (Winter 1978): 25. For Catholic efforts to promote Bible reading in the nineteenth century, which Protestants almost never noticed, see Gerald P. Fogarty, S.J., "The Quest for a Catholic Vernacular Bible in America," in *The Bible in America*, ed. Nathan O. Hatch and Mark A. Noll (New York: Oxford University Press, 1982), 164–69.

26. A good study of these Catholic converts is Jenny Franchot, *Roads to Rome: The Antebellum Protestant Encounter with Catholicism* (Berkeley: University of California Press, 1994).

evangelicalism, nonetheless included several stringent attacks on Rome. The contribution of Bostonian J. M. Foster was typical. His complaint was as much social and political as theological:

> [The Catholic Church is] the essential and deadly foe of civil and religious liberty. . . . The Roman hierarchy owns $300,000,000 in America. They have a parochial school system and clamorously demand a share in the public school fund. Their policy is the refinement of duplicity. They join the Jews, infidels and skeptics in driving the Bible from our public schools, on the ground that the State is only a secular corporation and has no right to teach morals and religion. . . . The answer which the organic people should return is: "This is a Christian State; the public school system is its agency for building up a Christian citizenship; morals and religion, so far as they are essential for discharging the functions of Christian citizenship, shall be taught in our public schools; and the school funds shall not be divided."[27]

As indicated by the 1960 quotations from evangelical leaders cited in the previous chapter, the charge that Catholics could not be fully American, because of their allegiance to the pope and their promotion of religious error, long influenced the way Protestants voted.[28] During the presidential elections of 1928 and 1960, when Catholic candidates Al Smith and John F. Kennedy led the Democratic ticket, interreligious suspicion ran high. Just after the election of 1960, Loraine Boettner's evangelical attack on Catholicism featured the charge that "Roman Catholicism [is] a poor defense against communism." Very near the conclusion of his book, Boettner repeated the stock evangelical assertion that "in general it [the Catholic Church] has sought to weaken or destroy free governments."[29]

In sum, the fixed Protestant opinion was that Catholicism was such a flawed version of Christianity that it was hardly Christian at all. In the United States, moreover, evangelical Protestants were full participants in arguing that Catholicism not only was a religious threat but also subverted the free political institutions of the United States. Well after World War II, the anti-Catholic polemic went on. Into the late 1950s, almost no one could have predicted that change was in the air.

27. J. M. Foster, "Rome: The Antagonist of the Nation," *The Fundamentals: A Testimony to the Truth*, 4 vols. (Grand Rapids: Baker, 1972), 3:301, 313–14.

28. See Lyman A. Kellstedt and Mark A. Noll, "Religion, Voting for President, and Party Identification, 1948–1984," in *Religion and American Politics*, ed. Mark A. Noll (New York: Oxford University Press, 1990), 361–62, 374–75.

29. Boettner, *Roman Catholicism*, 7, 459.

Signs of Peace during Times of War

Before sketching evangelical attitudes as they existed shortly before the unexpected developments of the 1960s, it is helpful to pause for another series of historical snapshots. Especially for those interested in recent changes, it is possible to find minority opinions scattered throughout the centuries since the Council of Trent that undercut the unanimity of suspicion. They have now an even greater significance than when they were first expressed.

Strife, in fact, was never the only reality in Catholic-Protestant exchange, even though it certainly was predominant. Simply noting that, even in the centuries of intense controversy, an occasional Catholic could commend an occasional Protestant, and vice versa, is to catch hints as to why Catholic-evangelical communication could blossom so rapidly after the 1960s. The key seems to have been that when "the other" manifested something self-evidently Christian (though not necessarily in the shape prescribed by the opposing party), polemics could give way to dialogue and even mutual edification. Enough of these moments pop up without looking for them that a thorough search for Catholic-Protestant engagement, even in the darkest years of strife, might yield many more edifying exceptions than the image of total war suggests.

An early instance of such an exemption was the Council of Regensburg in 1541. Remarkably, the Catholic and Protestant leaders assembled at that meeting actually reached an agreement on the contentious issue of justification by faith. This agreement stated that God's free grace was, strictly considered, the only foundation for the salvation of sinners, but also that it was wrong to separate justifying faith from works of love. Not all on both sides thought this was a breakthrough, but John Calvin (though expressing what had already become a standard anti-Catholic attitude) could yet point out that something significant had occurred:

> You will marvel [Calvin wrote to William Farel] when you read the copy [of the article on justification] . . . that our adversaries have conceded so much. For they have committed themselves to the essentials of what is our true teaching. Nothing is to be found in it which does not stand in our writings. I know that you would prefer a more explicit exposition and in this you are at one with myself. But if you consider with what sort of men we have to deal, you will acknowledge that a great deal has been achieved.[30]

Also in those early years, even when Roman Catholics and the early Protestants were engaged in their most brutal debates, leaders of both

30. Quoted in Matheson, *Cardinal Contarini at Regensburg*, 109.

sides continued to draw on the Christian insight of exemplary theologians from the Catholic Middle Ages such as Bernard of Clairvaux, Thomas à Kempis, and, above all, Augustine. Calvin, for example, quoted (almost always favorably) from eleven different works by Bernard of Clairvaux in his *Institutes of the Christian Religion,* and the American edition of Martin Luther's works contains generally positive use of twenty works by Bernard.[31]

Somewhat later, a long line of Protestants found inspiration in the bracing Christian vision of Blaise Pascal (1623–62), who was treasured for both his attacks on the Jesuits and his positive Christian statements. Evangelicals, to be sure, avoided the aspects of Pascal's writings that expressed his distinctly Catholic convictions, but Pascal nevertheless remained a favorite of many, including the seventeenth-century Puritan Theophilus Gale and the eighteenth-century awakeners George White-field, John Newton, Jonathan Edwards, and Charles and John Wesley.[32] In 1739, when Charles Wesley was taken to task by his fellow Protestant, Dean Conybeare of Christ Church, Oxford, he urged the dean to read the Catholic Pascal, among other authors, as a means for understanding "justification by faith" and "vital religion."[33]

Charles's brother, John, presents an even more interesting case of mixed attitudes toward Catholicism. This Wesley, who associated Pascal with the evangelical emphases outlined in Henry Scougall's seventeenth-century Scottish devotional classic *The Life of God in the Soul of Man,* was on occasion remarkably sanguine about Catholicism. Less than a year before his death, he wrote in 1790 to a nephew who had become a Catholic but who was now slipping away from all religion. To Wesley, the brand name was far less important than that the nephew practice the faith:

> What do you want [i.e., lack]? Not clothes or books or money. If you did, I should soon supply you. But I fear you want (what you least of all suspect), the greatest thing of all—religion. I do not mean external religion, but the religion of the heart; the religion which Kempis, Pascal, Fénelon enjoyed: that life of God in the soul of man, the walking with God and having fellowship with the Father and the Son.[34]

31. John Calvin, *Institutes of the Christian Religion,* 2 vols., ed. John T. McNeill, trans. Ford Lewis Battles (Philadelphia: Westminster, 1960), 2:1601; and Joel W. Lundeen, ed., *Luther's Works,* vol. 55, index (Philadelphia: Fortress, 1986), 27–28.

32. John Barker, *Strange Contrarieties: Pascal in England during the Age of Reason* (Montreal: McGill-Queen's University Press, 1975), 17 (Gale), 186 (Whitefield), 191 (John Newton), 181–95 (the Wesleys). On Jonathan Edwards's reading of Pascal, see Norman Fiering, *Jonathan Edwards's Moral Thought and Its British Context* (Chapel Hill: University of North Carolina Press, 1981), 176.

33. Barker, *Strange Contrarieties,* 185.

34. Ibid., 191.

Earlier, in 1749, Wesley had written *A Letter to a Roman Catholic*, in which he expressed the hope that, even if Protestants and Catholics maintained their sharpest disagreements, they might in the future avoid the abominable polemics of the past. Those polemics, in his view, showed "brotherly love . . . utterly destroyed." When they take place, "each side, looking on the other as monsters, gives way to anger, hatred, malice, to every unkind affection; which have frequently broke out in such inhuman barbarities as are scarce named among the Heathens." To Wesley, at this time, it was of first importance not that Catholics leave their church but that they "follow after that fear and love of God without which all religion is vain. I say not a word to you about your opinions or outward manner of worship."[35] A few years later Wesley translated for the benefit of his itinerants the tract of a pious French Jansenist from the early eighteenth century, which led him to observe, "What a multitude of wrong opinions are embraced by all the members of the Church of Rome? Yet how highly favoured have many of them been!"[36]

To remember that Wesley was still very much a Protestant of his age, it is necessary to recall that he wrote several works designed to refute Catholic understandings of Christianity, including one that he published to show "how far that church hath erred from truth and reason."[37] Especially during his many trips to largely Catholic Ireland, Wesley displayed a much more traditional anti-Catholicism. But even in Ireland, though much more in England and Wales, he was moved to play down traditional Catholic-Protestant differences in order to promote the practice of what he often called "true Christianity" marked by faith in Christ and resolute good works.[38]

As evangelicals have borrowed from the reasoning of Pascal, they have also embraced with affection the Catholic mystical tradition of François Fénelon (1651–1715) and Madam Guyon (1648–1717). When the Holiness preacher Thomas Upham published a life of Madam Guyon in the mid-nineteenth century, denomination was far less important to him than that Fénelon and Guyon had rightly proclaimed "the doctrine of pure or unselfish love, in the experience of which . . . the sanctification

35. John Wesley, *A Letter to a Roman Catholic* (1749), in *The Works of John Wesley*, 14 vols., ed. Thomas Jackson (London: Wesleyan Conference Office, 1872), 10:80, 83.

36. John Wesley, February 27, 1768, in *The Works of John Wesley*, vol. 22, *Journals and Diaries V (1765–1775)*, ed. W. Reginald Ward and Richard P. Heitzenrater (Nashville: Abingdon, 1993), 120.

37. John Wesley, *A Roman Catechism, faithfully drawn out of the allowed writings of the Church of Rome: with a Reply thereto*, in *The Works of John Wesley*, 3rd ed., vol. 10, *Letters, Essays, Dialogs, and Addresses* (Grand Rapids: Baker, 1996), 86–128 (quotation on 128).

38. See David Hempton and Myrtle Hill, *Evangelical Protestantism in Ulster Society, 1740–1890* (London: Routledge, 1992), 8; and Henry D. Rack, *Reasonable Enthusiast: John Wesley and the Rise of Methodism* (Philadelphia: Trinity Press, 1989), 309–12.

of the heart essentially consists."[39] Throughout the twentieth century, even in decades of intense interreligious strife, evangelical Protestant publishers, more than any others, kept the works of these Catholic mystics alive.[40]

A surprising number of others, from both sides of the polemical divide, multiplied instances of truce. In the mid-nineteenth century, the unselfish character and faithful Christian commitment of François Guizot, a notable historian and statesman of Huguenot Protestant conviction, became so much admired in some Catholic circles that a solidly Roman periodical from Munich could publish a glowing transdenominational tribute: "Guizot is a Christian, through and through. Although Protestant, he judges events and personalities in Catholic regions with such fairness—with such insight—that one is often astonished. And it makes one ask almost instinctively how it could be possible that this man, for whom religion is so important, still remains outside of the church?"[41]

Another century later, the evangelical Protestant historian Kenneth Scott Latourette enjoyed unusually good relations with Catholics. During his long tenure at Yale, Latourette was notable both as a scholar and as a discipler of young men for evangelical missionary service. The cordial reception of his pioneering *History of Christian Missions in China* (1929) by Catholics, among whom he had done some of the research for the volume, began a long and friendly relationship that lasted until his death many decades later. Latourette was especially pleased to discover that this book, all 930 pages of it, had been read aloud at meals to the students at the Catholic missionary seminary in Maryknoll, New York. During work on that volume, he also became friends with Father John J. Considine, whom Latourette described as "a priest of complete commitment to Christ." Some years later he entered into "a compact of prayer" with a Belgian priest and continued to nurture a wide range of Catholic friendships. When Latourette, as president of the American Historical Association, delivered his presidential address in 1949, "The Christian Understanding of History," many of his listeners "were disgusted" and reportedly groused that if they wanted to hear a sermon they would go to church. By contrast, "the Catholic priests who were present rushed up and said, 'The theology was perfect.'" With his broad interests in the

39. Thomas C. Upham, *Life and Religious Opinions and Experience of Madame de la Mothe Guyon: Together with Some Account of the Personal History and Religious Opinions of Fénelon, Archbishop of Cambray* (New York: Harper & Brothers, 1846), vi.

40. See especially Patricia A. Ward, "Madame Guyon and Experiential Theology in America," *Church History* 67 (September 1998): 484–98.

41. Karl von Moy de Sons, "Liberalen Katholiken und conservativen Protestanten zur Beherzigung," *Historich-politische Blätter für das katholische Deutschland* 58 (1866): 31.

spread of Christianity around the world, Latourette succeeded in avoiding most of his era's still active Catholic-evangelical antagonisms.[42]

When searching for moments of eased Catholic-Protestant tension, it is even possible to find a few episodes when the hereditary Protestant mistrust of Catholic political influence was set aside. Surprisingly, in light of how strongly anti-Catholicism contributed to the Puritan tradition in New England, events during the unfolding of the American Revolution created just such a moment.[43] When an American patriot army led by New Englanders invaded Quebec in late 1775 and early 1776, many French-Canadian habitants welcomed the invaders. When they did so, the New Englanders—despite historic suspicion of all Catholics—responded warmly in return. The shift of attitudes was never total, especially for New England clergymen who accompanied the troops or who commented on their movement into Canada. But with a rapidity especially surprising in light of the intense anti-Catholicism generated by the Parliament's Quebec Act of 1774, the prospect of incorporating Quebec into the new United States defused much of New England's historic anti-Catholicism, at least for the short term. Also during this same war, the patriots' alliance with France, which was established in February 1778 and which eventually led to the conclusive American victory at Yorktown in 1781, resulted in another case when political necessity moderated strong anti-Catholic and anti-French traditions. These political emergencies did not completely overwhelm residual Protestant antagonism, which returned powerfully when more and more Catholic immigrants began to arrive in the new United States. But at least for the short term, political alliances were trumping Catholic-Protestant suspicion. When Boston's first Roman Catholic parish was established in 1788, it had a much easier course in its earlier years than would have been the case without the political-religious history of the Revolution.

Finally, it is appropriate to note that, in more reflective moments, even battered veterans of the Catholic-Protestant wars could view the struggle above the battle lines. So it was with John Henry Newman, who, though raised an evangelical Anglican, became the most famous English convert to Catholicism in the nineteenth century.[44] Late in his life, after decades of sharp polemic with Protestants, an acquaintance from deep in his past,

42. Kenneth Scott Latourette, *Beyond the Ranges: An Autobiography* (Grand Rapids: Eerdmans, 1967), 78–79, 110–15 (quotations from 78, 112, 115).

43. This paragraph is dependent on Charles B. Hanson, *Necessary Virtue: The Pragmatic Origins of Religious Liberty in New England* (Charlottesville: University Press of Virginia, 1998).

44. A probing if controversial account of Newman's early career as dominated by evangelical and then anti-evangelical motives is Frank M. Turner, *John Henry Newman: The Challenge to Evangelical Religion* (New Haven: Yale University Press, 2002).

the evangelical Edward Bickersteth, sent Newman the copy of a poem he had written on the last judgment. Newman's reply spoke for a reality that may have been more common than antagonists were usually prepared to acknowledge: "I can but bow before the great mystery that those are divided here and look for the means of grace and glory in such different directions, who have so much in common in faith and hope."[45]

Beyond question, disengagement and polemic were the prevailing moods of evangelical-Catholic relationship in the four centuries before 1960. It may just be, however, that beneath the alarums of battle, even in the days of war, there existed voices that, could they only have been heard, might have heralded the changes that have now come to pass.

On the Eve of Change

In the fall of 1953, Catholic protests against the Martin Luther movie produced by Lothar Wolff and Protestant responses to those protests gave national media an occasion to highlight the ongoing tension between Protestants and Catholics.[46] Evangelicals, many of whom still shunned the cinema as worldly entertainment, paid only passing attention to contentions over the Luther film. But as a survey of leading evangelical periodicals from that period shows, public debate about a movie was not required to keep evangelical suspicion of Roman Catholicism at a high level. Sampling from three widely circulated magazines—the *Sunday School Times, Moody Monthly,* and *Eternity*—provides a flavor of prevailing evangelical attitudes.[47]

The most extensive attention to Roman Catholicism in the *Sunday School Times* during the autumn of 1953 was provided by a five-part article on "Charles Chiniquy—Apostle of Temperance." Chiniquy (1809–99) had been ordained as a Catholic priest in his native Quebec, became active as a temperance advocate, moved to Illinois to serve the expatriate Quebec community there, and then converted to evangelical Protestantism and embarked upon a long career as a Protestant temperance advocate and anti-Catholic crusader. These articles passed on Chiniquy's own (absurd) claim that the Catholic Church played a role in the assassination of Abraham Lincoln. The fact that Chiniquy's own missteps were as responsible for his alienation from the Catholic Church as his change of theological opinions was never mentioned. The articles fea-

45. Quoted in Sheridan Gilley, *Newman and His Age* (Westminster, MD: Christian Classics, 1990), 372.
46. For samples, see *New York Times*, September 10, 1953, 22; and September 12, 1953, 13.
47. Our thanks to Peter Swarr for compiling this material.

tured, rather, Chiniquy's statement about why he left Catholicism: "My Church was the deadly, the irreconcilable enemy of the Word of God, as I had often suspected! I was not allowed to remain a single day longer in that Church without positively giving up the Gospel of Christ!"[48]

Other Catholic-related stories from that fall included a news item about a French bishop who urged the faithful to pray to Mary as their Mother, a short article linking a Catholic church in Cleveland with the infernal liquor traffic, and another news item about the Paulist fathers, who maintained an office in Boston, "where the net is spread for Unitarian and Episcopalian members of old Boston families."[49] A lengthy article, reporting on dissatisfaction among Catholic laypeople and priests in France, concluded that many of them were following prominent ex-Catholics such as Angel Béart in embracing the Bible and becoming Protestants as they sought the truth they could not find in "the Roman Institution." According to the *Sunday School Times*, "the Institution will not let itself be reformed save in a few diplomatic changes in the Roman Curia, some modifications of rubric, or in the disappearance of some outmoded ecclesiastical garment. The wind of the Spirit does not blow over the Seven Hills."[50]

The viewpoint was similar in *Moody Monthly*, which in December 1953 carried a substantial news story about a Protestant family in Colombia. The father was "murdered by Roman Catholic fanatics," and the mother was losing her children because of her Protestant faith. The next issue editorialized on the problem by noting how the Vatican was conspiring with the Colombian government in "an underhanded attempt to suppress religious liberty."[51] Also in December the magazine printed a letter from a reader who, while praising the magazine for its efforts at "ferreting out the Reds [Communists]" in liberal Protestant churches, warned that this effort may be "playing into the hands of the Roman Catholic system" by drawing attention away from the more serious evils worked by Rome.[52] At least in these months, *Moody Monthly* was reflecting the

48. George Hugh Seville, "Charles Chiniquy—Apostle of Temperance," *Sunday School Times*, September 26, October 3, October 10, October 24, and October 31, 1953, 815–16, 839–40, 870–71, 909–10, 928–29, 940 (quotation from 909). For a modern and more balanced treatment, see Richard Lougheed, *La Conversion Controversée de Charles Chiniquy: Prêtre Catholique devenu Protestant* (Quebec: La Clairière, 1999).

49. News item, *Sunday School Times*, August 8, 1953, 682; "The Busy Men's Corner" (liquor traffic), *Sunday School Times*, October 10, 1953, 874–75; and news item, *Sunday School Times*, November 29, 1953, 981.

50. Ernest Gordon, "Ferment in French Catholicism," *Sunday School Times*, October 24, 1953, 905–6, 910; and October 31, 1953, 925–26, 941 (quotation from 926).

51. "This Happened in Colombia," *Moody Monthly*, December 1953, 38; and "How Catholic Is Colombia," *Moody Monthly*, January 1954, 9.

52. Pastor George G. Nika, "Chance for Misunderstanding?" *Moody Monthly*, December 1953, 4.

widespread evangelical concern about the Catholic civil threat as much as long-standing concerns about doctrinal errors.

Articles in *Eternity*, under the editorial direction of the formidable Donald Grey Barnhouse, presented the only nuance to be found in this quick survey of evangelical periodicals, though compared to what came short years later, the nuance was modest. In September 1953, a longtime missionary to Korea who was then serving as a chaplain to U.S. forces published a lengthy article on the Catholic chaplains with whom he was working. This evangelical had positive things to say about the German Benedictines he had known in Korea and also acknowledged that some of the Catholics' short "talks" on subjects such as "the deity of Christ, the cross, the Holy Spirit, etc." would work well, if expanded, as Protestant sermons. But for the rest, all was negative: The priests were not interested in evangelism, even those who had been in Korea for several years spoke the language poorly, they never read anything apart from their breviaries, and they would recite only the psalms (in Latin!) when called upon for extempore prayers. Most of all, the priests in Korea suffered from the stultifying constraints of their own church:

> It is this constant self-intoxication with the divinity of the church organization, the finality of their neatly-packaged doctrine, and the necessity of opposing any and all who question in the tiniest detail their authoritative custody of the truth, that precludes a Catholic from a quiet and calm Biblical or theological discussion with anyone who differs from him. . . . The low ethical standards of Catholicism, the condoning of drunkenness and other inconsistencies, and the simplicity of quieting one's conscience at the confessional, make it "easy" for a Catholic to be "religious." It presents a tempting appeal for the unlearned, but it is essentially unsatisfying, and a virile Gospel confirmed by holy lives, I am convinced, will lead many spiritually-hungry Catholics out into the light and liberty of Christ.[53]

Other *Eternity* articles reflected this same stance: a willingness to acknowledge some positive aspects of contemporary Catholicism but only within the larger context of profound suspicion. Thus, it may have been good for Catholic churches in North Carolina and Mississippi to integrate their services, but the major reason for reporting such stories in the magazine was concern about the number of African Americans who might be drawn to Rome.[54] The magazine praised the Catholic Church in France for promulgating a new code of professional standards

---

53. Harold Voelkel, "My Roman Catholic Partners," *Eternity*, September 1953, 16–17, 35.

54. "Non-segregation Policy," and "Negro Bishop Consecrated," *Eternity*, August 1953, 19, 35.

for Catholic journalists yet worried about those "parts of the statement
. . . which express the supreme absolutism and final authority of the
church, and the expression is in the arrogant tone which usually carries such claims."[55] Another story is unusually interesting in light of
later pro-life coalitions between Catholics and evangelicals. While the
magazine applauded the principles expressed by fifty-three Roman
Catholic organizations that resigned from the New York Welfare and
Health Council when that council admitted Planned Parenthood as a
member, it also opined that it was probably a good thing for the council
to be rid of such Catholic influences.[56]

In sum, although hints could be found about a more discriminating
approach by evangelicals to Catholicism, this sampling of attitudes from
the mid-1950s demonstrates the overwhelmingly negative stance that
evangelicals then maintained toward Rome. The fact that reports of the
worst Catholic evils, such as persecution of Protestants in Colombia,
rested on well-ascertained facts was all the proof needed to maintain
the evangelical indictment of a church that in its arrogance, despotism,
and callousness toward the gospel would never change.

55. "Code for Journalists," *Eternity*, August 1953, 16.
56. "Catholic Pull Out," *Eternity*, October 1953, 13.

3

WHY DID THINGS CHANGE?

In retrospect, evangelical opinions from the 1950s were mistaken about two important matters. First, even before the Second Vatican Council, the Roman Catholic Church was far from a monolith. Though joined in fellowship with the pope, Catholic churches were not the same throughout the world. The German Benedictines in Korea, whom the *Sunday School Times* commended with a few words of backhanded praise, represented a local version of Catholicism very different from the harsh church-state hegemony exercised by Catholics in Colombia. Second, the Catholic Church could in fact change.

But why did changes occur in the Catholic Church and then between Catholics and evangelicals? The final answer to this question must be that God willed the changes to take place. But here, as usual, the role of divine providence with respect to ordinary human events is mysterious, or subject to radically different interpretations. It is, therefore, appropriate to consider the level of events where documentation, public testimony, and observation of circumstances offer clues. Lengthy books have already been written in an effort to probe the historical mysteries of the recent past, and many more will follow. Here our efforts are more modest. We hope to provide a few suggestions as to why, over the course of only a few years, camps of warring Christians who for centuries had been hurling anathemas at each other began to interact more positively, why once implacable enemies began to edge toward new relationships.

59

To organize a rapidly changing history, it is useful to group developments into several general categories, although no simple division corresponds to what individuals and churches actually experienced. For the sake of simplifying, we can point to changes within the Catholic Church, changes in world Christianity, changes in American politics and society, changes in the exercise of personal agency, and changes within evangelicalism.

Changes within the Catholic Church

Most important was the Second Vatican Council of 1962–65, which was convened by Pope John XXIII (1958–63) but which he did not live to see completed. Those few evangelicals who in the early 1960s hoped for something better from Rome were given much to ponder by the council, including its willingness to address non-Catholic Christians as "brothers," to acknowledge that blame lay on both sides for the ecclesiastical ruptures of the Reformation, to stress the unique role of Christ as mediator between God and humanity, and to urge ordinary lay Catholics to live lives of practical Christian holiness.[1] When considering much of the ink spilled in later decades, it may be asked how many evangelicals were actually paying attention to what was happening in Rome during the early 1960s. But for those who were, most could concede, as David Wells put it in 1972, that the council's "change of mind in matters as . . . fundamental as revelation, the relation of the natural and the supernatural, salvation and doctrines of the Church and papal authority has rendered the vast majority of Protestant analysis of Catholic doctrine obsolete. It has also placed on Protestants an obligation to revise their thinking about Rome."[2]

David Wells's own conclusion was that the council opened Catholicism to greater influence from Scripture and more concentration on Christ-centered faith but also to greater influence from theological liberalism and less emphasis on Christ as the unique author of salvation. Writing in 1972, Wells wondered which of several forces would win out in the church, for he saw parties of scriptural renewal, theological liberalism, traditional papalism, engaged social action, and Rome-centered bureaucracy all taking heart from the council's deliberations. From a Protestant perspective early in the twenty-first century, it would seem as if the pontificates of Paul VI (1963–78) and John Paul II (1978–) have

1. We are here abridging the helpful summary in Cecil M. Robeck Jr., "Evangelicals and Catholics Together," in *Catholics and Evangelicals: Do They Share a Common Future?* ed. Thomas P. Rausch (Downers Grove, IL: InterVarsity, 2000), 23–24.

2. David F. Wells, *Revolution in Rome* (Downers Grove, IL: InterVarsity, 1972), 117.

given an advantage to the parties of tradition and scriptural renewal but also that all of the party groupings energized by the council—and more—continue to be active in the church.

Relations between Catholics and evangelicals represent a subset of a much larger reorientation of inter-Christian relationships. Ripple effects from the new ecumenical spirit promoted by Pope John XXIII were not long in coming. Even before he convened the council in 1962, the pope had sent Catholic observers to the 1960 assembly of the World Council of Churches in New Delhi and had established in the Vatican a Secretariat for Promoting Christian Unity. In the wake of the council's *Decree on Ecumenicism,* which "commends this work to the bishops everywhere in the world for their diligent and prudent guidance," the Conference of American Bishops in November 1964 set up its own Ecumenical Commission. This agency, in turn, sponsored subcommissions that soon were deep in discussion with the Orthodox Church in the United States and several of the major Protestant denominations.[3] Of these meetings, the American—and then worldwide—discussions between Lutherans and Catholics produced the richest fruit, with a series of agreements on the Nicene Creed, baptism, the Eucharist, and, most importantly, justification by faith. The American dialogue on justification (final report published in 1985) contributed to the ongoing deliberations of the Lutheran World Federation and the Vatican, which in 1999 culminated in "The Joint Declaration on the Doctrine of Justification."[4]

Although the Catholic Church has never joined either the National Council of Churches or the World Council of Churches, it takes an active observer's role in the deliberations of these bodies. Moreover, it has become a member of the National Council's Commission on Faith and Order, an agency whose staff now regularly includes Catholics.[5]

3. John B. Sheerin, "American Catholics and Ecumenism," in *Contemporary Catholicism in the United States,* ed. Philip Gleason (Notre Dame: University of Notre Dame Press, 1969), 75–78. The texts from these discussions are collected in Harding Meyer and Lukas Vischer, eds., *Growth in Agreement: Reports and Agreed Statements of Ecumenical Conversations on a World Level* (New York: Paulist Press, 1984); and Jeffrey Gros, Harding Meyer, and William G. Rusch, eds., *Growth in Agreement II: Reports and Agreed Statements of Ecumenical Conversations on a World Level, 1982–1998* (Grand Rapids: Eerdmans, 2000; Geneva: World Council of Churches, 2000). Our interpretation of these dialogues is found in chapter 4.

4. Completed American "Dialogues," as published by Augsburg Press in Minneapolis, include *The Status of the Nicene Creed as Dogma of the Church* (1965), *One Baptism for the Remission of Sins* (1965), *The Eucharist as Sacrifice* (1967), *Eucharist and Ministry* (1970), *Papal Primacy and the Universal Church* (1974), *Teaching Authority and Infallibility in the Church* (1980), *Justification by Faith* (1985), and *The One Mediator, the Saints, and Mary* (1992). The report on justification is discussed below in chapter 4.

5. "Faith and Order U.S.A.," pamphlet from the National Council of the Churches of Christ in the U.S.A. (n.d.).

Catholic-Protestant discussions, instructions, debates, and dialogue are now a regular feature at nearly all major interfaith forums on almost every imaginable issue.

The new interest in ecumenicity reflects even deeper changes in the Catholic Church since the 1960s. The council's focus on the importance of the laity as "the people of God" has made at least some parts of the church's structure and some aspects of its day-to-day life less clerical and ecclesiastical. Emphasis on the privileges of all Christians in living out the gospel has encouraged ordinary Catholics to be more active in public worship, private devotion, evangelization, and service to the world. As a result, the last decades have witnessed a bewildering array of local Catholic initiatives—Bible studies, workshops for peace, coalitions for the right to life, base communities practicing a theology of liberation (especially in Latin America), masses with guitars and contemporary music, traditional masses in Latin, and on and on. To outsiders, these developments look like a Catholic acceptance of some aspects of the Protestant emphasis on the priesthood of all believers, though Catholic insiders can explain how the newer tendencies grew from long-standing, though hitherto obscure, elements of Catholic tradition.

Since 1978, the papal leadership of John Paul II has also reflected significant changes in the Catholic Church.[6] Although Catholics debate among themselves whether this pope is bringing to fulfillment or violating the spirit of the council, outsiders note that his great range of activities would have been much more difficult to execute without the general loosening that followed the council. The pope has pioneered in ecumenical activity, especially with the Orthodox Church and Jews. He has acted boldly in support of religious and civic freedom, at first with attention fixed on his native Poland and the rest of the communist world but then as a worldwide priority. He has traveled incessantly, particularly to the two-thirds world, where the bulk of the Catholic faithful now live. He has published encyclicals of an intellectual gravity all but unprecedented in the pronouncements of modern public figures; even those who disagree with what the pope has said in these encyclicals must acknowledge that he has addressed a remarkably broad set of concerns and analyzed them with extraordinary depth.

In his own mind, John Paul II has followed the guidelines for church renewal outlined by the Second Vatican Council. Later historians and theologians will certainly express their own judgments on the relationship between the council and John Paul II's pontificate. For our purposes,

6. See George Weigel, *Witness to Hope: The Biography of Pope John Paul II* (New York: HarperCollins, 1999); as well as the plethora of reports in 2003 assessing the twenty-five-year tenure of the pope.

however, it is enough to see that the jolt administered to the church by the council led to dramatic innovations, dramatic initiatives, and dramatic contests within Roman Catholicism over the future of the church—and also to dramatically altered relations with Protestant evangelicals.

Changes in World Christianity

Increasingly obvious changes in the worldwide circumstances of Christianity have also played a role in altering the once apparently fixed gulf between Catholics and evangelicals. In the first instance, the shift to the south in the center of gravity for world Christianity has relativized the antagonism inherited from European church history.[7] The rapid, recent expansion of Christianity in Africa, Asia, and the Pacific—combined with the ferment of renewal in the Americas and the rapid decline of historic Christendom in Europe—has pushed Catholic-evangelical relationships into unknown territory. European Christendom—or the organic society created by historic links between one magisterial church and an entire society—necessitated a certain degree of intolerance to other faiths. But as Christianity—whether Catholic, Protestant, or indigenous—spreads beyond the borders of European Christendom, there is no platform or cause for intolerance.[8]

To be sure, where the weight of traditional European divisions, with attendant civil and political tensions, remains strong (mostly in Latin America and southern Europe), Catholic-evangelical relations remain cool. Where traditional European forms are now thoroughly intermixed with post-Christendom realities (North America and parts of Africa and Asia), Catholic-evangelical relations are cordial, if still cautious. Where traditional European Christendom is only a vague reference to an unexperienced past (most of Africa, Asia, and the Pacific), Catholic-evangelical relations are much more relaxed.

The missiologist and scholar of Islam, Lamin Sanneh, has pointed out how Africa's first Anglican bishop, the evangelical Samuel Ajayi Crowther

7. On that shift, see Andrew F. Walls, *The Missionary Movement in Christian History* (Maryknoll, NY: Orbis, 1996); Dana Robert, "Shifting Southward: Global Christianity since 1945," *International Bulletin of Missionary Research* (April 2000): 50–58; Philip Jenkins, *The Next Christendom: The Coming of Global Christianity* (New York: Oxford University Press, 2002); Andrew F. Walls, *The Cross-Cultural Process in Christian History* (Maryknoll, NY: Orbis, 2002); and Lamin Sanneh, *Whose Religion Is Christianity? The Gospel beyond the West* (Grand Rapids: Eerdmans, 2003).

8. On that spread and with specific attention to Christian conditions beyond Christendom, see David Martin, *Pentecostalism: The World Their Parish* (Oxford: Blackwell, 2002).

(1806?–91), could establish friendly relations with Catholics in the Niger River region at a time when such friendships were nearly impossible in Europe.[9] The ecumenical bridgehead represented by Crowther's kind of evangelicalism has broadened considerably as Crowther's kind of evangelicalism has come to make up an ever-increasing portion of the Protestant world.

An interesting recent illustration of how Crowther's relative unconcern about Catholic-evangelical distinctives has developed is provided by a Nigerian Dominican, Chika-Odinaka, who recently published a substantial booklet titled *Catholic and Born Again*. The burden of Chika-Odinaka's argument is twofold: First, the Catholic Church needs more of what the charismatic movement has brought to worldwide Christianity, and, second, Catholics who have received the special gifts of the Holy Spirit should stay in that communion to move it more rapidly in a charismatic direction. To this charismatic Dominican, the Catholic Church "is in need of a new evangelization," because "within her are many who have been merely 'sacramentalized' [who] . . . now need to become 'spiritualized.'" And he prays for an infusion into the Catholic Church of "priests holy and humble . . . men whose only credentials—divine accreditation—like the Lord Jesus, would be miracles, signs and wonders (Acts 2:22)."[10] Entirely absent from the pamphlet is the sense that anything could be amiss with incorporating a pure dose of Protestant-birthed charismatic Christianity into the Catholic Church.[11]

As Chika-Odinaka's testimony suggests, a second worldwide Christian development that has eased the way for Catholic-evangelical connection is the charismatic movement.[12] Even before the Second Vatican Council, charismatic practices and even organizations such as the Full Gospel Business Men's Fellowship International were bringing together increasing numbers of Catholics and evangelicals. Charismatic renewal

9. Sanneh, *Whose Religion Is Christianity?* 90.

10. Chika-Odinaka, *Catholic and Born Again* (Lagos, Nigeria: Oracle Books, 1997), 35, 40.

11. Other examples of Catholic-evangelical cooperation in contemporary Africa include a successful joint contribution made toward ending the Angolan civil war and a jointly sponsored prayer initiative for peace in Liberia. On the efforts of the Inter-Ecclesiastic Committee for Peace in Angola, see Ofeibea Quist-Arcton, "AAGM: We Must 'Disarm Our Minds,' Says Church Leader," *Financial Times Information—Global News Wire*, June 21, 2002; and "Concrete Action Required to Skip the Emergency," *Africa News*, February 18, 2002.

12. For surveys, see Donald Bloesch, *The Future of Evangelical Christianity: A Call for Unity amid Diversity* (New York: Doubleday, 1983), 38–42; Robeck, "Evangelicals and Catholics Together," 24–25; and Peter Hocken, *The Spirit of Unity: How Renewal Is Breaking Down Barriers between Evangelicals and Roman Catholics* (Cambridge: Grove Books, 2001).

blurred lines of distinction between Protestants and Catholics as they sang common worship songs, spoke in tongues, developed a "personal relationship with Jesus," and praised God together. Beginning in 1960 at St. Mark's Episcopal Church in Van Nuys, California, the movement continued through the 1960s mostly in mainline Protestant churches but less often among evangelical groups. Then in early 1967, a prayer group of faculty and students at Pittsburgh's Duquesne University, a Catholic school, experienced similar manifestations of God's Spirit. Ralph Keifer, a lay instructor in the department of theology at Duquesne, became convinced that this experience of Pentecost-like gifts made him a better Catholic. He visited Catholic friends at Notre Dame and Michigan State University, where there had been a similar Pentecostal outpouring. In the summer of 1967, three thousand Catholic students from all over the country gathered at Notre Dame. The Catholic charismatic renewal was born. In 1975, twenty-five thousand Catholics gathered for Pentecostal conferences sponsored by the Word of God community at the University of Michigan. From Rome, Pope Paul VI spoke his appreciation.[13] Just as the first Pentecost of Acts 2 drew together God-fearing Jews, Galileans, Greeks, Africans, and Arabs, the new charismatic movement blurred the barriers of Protestant-Catholic demarcation as participants together followed the wind of the Spirit.

Especially important for eroding old barriers and building new bridges were the new music, affective worship, and expressive spirituality that the charismatic movement unleashed over huge tracts of both evangelical and Catholic terrain. As only one indication of this dynamic at work, a trip to Lourdes in France was organized for mainline Protestants from the western United States. When the group arrived at this very Catholic pilgrimage site, the evangelicals among the American Protestants felt immediately at home because they knew almost all of the worship songs that the Catholic pilgrims to Lourdes were singing. The languages were different—French, English, other European tongues—but the music, of broadly charismatic origin, was the same.[14] More generally, charismatic emphasis on the direct work of the Holy Spirit has made doctrine, traditional church practices, and inherited authority structures less prominent among Catholic and evangelical charismatics but also among the much broader circles that have been touched in some way by charismatic influences.

13. Donald W. Sweeting, "From Conflict to Cooperation? Changing American Evangelical Attitudes towards Roman Catholics: 1960–1998" (Ph.D. diss., Trinity Evangelical Divinity School, 1998), 166–75.
14. Related in conversation to Mark Noll, spring 1998.

Evangelical youth movements, which are organized to reach specific Christian but not ecclesiastical goals, have also promoted positive interactions between Catholics and evangelicals. To take an example that speaks for many, YWAM (Youth with a Mission), which was founded in 1950, at first took for granted that Catholics were uniformly unbelievers in need of evangelization. Today, YWAM works with Catholics cooperatively in many countries, and as of 1994, its Irish staff was three-fourths Catholic.[15] Similar contacts between Catholics and evangelicals have developed on American college campuses, where, for example, workers for InterVarsity Christian Fellowship now cooperate in some localities with their Catholic counterparts. These contacts were not necessarily sought deliberately but developed as campus workers discovered that their goals, strategies, and practices were sometimes making former Catholic-evangelical divisions irrelevant.

The engines of celebrity creation, which are so active in a modern world of hyperactive media, have also contributed to eroding historic Catholic-evangelical suspicion. Evangelicals who witnessed television reports or read later accounts of John Paul II's first return to his native Poland in 1979, when millions of Poles defied governmental authorities to listen raptly and then to chant "We want God, we want God," could not help but be impressed.[16] A similarly broad appeal has been witnessed when Billy Graham and Luis Palau have taken their evangelical proclamations of the gospel into Catholic regions of the world.

A different kind of celebrity creation attends literary and artistic works. Readers of authors such as G. K. Chesterton and J. R. R. Tolkien or listeners to the music of J. S. Bach do not usually have ecclesiastical issues in mind when they take up the works of such figures. But evangelicals recognizing the baptized imaginations at play in books by the former and Catholics responding to the gospel shape of the latter's compositions have built bridges between traditions. As the celebrity status of such figures has risen in recent decades because of new technologies, new productions, and new media, their transdenominational appeal has even more actively undermined the ancient standoffs.

Concerning such relationships, discussions in *Christianity Today* in the mid-1980s over the entrance of Thomas Howard into the Catholic Church may have been a straw in the wind. One of those who wrote a letter to this evangelical magazine after its lengthy, mostly critical treatment of this former evangelical's conversion to Rome noted the irony

15. Thomas P. Rausch, "Catholic-Evangelical Relations: Signs of Progress," in *Catholics and Evangelicals*, 43.

16. Weigel, *Witness to Hope*, 293.

that the same issue that provided this critique also included a laudatory article on the Catholic writer Flannery O'Connor.[17]

Yet another feature of modern world Christianity that has altered the historic situation is the increasing prominence of women in almost all activities of all the churches. Since close to 100 percent of the polemical literature in the centuries of Catholic-Protestant antagonism was authored by men, it is not surprising that as women have come to occupy more space in public religious activity, not as much energy has been poured into the contentious practice of defining boundaries against ecclesiastical opponents. More specifically, although documentation is hard to come by concerning the impact of neighborhood Bible studies, the considerable success of these grassroots organizations is due almost exclusively to the leadership of Christian women. At least since the 1960s, the participation of Catholics with evangelicals in such studies, and vice versa, has played a large part in lowering the temperature of Catholic-evangelical strife in many places throughout North America, Europe, and the rest of the world.

New directions from dominant themes, impulses, movements, and conditions in the recent world history of Christianity do not by themselves explain the new openings for Catholic-evangelical engagement. It is difficult, however, to find examples among these recent developments that fortify historic tensions, but it is easy to specify many that lead to their relaxation.

Changes in American Politics and Society

In light of how important the civic sphere has always been for Catholic-evangelical relations, especially in North America, it is not surprising that alterations in political perception have contributed greatly to religious change.

The most visible public signal of a shift in the United States was the election of a Catholic as president in 1960. John F. Kennedy's victory was itself a milestone for overcoming Protestant bias and fulfilling earlier trajectories of Catholic public service. That election marked the culmination of a long process begun during the Revolutionary period by the participation of the Maryland Catholic Charles Carroll in the Continental Congress as well as by George Washington's proclamation suppressing traditional antipapal demonstrations on November 5 (Guy Fawkes or Pope's Day). Kennedy's election was also the culmination of more than a century and a half of intensive Catholic involvement in

17. R. C. Woodcock, letter to *Christianity Today*, July 12, 1985, 8.

grassroots politics.[18] The circumstances of the 1960 campaign added even greater symbolic importance to Kennedy's election. A widely reported campaign speech before Protestant ministers in Houston seemed to convince them, and many others, that a Catholic president would not imperil the nation's safety. Kennedy's scrupulous record on church-state matters, particularly his opposition to government aid for parochial schools, silenced Protestant critics who feared that Catholics did not have proper national priorities. On this issue, Billy Graham spoke for others by bestowing the indelicate praise that Kennedy had "turned out to be a Baptist President."[19] Moreover, the apotheosis that occurred after Kennedy's assassination left him, a Catholic, one of the most popular American presidents among the public at large. The "religious issue" in American politics, though not yet dead, had suffered a crushing blow. Even later revelations about Kennedy's misdeeds helped defuse inter-religious antagonisms, for his womanizing and power-grabbing were "ecumenical" in that they resembled similar misdeeds of other politicians who happened to be Protestant.

Much more important in the political and social sphere, however, has been what Timothy George once called an "ecumenism of the trenches." On many moral issues—"support for parental choice in education; advocacy of the traditional values of chastity, family, and community; opposition to abortion on demand; and repudiation of pornography"— more and more evangelicals have found themselves joining more and more frequently with more and more Catholics. The result has been a growing conviction that behind this common public testimony lay, again in George's phrases, a "coalescence of believing Roman Catholics and faithful evangelicals who both affirm the substance of historic Christian orthodoxy against the ideology of theological pluralism that marks much mainline Protestant thought as well as avant-garde Catholic theology."[20]

More generally, several developments since the 1960s have conspired to extinguish (or at least greatly diminish) the evangelical fear of Ca-

18. The historical background of Catholic political efforts is ably treated in John Tracy Ellis, ed., *Documents of American Catholic History*, 2nd ed. (Milwaukee: Bruce, 1962); James Hennesey, S.J., *American Catholics: A History of the Roman Catholic Community in the United States* (New York: Oxford University Press, 1981); Jay P. Dolan, *The American Catholic Experience* (Garden City, NY: Doubleday, 1985); and John T. McGreevy, *Catholicism and American Freedom: A History* (New York: Norton, 2003).

19. Theodore C. Sorensen, *Kennedy* (New York: Harper & Row, 1965), 188–95, 357–65; and Marshall Frady, *Billy Graham: A Parable of American Righteousness* (Boston: Little, Brown, 1979), 446.

20. Timothy George, "Catholics and Evangelicals in the Trenches," *Christianity Today*, May 16, 1994, 16; and idem, "Evangelicals and Catholics Together: A New Initiative. 'The Gift of Salvation': An Evangelical Assessment," *Christianity Today*, December 8, 1997, 34.

tholicism as a civil threat. In a development large with implications for the home front, American Catholics were led by the Jesuit scholar John Courtney Murray in urging the Second Vatican Council to make strong affirmations about the necessity of civil and religious liberty. Although most American evangelicals did not know much about Murray and other such American Catholic proponents of civil liberty, their work nonetheless undermined historic evangelical fears of Catholic despotism.[21]

In the international arena, even more damage was done to Protestant notions of Catholic tyranny by the contribution of the Catholic Church to the Solidarity movement in Poland, the public leadership of Pope John Paul II in combating communism in Europe, and the pope's temperate statements on explosive political situations in Latin America, Africa, and Asia.[22] These political actions did not address doctrinal issues directly, but they did strip away much of the civil anxiety with which American Protestants had always looked upon Roman Catholics.

The practicalities of local political action have also done much to open doorways. Over the last several decades, contemporary political affairs have become so passionately tangled that Christian faiths and public stances on moral issues now collide in nearly every conceivable combination. The crucible effect wrought by this situation explains why many Catholic-evangelical barriers have fallen: Committed toilers in the public vineyard have glanced up in surprise to find previously despised Catholics or evangelicals laboring right alongside them.

The complex controversies surrounding three of America's fundamental social concerns—sex, national self-defense, and the economy—have contributed a great deal to the withering of old interreligious antagonisms. Political debates on these issues, particularly controversy concerning how moral beliefs are to shape education, regularly reflect the passionate commitments of Americans from all points on the religious compass. Morally infused arguments over abortion—but also over many other issues, including health care reform, tax policy, specific military actions, United States foreign policy, or the character of candidates for public office—fill the air. The significant fact for contemporary interreligious relations is that allegiance to a general Protestantism or Catholicism is no longer a reliable indicator of commitments on public policy. Both theoretical questions and practical dilemmas, both theological applications and religious reflexes, are so diverse that whatever systematic differences still

21. See especially John Courtney Murray, *We Hold These Truths: Catholic Reflections on the American Proposition* (New York: Sheed & Ward, 1960).

22. A good treatment of the role of Catholicism in the fall of communism in Poland and Czechoslovakia is George Weigel, *The Final Revolution: The Resistance Church and the Collapse of Communism* (New York: Oxford University Press, 1992). For a responsible effort at biography, see Weigel, *Witness to Hope.*

separate Catholics and Protestants are lost in the public shuffle. In this new situation, Catholics and evangelicals often find themselves arguing the same or similar positions on public issues.[23]

Changed attitudes toward public education figure prominently in this process of civic engagement. Into the 1960s, Protestants of all sorts, including evangelicals, defended public schools in large part because of their fear that Catholic parochial education subverted one of the core ingredients of American democracy. As many scholars have shown conclusively, however, public education in the United States for a very long time meant schools dominated by a Protestant ethos, a Protestant Bible (the King James Version), a Protestant frame of mind, and a historic Protestant anti-Catholicism.[24] Over the last half century, this situation has changed with breathtaking speed. Evangelicals are now numbered among those who criticize public education as a stalking horse for secularism, a promoter of godless evolution, and an advocate for immoral sexual values. Although many evangelicals still support the public educational system, other evangelicals have founded their own Christian schools or have begun to teach their children at home in order to protest what they regard as the weaknesses of the public system. In 1999, 1,271,000 children were schooled at home for education from kindergarten through grade twelve, and many of these students were from evangelical homes. These home-school students represented about 1.7 percent of the school population.[25] With such developments, suspicion of long-term Catholic support for parochial schools has vanished as a cause of evangelical-Catholic strife, and it has probably vanished for good.

Changes in the Exercise of Personal Agency

For an evangelical assessment of contemporary Roman Catholicism, it is certainly important to consider broad social and religious move-

23. Those arguments are frequently found in the pages of *First Things*, a periodical edited by the Catholic priest Richard Neuhaus, who was once a Lutheran, and (with Neuhaus for many years) the still-Lutheran James Nuechterlein.

24. See especially Andrew M. Greeley, *An Ugly Little Secret: Anti-Catholicism in North America* (Kansas City: Sheed Andrews & McMeel, 1977); Rockne M. McCarthy, James W. Skillen, and William A. Harper, *Disestablishment a Second Time: Genuine Pluralism for American Schools* (Grand Rapids: Eerdmans, 1982); Philip Hamburger, *Separation of Church and State* (Cambridge: Harvard University Press, 2002); Philip Jenkins, *The New Anti-Catholicism: The Last Acceptable Prejudice* (New York: Oxford University Press, 2003); Mark S. Massa, S.J., *Anti-Catholicism in America: The Last Acceptable Prejudice* (New York: Crossroad, 2003); and McGreevy, *Catholicism and American Freedom*.

25. U.S. Department of Commerce, *Statistical Abstract of the United States: 2003*, National Data Book, 123rd ed., December 2003, 162 (Education).

ments, but it is also important not to forget the individuals and specific groups whose actions made a decisive difference. Such agents now make up an extensive roster: for example, the Vatican officials who set up meetings with Pentecostals, evangelicals, and Baptists; the church and seminary leaders who in 1987 founded the Los Angeles Catholic/ Evangelical Committee as the nation's first dialogue of its kind; Billy Graham, who arranged for increasing cooperation with Catholics in his evangelistic efforts; Richard John Neuhaus and Charles Colson, who have stage-managed the Evangelicals and Catholics Together initiative (discussed in chap. 6); Father Theodore Hesburgh and Father Edward Malloy, who as presidents of the University of Notre Dame hired some of evangelicalism's brightest scholars to deepen the Christian intellectual witness of that university; and many, many more who in their local situations have taken the steps required for information, dialogue, mutual learning, and mutual edification.[26]

Changes within Evangelicalism

A more positive relationship between evangelicals and Catholics has also arisen as a by-product of actions taken by evangelicals who claim that evangelicalism is not all it should be. A tradition of vigorous self-criticism is actually its own kind of testimony to evangelical vitality. But where evangelicals have been moved to admonish themselves and other evangelicals for weaknesses in ecclesiology, tradition, the intellectual life, sacraments, theology of culture, aesthetics, philosophical theology, or historical consciousness, the result has almost always been selective appreciation for elements of the Catholic tradition. Some of these critics have even, as it used to be phrased, gone over to Rome. Numbered among twentieth-century converts to Roman Catholicism have been several prominent evangelicals whose voices have continued to resonate with their former evangelical colleagues. They include, for example, the literary scholar Thomas Howard and the philosopher Peter Kreeft, whose stories are treated more fully in chapter 7.[27]

26. These others include Dennis Okholm and the late Timothy Phillips, whose patient labors over many years resulted in a path-breaking conference at Wheaton College called "Catholics and Evangelicals in Conversation" (April 11–13, 2002), where, among other papers, Mark Noll presented a few of the ideas that have been expanded in this book.

27. See, for example, Thomas Howard, *Evangelical Is Not Enough* (Nashville: Nelson, 1984); idem, *Lead Kindly Light: My Journey to Rome* (Steubenville, OH: Franciscan University Press, 1994); idem, *On Being Catholic* (San Francisco: Ignatius Press, 1997); Peter Kreeft, *Reading the New Testament: A Book-by-Book Guide for Catholics* (Ann Arbor: Servant Publications, 1992); idem, *Handbook of Christian Apologetics* (Downers Grove,

A different kind of Catholic intellectual influence has also been exerted by Catholic social teaching, particularly as found in the noteworthy encyclicals of Pope Leo XIII (e.g., *Rerum Novarum* in 1893) and several of the encyclicals of John Paul II. Surprisingly, various aspects of that social teaching have proven useful for evangelicals from the political left, right, and center as they seek to promote Christian values in their own public activity.

A recent essay by the evangelical Bible scholar Scot McKnight, to which we return for further insight in chapter 7, reflects on a number of McKnight's once-evangelical students who have become Catholics. McKnight suggests the type of issues that find some evangelicals looking to Rome for what they have not found in their own churches.[28] These converts seek more thoughtful liturgy, deeper grounding in Christian history, a fuller use of the sacraments, authoritative interpretations of Scripture, and (sometimes) the Catholic sex ethic with respect to contraception. But above all, McKnight describes a search for what they did not experience as evangelicals, that is, a search "to transcend the human limits of knowledge to find certainty . . . to transcend the human limits of temporality to find connection to the entire history of the Church . . . to transcend the human limits of interpretive diversity to find an interpretive authority."[29]

Most evangelicals who think about these questions, even those who strenuously criticize evangelical practices and traditions, do not become Roman Catholics. But consideration of such matters by those who do join the Catholic Church illuminates a situation in which evangelicals are more attentive to instruction from Catholics because they have perceived weaknesses in their own forms of faith. Ian Hunter is a Protestant and also a biographer of Malcolm Muggeridge, a figure much appreciated by some evangelicals who as an old man converted with his wife, Kitty, to Catholicism. Hunter has recently written about changes in recent decades that have created a situation in which evangelicals look to Catholic tradition for Christian instruction. In reviewing a book about the Catholic writer Flannery O'Connor, Hunter notes that O'Connor once told a friend that she thought it was her duty to read "modern Protestant

---

IL: InterVarsity, 1994); and idem, *How to Win the Culture War: A Christian Battle Plan for a Society in Crisis* (Downers Grove, IL: InterVarsity, 2002).

28. Scott McKnight, "From Wheaton to Rome: Why Evangelicals Become Roman Catholic," *Journal of the Evangelical Theological Society* 45 (September 2002): 451–72. For other recent accounts of similar conversions for similar reasons, see Dennis Martin, "Retrospect and Apologia," *Mennonite Quarterly Review* 77 (April 2003): 167–96; and Ivan Kauffman, "On Being Mennonite Catholic," *Mennonite Quarterly Review* 77 (April 2003): 235–56.

29. McKnight, "From Wheaton to Rome," 460.

theology." Because of his own disillusionment with the contemporary leaders of mainline Protestantism, Hunter is flabbergasted: "Think about that sentence. How astonishing, half a century later, to think that there was a time when 'Protestant theology' was not a contradiction in terms." But then he goes on to an assertion with which at least some evangelicals would agree: "The very first place every serious Protestant that I know turns today for guidance on Christian doctrine is the *Catechism* of the Roman Catholic Church; failing that, the Encyclicals of Pope John Paul II."[30] Our own examination of the *Catechism* in chapter 5 does not go that far. Yet Hunter's hyperbolic statement nonetheless indicates the extent of change in the recent past.

Hunter's reflections echo an assessment made by the Catholic historian James Turner of evangelical academics, mostly historians, whom he commends for taking a more active place in broader currents of American scholarship. Yet the commendation also comes with a question: "To what extent can the Evangelical intellectual revival be called Evangelical? The distinctives of Evangelicalism seem to survive more in religious than in intellectual behavior: the new Evangelical intellectuals pray as Evangelicals but think as Calvinists or Anglicans or sometimes even Catholics."[31] Like Ian Hunter, James Turner is recognizing altered conditions of evangelical self-perception as well as altered evangelical perceptions of Catholics. Such alterations have by no means spread to all corners of the evangelical world, but they are becoming increasingly common.

Taking Stock

The last several decades, in sum, have witnessed a major reorientation in relations between Protestant evangelicals and Roman Catholics. To be sure, echoes of old antagonisms still remain. A residual anti-Catholicism lives on in some areas of American civil life, but that anti-Catholicism is just as likely to arise from within cultural liberalism as Protestant evangelicalism. As shown in chapter 7, more specific religious hostility of the once common sort does linger among a few Protestant fundamentalists. In the early 1980s, for example, a California publisher issued two comic books, *Alberto* and *The Double Cross*, which illustrated such lingering hostility. These comics by Jack Chick purported to tell

30. Ian Hunter, "God's Grace Central on Solitary Path of Suffering," *Christian Week*, January 6, 2004, 14.

31. James Turner, "The Evangelical Intellectual Revival," in James Turner, *Language, Religion, Knowledge: Past and Present* (Notre Dame: University of Notre Dame Press, 2003), 127.

the story of a former Spanish Jesuit who was trained to subvert Protestantism through a number of ingenious schemes, and of his sister, who endured the terrors of Maria Monk in an English convent. The two tracts employed a language every bit as unreserved as the harshest polemics of the sixteenth or nineteenth centuries. The fairly wide sale of the comic books suggests that latent antagonisms remain in Protestant circles that the well-publicized Catholic-Protestant reengagements of recent years have not affected. It was an indication of changing times, however, that evangelicals joined other Protestants to denounce these books; that the Christian Booksellers Association, which represents largely a conservative evangelical constituency, expressed its regret over the publications; and that evangelical journalists contributed much of the hard information that exposed the comic books as fraudulent.[32] The hostilities that Jack Chick markets would have been well at home in the 1840s or 1890s. Then they were in the mainstream. Now they are on the margin.

This rapid survey of the recent past has, no doubt, missed many developments pertinent for explaining change. But what has been presented in this chapter should be enough to suggest substantial reasons why the relationship between Catholics and evangelicals is now so different from what it was fifty years ago.

---

32. Gary Metz, "Jack Chick's Anti-Catholic Alberto Comic Book Is Exposed as a Fraud," *Christianity Today*, March 13, 1981, 50–52; and "Bookseller's Group May Expel Chick," *Christianity Today*, October 23, 1981, 62. For an update on Chick's efforts, see Massa, *Anti-Catholicism in America*, 100–20.

4

ECUMENICAL DIALOGUES

L ess than two hundred years ago the idea of constructive evangelical-Catholic dialogue was unthinkable. What *was* thinkable was
mutual antagonism that could sometimes rise to a fever pitch. In 1835,
for instance, Lyman Beecher, father of the novelist Harriet Beecher Stowe
and a well-known minister in his own right, preached three sermons in
Boston that were so inflammatory against Catholics that they contributed to the formation of a mob that burned a convent to the ground.[1]
In the nation's public schools, Catholic children were chastised, sometimes physically, for not being willing to read from the Protestants' King
James Version of the Bible.[2] When Catholics asked if their version (the
Douay-Rheims) might be included in these daily readings, Protestants
not only exercised their majority voice with a resounding no but also
underscored their response with mob action. On several occasions in
Philadelphia and New York during the 1840s, rioting once again was
the answer. Shortly thereafter, a significant political movement—with
its main plank the exclusion of Catholics from the rights of citizen-

1. Nancy L. Schultz, *Fire and Roses: The Burning of the Charlestown Convent, 1834*
(New York: Free Press, 2000).
2. John T. McGreevy, *Catholicism and American Freedom: A History* (New York: Norton,
2003), 7–11.

75

ship—coalesced around the American Party (or Know Nothing Party) and won scores of elections for state and federal office.[3]

One hundred years later, by the mid-twentieth century, violence between Catholics and Protestants in North America was mostly a thing of the past. Yet subtle and not so subtle habits of mutual suspicion kept Protestants and Catholics in isolated, separate camps. Catholics feared excommunication if they worshiped in a Protestant church or read a Protestant Bible. Protestants feared that the devil lurked in the darkened corners of Catholic churches with their mysterious twinkling lights and smoldering incense. Many Protestants continued to believe that the book of Revelation defined the antichrist as the Catholic Church.

With remarkable speed, the Second Vatican Council (1962–65) created a new situation. Not since the Council of Trent (1545–63) had an ecclesiastical gathering exerted such a powerful influence on Protestant-Catholic relationships. But this time the impetus propelled Catholics and Protestants toward each other rather than apart. Of Vatican II's sixteen official documents, the one that meant most for this aspect of world Christian history was a decree on ecumenism that first paved the way for official conversations with the Eastern Orthodox and then with various Protestant bodies. Within a year from the conclusion of the council, the dialogues began. Some went on for nearly three decades; most continue to this day.[4]

If those who had experienced Catholic-Protestant history in the centuries before 1960 could have eavesdropped on these dialogues as they got under way, they would have been astounded. Meetings between Roman Catholics and representatives of the Disciples of Christ, which convened at intervals over a fifteen-year period from 1977 to 1992, illustrate a typical pattern. Each five-day conference examined critical differences but also looked for points of commonality leading toward unity. Representatives of each side presented coordinated papers addressing the same topics. Together they shared times of worship and prayer but also stepped outside their conference centers to worship with local congregations of both bodies. At the end of each meeting, they documented an "agreed account." Summarizing their experience, commissioners wrote words that

3. A useful general account is Ray Allen Billington, *Protestant Crusade, 1800–1860* (New York: Rinehart, 1938).

4. Ongoing ecumenical dialogues continue between the Catholic Church and the Anglican Communion, the Lutheran World Federation, the World Alliance of Reformed Churches, the World Methodist Council, the Baptist World Alliance, the Disciples of Christ, and some Pentecostal groups. Information from the Vatican's Pontifical Council for Promoting Church Unity as noted on the Vatican website: www.vatican.va/roman_curia/ pontifical_councils/chrstuni/documents/rc_pc_chrstuni_pro_200519996_chrstuni_pro _en.htm (accessed May 29, 2004).

no one in the age before Vatican II could have believed possible: "Above all, we have experienced [unity] together in our prayer, our reading of the Scripture, and the meditation which has seasoned all our work and given a special flavor and substance to this dialogue."[5]

Meetings and Minds

Official published summaries of the first thirty-five years of Catholic-initiated ecumenical dialogues fill two books totaling more than fourteen hundred pages. While this mountain of evidence about ecumenical relations could be approached from many angles, the aim of this chapter is simple. We are trying to inform. To do so, we provide (chronologically arranged) brief overviews of official conversations between delegates of the Vatican and eight Protestant bodies that can be viewed as evangelical or that include substantial evangelical elements. First, we briefly describe the time, place, and content of the meetings; then we canvass the agreements and disagreements produced by the dialogues. Finally, because of great evangelical concern for issues relating to personal salvation, we provide a slightly expanded discussion on the Lutheran-Catholic dialogues on justification by faith. At the end, we offer a brief assessment of what this unprecedented array of ecumenical discussions has—and has not—accomplished. Reports of conferences may bore readers, but we take that risk willingly in order to communicate the breadth and depth of these recent and serious conversations.

Anglicans (1966–96)

The Catholic-Anglican dialogue began with conversations at the highest possible level. Anglican archbishop Michael Ramsey met Pope Paul VI in Rome in March of 1966, and together they issued a "Common Declaration" that challenged their two churches to take up the task of mutual discussion. The pope and the archbishop announced the startling and unprecedented goal of "restoration of complete communion in faith and sacramental life."[6]

Five times during the course of this dialogue, the Anglican archbishop and the Roman Catholic pope met together to worship, pray, and promulgate versions of their "Common Declaration" (Rome 1966,[7] Vatican

5. Harding Meyer and Lucas Vischer, eds., *Growth in Agreement: Reports and Agreed Statements of Ecumenical Conversation on a World Level* (New York: Paulist Press, 1984; Geneva: World Council of Churches, 1984), 165.

6. Ibid., 63.

7. Ibid., 125.

1977,[8] Canterbury 1982,[9] Vatican 1989,[10] Vatican 1996).[11] Each declaration spoke of current progress, future goals, and mutual charity. Each was signed by the archbishop and the pope. These declarations, created as they were by the chief authorities in each church, provided powerful motivation to the teams of theologians who actually carried out the dialogues in an effort to overcome differences and come to agreements.

The first Anglican–Roman Catholic International Commission (ARCIC I) met from 1970 to 1981 and produced four reports: "Eucharistic Doctrine," "Ministry and Ordination," and "Authority in the Church," parts 1 and 2. ARCIC II held four meetings between 1983 and 1986 and produced a statement titled "Salvation and the Church." It then met four more times between 1987 and 1990 and published "Church and Communion." Predictably, when information about the dialogues reached the broader membership of both churches, not all were overjoyed. Criticisms and questions from both constituencies resulted in further honing of the ARCIC documents. Responses to ARCIC I resulted in three "Elucidation" reports (1979, 1979, 1981). ARCIC II issued clarification documents in 1993 and 1994.[12] On some questions, such as the nature of the priesthood, early statements of agreement were later softened in response to criticism.[13]

In general, the Protestant-Catholic ecumenical dialogues produced a common list of ongoing disagreements, including questions concerning the authority of the church, the importance of Peter and his successors, the infallibility of the pope, and the veneration of Mary. Some of these items also factored large for Anglicans and Catholics, but by comparison with the other dialogues, disagreements here were more modest. On a few issues that had divided the churches for centuries, such as the sacraments,[14] papal authority,[15] and priesthood of the laity,[16] the Anglican-Catholic statements came close to complete agreement.

Methodists (1967–96)

Chronologically parallel to Catholic-Anglican dialogues were meetings between Methodists and Catholics. They took their initiative from the

8. Ibid., 127.
9. Jeffrey Gros, Harding Meyer, and William G. Rusch, eds., *Growth in Agreement II: Reports and Agreed Statements of Ecumenical Conversations on a World Level, 1982–1998* (Grand Rapids: Eerdmans, 2000; Geneva: World Council of Churches, 2000), 313.
10. Ibid., 326.
11. Ibid., 371.
12. Ibid., 312.
13. Meyer and Vischer, *Growth in Agreement*, 85, par. 2.
14. Ibid., 75, par. 7.
15. Ibid., 97, par. 23; 108, par. 7.
16. Ibid., 89, par. 7.

Second Vatican Council and from decisions the World Methodist Council made in London in 1966. But they also reached back into Methodist history, specifically to a letter dated July 18, 1749, from John Wesley to "a Roman Catholic."[17] In that letter, Wesley, in admitted defiance of other Protestants who "will be angry at me . . . for writing to you in this manner," outlined key elements of the Nicene Creed (giving his full assent), set out standards of holy living as a test of what is "a true Protestant" (thus discarding detractors who did not live out the faith they professed), and invited his Catholic reader to "come, my brother, and let us reason together." Wesley then proposed four resolutions: that this Catholic and this Methodist not hurt each other, that they speak nothing harsh or unkind to each other, that they harbor no unkind thoughts toward each other, and that they help each other "in whatever way we agree leads to the kingdom."[18]

Two hundred years later, Wesley's ecclesial descendants sat down with Catholics and went to work fleshing out his proposal for an ecclesiastical cease-fire. These dialogues produced six major documents: The Denver report (1971) covered Christianity and the contemporary world, spirituality, Christian home and family, the Eucharist, and ministry and authority.[19] The Dublin report (1972–76) studied in more depth spirituality and moral issues along with the Eucharist and ordained ministry.[20] The Honolulu report (1977–81) continued work on Christian experience and moral decisions and began to study the potentially divisive issue of authority.[21] In Nairobi (1982–86), the focus was "The Nature of the Church."[22] Paris (1986–91) represented a natural outgrowth of previous dialogues with a statement titled "The Apostolic Tradition."[23] In Baar, Switzerland (1991–96), thirty years of Methodist and Catholic discussion led to a statement exploring the ways in which God revealed himself to his people and the nature of their responses to him. This document was called "The Word of Life."[24]

17. Ibid., 308, pars. 1–3. We quote another section of this letter in chapter 2.

18. *The Works of John Wesley*, 3rd ed., vol. 10, *Letters, Essays, Dialogs, and Addresses* (Grand Rapids: Baker, 1996), 80–86. Readers should be careful not to read this letter in isolation. Wesley was a good English Anglican who guarded his religious turf from "popery." In spite of this conciliatory letter to a Roman Catholic, he also wrote a systematic refutation of the Roman *Catechism* as well as a tract titled "A Short Method of Converting All the Roman Catholics in the Kingdom of Ireland."

19. Meyer and Vischer, *Growth in Agreement*, 308–39.

20. Ibid., 340–66.

21. Ibid., 367–87.

22. Gros, Meyer, and Rusch, *Growth in Agreement II*, 583–96.

23. Ibid., 597–617.

24. Ibid., 618–46.

Pentecostals (1969–97)

In 1969, the efforts of two spiritual visionaries opened up a quarter century of dialogue between Pentecostals and Roman Catholics. The visionaries were David du Plessis, an international Pentecostal leader as well as an observer at the Second Vatican Council, and Killian McDonnell, O.S.B., of Collegeville, Minnesota. After several exploratory meetings, the first set of dialogues began in 1972 and continued with a total of five annual meetings through 1976.[25] These first dialogues spanned some of the most fervent years of the early charismatic movement. Sample topics included baptism in the Holy Spirit, the role of the Holy Spirit in the mystical tradition, discernment of spirits, and the exercise of spiritual gifts.[26] Cautious wording throughout and frequent reference to the fact that discussants were not able to reach complete agreement testified to the difficulties inherent in such work.

Pentecostals and Catholics held three more sets of meetings, the second of which (1977–82) focused on faith and religious experience, speaking in tongues, and the role of Mary. Closing comments at the end of these sessions spoke of "candour and earnestness" in the exchange but also of "serious disagreements" that still remained.[27] The third set of dialogues (1985–89) focused on koinonia: Christian community and fellowship.[28] Here, as in most of the dialogues, contrasting convictions concerning the nature of church made it difficult to draft a united statement. The final set of dialogues (1990–97) focused on missions and evangelism. The closing sessions of this last round took up the sensitive issues of proselytism and common witness. On these matters, as we will see later in this chapter, significant progress was made.

Reformed (1970–90)

Representatives of Roman Catholic and Reformed churches met in two series of meetings spanning 1970–90. Reformed delegates were sponsored by the World Alliance of Reformed Churches, and Catholics were sponsored by the Pontifical Council for Promoting Christian Unity. Their purpose was "to deepen mutual understanding and to foster the eventual reconciliation of our two communities."[29] During the first set of meetings, each side was represented by five delegates, a staff person, and one consultant expert on the subject at hand. Four position papers, two from each team, circulated in advance. After discussion, the partici-

---

25. Meyer and Vischer, *Growth in Agreement*, 422, par. 1.
26. Gros, Meyer, and Rusch, *Growth in Agreement II*, 721–22, pars. 5–6.
27. Ibid., 733, pars. 92–94.
28. Ibid., 754, par. 5.
29. Ibid., 780, par. 1.

pants issued a joint statement.[30] Under a general theme, "The Presence of Christ in Church and World," the first meetings covered four topics: the relationship of Christ to the church, the church as a teaching authority, the Eucharist, and ministry.[31]

A second phase of meetings between Catholic and Reformed churches extended from 1984 to 1990. This series was distinctive in two ways. It first engaged in a "reconciliation of memories" in which each party reviewed events of the Reformation and subsequent years. Second, it led to the composition of a "common confession of faith." Finally, as other meetings had done, this one specified continued disagreements, including topics for future discussion.[32]

Lutherans (1972–99)

Twenty-seven years of dialogues between Roman Catholics and Lutherans produced published reports composed of 175,000 words filling 282 pages in the two volumes of *Growth in Agreement*. This was by far the fullest of all the dialogues covered in this chapter. Of the major principles of the Protestant Reformation—*sola fide, sola gratia, sola scriptura*, and the priesthood of all believers—Lutherans had especially stressed the issue of justification. Hence, Lutheran and Catholic representatives worked hardest on *sola fide* (salvation by faith alone) and *sola gratia* (salvation through grace alone). Of course, in trying to reach agreement on justification, they also had to treat the other two distinctives of the Reformation, though more briefly. The result was excellent work on all four areas and basic agreement (though nuanced) concerning the first two *solas*. In the process, the delegates also achieved significant progress concerning the Eucharist and ecclesiology. But as we try to indicate at the end of this chapter, Catholic-Lutheran dialogue on justification was most important.

Disciples of Christ (1977–93)

The Roman Catholic Church and the Disciples of Christ engaged in two series of dialogues spanning fifteen years. The first series (1977–81) followed the theme "Apostolicity and Catholicity in the Visible Unity of the Church." Each body sent officially approved delegates to make up an eighteen-member commission guided by cochairs: Stanley J. Ott, who represented the Catholics, and Paul A. Crow Jr. representing the Disciples. The commission met five times, five days for each gather-

---

30. Meyer and Vischer, *Growth in Agreement*, 435–36, pars. 7–8.
31. Gros, Meyer, and Rusch, *Growth in Agreement II*, 780, par 2.
32. Ibid., 780–818.

ing.[33] Discussions during the first set of meetings revealed the need for more focused work on the nature of the church. Therefore, a second series of dialogues began in 1983 and met ten times over the next decade. Crow continued his role as cochair representing the Disciples. Samuel E. Carter, S.J., became his Roman Catholic counterpart. This decade of meetings focused entirely on ecclesiology, including various subtopics under the general heading "The Church as Communion in Christ."[34]

By this time, in the various ecumenical dialogues, questions about the church (or ecclesiology) were already emerging as the most significant divide between Catholics and Protestants. Because of the strong emphasis Disciples have always placed on individuality (for people and for congregations), this series of dialogues focused pointedly on many church-related questions that other Protestant-Catholic dialogues tried to address as well.

Evangelicals (1977–84)

Generically designated evangelicals met with Roman Catholics three times over a period of seven years. One distinctive of this series of dialogues was that those on the Protestant side did not come with the official sanction of an individual denomination. Rather, they were Protestants identified by their evangelical theological convictions and their interest in missions. Instead of addressing various theological distinctives of a particular denomination, this dialogue focused primarily on carrying the good news of Christ to those who have not yet heard. The delegations were composed of three theologians and missiologists from each side who attended all the meetings, along with other individuals for each specific meeting. The evangelicals came from various church and parachurch groups and subscribed to basic evangelical statements of theology as well as the Nicene Creed. Catholic delegates were appointed by the Vatican Secretariat for Promoting Christian Unity. Meetings were held in Venice (1977), Cambridge (1982), and Landevennec, France (1984).[35] Since reaching the lost for Christ has always been a strong mandate for evangelicals, this particular set of discussions, though short and unofficial, made at least some progress on issues touching the heart of long-standing evangelical concerns.

33. Meyer and Vischer, *Growth in Agreement*, 154.
34. Gros, Meyer, and Rusch, *Growth in Agreement II*, 386.
35. Ibid., 399–400.

Baptists (1984–88)

Because Baptists by definition are independent in regard to ecclesiology, it was impossible to gather a group able to represent the broad variety of Baptist churches. Even so, a brief Baptist-Catholic dialogue took place as sixteen representatives met at five gatherings between 1984 and 1988. They were sponsored by the Commission on Baptist Doctrine and Interchurch Cooperation of the Baptist World Alliance and the Vatican Secretariat for Promoting Christian Unity. Meetings were held in West Berlin (discussing evangelism and evangelization), Los Angeles (conversion and discipleship), New York (ecclesiology), Rome (common witness), and Atlanta (where a summary report was issued).

Baptists and Catholics engaged in theological discussion through scholarly papers, Bible studies, visits to local congregations, and visits from local Baptist and Roman Catholic leaders. At the close, cochairs Bede Heather and David Shannon were able to write, "The sixteen of us . . . have been conscious of the Spirit of God at work among us, and formed in the course of three years friendships that have been full of encouragement and edification. . . . [We] regard our experience together as a great gift from God."[36]

Reflections on the Dialogues

Decades of ecumenical dialogue between Catholics and various Protestant groups drew little attention in the popular press. Most people in the pews knew nothing of what they were discussing—or even that they were taking place. Yet month by month, at various sites throughout the world, Protestants and Catholics were sitting across tables from each other, where they pushed back the harsh edges that divided them, puzzled about the different ways they used the same Christian terms, sharpened their sense of enduring differences, and, on many occasions, arrived at startling agreements that would have amazed their counterparts in the sixteenth century.

Taken together, several common themes emerged from the dialogues. Most importantly, it became obvious that Catholics view all of theology through the lens of the church. The long shadow of Bishop Cyprian from the third century ("He who does not have the Church as mother does not have God as Father") extends over all Catholic theology. "People of God" and "body of Christ" are important Catholic images for the church; they emphasize a corporate sense of belonging to God. Anglicans, with

36. Ibid., 373–74.

their roots in England's sixteenth-century effort to reform an entire national church, could express similar commitments to Mother Church and a corporate faith.

Most other Protestant bodies, however, particularly those that developed on the broad plains of American democracy, placed much more stress on the individual Christian. For these bodies, the emphasis was on believers who made "personal decisions for Christ" or on church government as expressing the democratic principles of majority vote. The difference between a corporate and an individual approach to faith colors how Protestants and Catholics read Scripture and interpret theology. Most importantly, it shapes how they define the nature and function of the church. Thus, ecclesiology was always central in the dialogues.

Even so, the thirty-five years of ecumenical discussion revealed a surprising range of agreements between Protestants and Catholics. Even where disagreement remained, the dialogues created a large measure of mutual understanding and respect. A constant refrain in the records of these meetings was reference to the prayer of Jesus for his disciples: "I pray also for those who will believe in me . . . that all of them may be one . . . so that the world may believe that you have sent me" (John 17:20–21). Mere decades of meetings, however cordial, could not overcome many centuries of antagonism. Yet those who desire the kind of unity for which Jesus prayed can find in the dialogues encouraging signs of an answer to that prayer.

Agreements

Challenges that faced the dialogues between Catholics and the Disciples of Christ were typical of core differences between the Catholic Church and many Protestant bodies. On the surface, Catholics and Disciples make an unlikely pairing. Regarding textual authority, Catholics adhere to creeds and confessions as definitive for doctrinal truth and necessary for unity within the church. Disciples cling to the New Testament alone, claiming that creeds and confessions are human standards that have led to divisions among Christians. Catholics emphasize sacraments, liturgy, and the corporate character of faith. Disciples emphasize proclamation of the Word aimed at individual appropriation and individual responsibility. As one of the documents from this dialogue phrased it:

> [Regarding church] they differ on the relative weight given, on the one hand, to individual discernment and conscience and, on the other hand, to the communal mind. It can be said that Roman Catholics are convinced that, although they must decide *for* themselves, they cannot decide *by*

themselves. Disciples, on the other hand, are convinced that, although they cannot decide *by* themselves, they must decide *for* themselves." (emphasis added)[37]

Sacraments raised tensions. Catholics baptize infants by sprinkling. Disciples baptize believers by immersion. (During the discussions, however, they recognized that both groups baptize with water in the name of the Trinity by a duly authorized minister, and both believe that rebaptism is never necessary.) As for the Eucharist or the Lord's Supper, both groups celebrate Communion weekly, though Disciples are quite happy to have a layperson preside over the service if a minister or elder is not available. By contrast, the Catholic Eucharist must be celebrated by an ordained priest under the authority of a bishop. These differences over the sacrament reflect differences concerning the nature of the church. Disciples see the church (even their own) as quite fallible. Catholics, however, while aware of individual human finitude, see the church as belonging to Christ and therefore preserved in holiness and truth by God's Spirit.

Another difference concerns accounts of beginnings. Catholics trace their origin from the first apostles. Disciples, by comparison, are latecomers who emerged only in the early years of American Protestantism; they lack even the standard Protestant history of a deliberate break from the Catholic Church. Clearly, conversation between these groups would not come easily—nor did it.[38]

Yet in spite of these manifold historical disagreements, fifteen years of patient dialogue led to startling agreements. Disciples said that they better appreciated tradition and corporate faith.[39] Catholics came to respect individual salvation and the priesthood of all believers.[40] Meanwhile, across other tables in other cities, similar delegations of Protestants and Catholics were also finding it possible to move toward common ground.

THE PLACE OF THE CHURCH IN SALVATION

All of the Protestant-Catholic dialogues addressed the question of the church and its connection to salvation. The dialogue in which evangelicals and Catholics focused on the work of missions possessed a special interest on this score, in large part because many evangelical organizations, though passionately concerned about winning the lost to Christ, are parachurch groups only loosely connected to an ecclesi-

37. Ibid., 390, par. 16.
38. Ibid., 387–90.
39. Ibid., 393, par. 37.
40. Ibid., 395, par. 45.

astical structure. Yet here dialogue with Catholics may have resulted in a needed correction for both sides. The group agreed that the Christian community needs to be viewed as part of the gospel, fruit of the gospel, embodiment of the gospel, and agent of the gospel. "To sum up, the church and the gospel belong indissolubly together. . . . Unless the church embodies the gospel, giving it visible flesh and blood, the gospel lacks credibility and the church lacks effectiveness in witness."[41] To live up to the high ideals of this joint statement, both evangelicals and Catholics would have to make changes in how they approached missions. Evangelicals who agreed with this statement would have to do mission work within the context of the church with the primary goal of creating and sustaining churches. But doing so would challenge some parachurch mission groups. The stated agreement also defined spreading the gospel as a major responsibility of the church, and this emphasis would challenge some Catholics.

Catholics and the Disciples of Christ agreed to the following statements about salvation as it relates to and within the church:

- "Each Christian's faith is inseparable from the faith of the community. Personal faith is an appropriation of the Church's faith and depends on it for authenticity as well as for nurture."[42]
- "Through word and sacraments the church is the servant or instrument of God's plan of salvation."[43]
- "The communion that is the church allows people to witness what Christian faith confesses: there is salvation and it comes from God through Christ."[44]

Each of the above statements reveals concessions and contributions from both sides. Phrases sacred in evangelical Protestant history, such as "personal faith" and "word and sacraments," dot the page. But Cyprian's influence is also present where the church is called the "servant or instrument of God's plan for salvation."

Apostolic Succession

As expected, Protestant-Catholic groups had genuine difficulty with apostolic succession. At best they worked toward a measure of agreement on definitions and history. For example, Disciples and Roman Catholics could agree "that the church is the company of all the baptized, the com-

41. Ibid., 426–27.
42. Meyer and Vischer, *Growth in Agreement,* 161.
43. Gros, Meyer, and Rusch, *Growth in Agreement II,* 395, par. 46.
44. Ibid., 397, par. 52.

munity through which they are constantly kept in the memory of the apostolic witness and nourished by the Eucharist."[45] Catholics in this dialogue did admit the historical possibility that the concept of apostolic succession was initially geographical and only later chronological: "The intention of the apostolic community in establishing ministries in other places was initially to establish collaborators rather than to choose successors: what began as an expansion of communion over distance became later on an expansion over time."[46]

The dialogue between Catholics and the Reformed settled for language on the subject of apostolic succession that featured the phrase "at least." For example, they agreed that apostolic succession consists "at least" in continuity of apostolic doctrine, but such agreement did not necessarily rule out succession through continuity of ordained ministry. The same partners also agreed that no one assumes special ministry solely on the basis of personal initiative. The ministry of Word and sacrament comes through the calling of a community and the act of ordination by other ministers.[47]

Dialogue statements about the church and apostolic succession reflect especially the broadened understanding of the church as defined by the Second Vatican Council. In what is now official Catholic teaching, Protestants, indeed all Christian believers throughout history, are included in the church. Protestants accept a cultivated memory of the apostles as key agents in God's work, even if they do not accept Catholic teaching on apostolic succession. Meanwhile, Catholics conceded that succession may have been an afterthought, an expedient for managing a quickly spreading church.

THE PRIESTHOOD OF ALL BELIEVERS

Dialogues between the Disciples of Christ and Catholics made an initial foray into the area of universal priesthood, one of the major dividing points of the Reformation. "Both Disciples and Roman Catholics affirm that the whole church shares in the priesthood and ministry of Christ. They also affirm that ordained ministers have the specific charisma of representing Christ to the church."[48]

But because Anglican-Catholic dialogue began with the goal of structural unity, the priesthood of all believers received even more serious attention in their discussions. Early statements from this dialogue showed surprising concessions on both sides. Catholics stretched to say:

45. Ibid., 396, par. 49.
46. Ibid., 394–95, par. 44.
47. Meyer and Vischer, *Growth in Agreement*, 458, pars. 100–101.
48. Gros, Meyer, and Rusch, *Growth in Agreement II*, 395, par. 45.

All Christians are called to serve . . . by their life of prayer and surrender to divine grace, and by their careful attention to the needs of all
human beings. They should witness to God's compassion for all man-
kind and his concern for justice in the affairs of men. They should offer
themselves to God in praise and worship, and devote their energies to
bring men into the fellowship of Christ's people; and so under his rule
of love. The goal of the ordained ministry is to serve this priesthood of
all the faithful.[49]

Martin Luther could only agree. Most Baptists could affirm the
next statement, even though it came from the same Catholic-Anglican
dialogue:

Since the ordained ministers are ministers of the gospel, every facet of
their oversight is linked with the word of God. In the original mission and
witness recorded in Holy Scripture lies the source and ground of their
preaching and authority. By preaching of the word they seek to bring those
who are not Christians into the fellowship of Christ.[50]

Not surprisingly, after these statements reached their respective constituencies, the wording required some elucidation.[51]

For their part, Anglicans gave away similar territory in an amazing
statement about papal authority:

The only see [domain of a bishop] which makes any claim to universal
primacy and which has exercised and still exercises such *episcope* is the
see of Rome, the city where Peter and Paul died. It seems appropriate
that in any future union a universal primacy such as has been described
should be held at that see. . . .[52]

It is possible to think that a primacy of the bishop of Rome is not contrary to the New Testament and is part of God's purpose regarding the
Church's unity and catholicity, while admitting that the New Testament
texts offer no sufficient basis for this. . . .

We nevertheless agree that a universal primacy will be needed in a
reunited Church and should appropriately be the primacy of the bishop
of Rome.[53]

To sum up, Catholics affirmed a prize Reformation doctrine: the
priesthood of all believers. Some Protestants affirmed what Catholics
call the specific charisma of ordination, with the priest representing

49. Meyer and Vischer, *Growth in Agreement,* 80, par. 7.
50. Ibid., 81, par. 10.
51. Ibid., 85, par. 2.
52. Ibid., 97, par. 23.
53. Ibid., 108, pars. 7, 9.

Christ to the church. Anglicans even hinted at some kind of submission to the bishop of Rome as pope.

SALVATION

It comes as no surprise to those who know anything about Baptist history that the issue of salvation was an important subject in Baptist-Catholic dialogues. The Baptist emphasis on salvation as a onetime event and the Catholic belief that salvation is a lifelong process required the two sides to come together on basic definitions—which, in fact, they were able to do. To achieve that goal, this dialogue distinguished between conversion and discipleship, thereby attempting to bridge traditional differences between event and process, individual faith and corporate faith:

> Conversion is turning away from all that is opposed to God, contrary to Christ's teaching, and turning to God, to Christ, the Son, through the work of the Holy Spirit. It entails a turning from the self-centeredness of sin to faith in Christ as Lord and Savior. Conversion is a passing from one way of life to another new one, marked with the newness of Christ. It is a continuing process so that the whole life of a Christian should be a passage from death to life, from error to truth, from sin to grace. Our life in Christ demands continual growth in God's grace. Conversion is personal but not private. Individuals respond in faith to God's call, but faith comes from hearing the proclamation of the word of God and is to be expressed in the life together in Christ that is the church.[54]

Likewise, "discipleship consists in personal attachment to Jesus and in commitment to proclamation of the gospel and to those actions which bring the healing and saving power of Jesus to men and women today." With this definition in place, the group could recommend various spiritual disciplines along with growth within the church community and tireless mission "to call all people to repentance and faith."[55] Substantial as such common statements were, however, significant differences remained as to how such definitions should be applied to evangelism, or the calling of nonbelievers to Christian faith.[56]

Catholic dialogue with Reformed Protestants resulted in a common confession of faith that treated doctrines of Christ, justification, and the church. Its extensive agreed statements regarding salvation included the following:

54. Gros, Meyer, and Vischer, *Growth in Agreement II*, 376, par. 15.
55. Ibid., 377, par. 17.
56. Ibid., 384–85, pars. 54–55.

- "Jesus Christ, in whose name our forbears separated themselves from one another, is also the one who unites us in a community of forgiveness and of kinship."[57]
- "Before all human kind, our sisters and brothers, we announce the death of the Lord . . . and proclaim his resurrection from the dead."[58]
- "God is the one who 'chose us (in Christ) before the foundation of the world. He destined us in love to be his sons through Jesus Christ.'"[59]
- "The death and resurrection of Jesus finally reveal who Jesus himself is, the one Mediator between God and humanity."[60]
- "Nothing and nobody could replace or duplicate, complete or in any way add to the unique mediation accomplished 'once for all' . . . by Christ."[61]
- "Justification by faith brings with it the gift of sanctification, which can grow continuously as it creates life, justice and liberty."[62]
- "Together we confess the church, for there is no justification in isolation. All justification takes place in the community of believers or is ordered towards the gathering of such a community. Fundamental for us all is the presence of Christ in the church."[63]
- "The justification of Jesus' disciples, sinful individuals freely justified by grace without any merit on their part, has been one of the constitutive experiences of the Christian faith since the foundation of the church. Justification by grace through faith is given us in the church."[64]
- "If God chooses to act through the church for the salvation of believers, this does not restrict saving grace to these means."[65]

In light of historic Protestant-Catholic differences on the question of justification by faith and also in light of the discussions going on at the same time between Lutherans and Catholics, treated below, it was especially significant that participants in the Reformed dialogue made the following explicit statement: "We recognize that our justification is

57. Ibid., 795, par. 65.
58. Ibid., 795, par. 68.
59. Ibid., 796, par. 69a.
60. Ibid., 796, par. 69c.
61. Ibid., 797, par. 72.
62. Ibid., 799, par. 79.
63. Ibid., 799, par. 80.
64. Ibid., 800, par. 86.
65. Ibid., 800, par. 87.

a totally gratuitous work accomplished by God in Christ. We confess that the acceptance in faith of justification is itself a gift of grace. . . . To rely for salvation on anything other than faith would be to diminish the fullness accomplished and offered in Jesus Christ."[66] With this lengthy list of agreements appearing in one dialogue, it is not surprising that other dialogues could come to similar conclusions.

Thus, the Anglican-Catholic dialogue also treated salvation by discussing four major areas of historic tension: the role of faith, the understanding of justification, the place of good works, and the function of the church.[67] In the end, Catholics and Anglicans concluded, "We are agreed that this [salvation] is not an area where any remaining differences of theological interpretation or ecclesiological emphasis, either within or between our communions, can justify our continuing separation."[68]

The clash of convictions concerning salvation, conversion, justification, and sanctification is by no means totally resolved between Catholics and Protestants, but significant steps have been made through the dialogues in finding agreement on some critical issues and in narrowing differences on others. Further examples of this coming together are explored later in this chapter through attention to the Lutheran-Catholic dialogue.

SACRAMENTS

All of the dialogues struggled with differences concerning the sacraments. Catholics assume seven sacraments. Most Protestants practice only Communion (the Lord's Supper or Eucharist) and baptism—with (of course) differing views among Protestants on the meaning of each. Some Protestant groups use the term *ordinance* rather than sacrament and do not view the two as synonyms. Most Protestant-Catholic dialogues on the sacraments focused on baptism and the Lord's Supper rather than on the five additional rites that Catholics practice.

In regard to the Eucharist, the Reformed-Catholic dialogue again employed the phrase "at least" to soften differences, even as its documents admitted that full agreement on this sacrament was not likely. They agreed on the Real Presence of Christ in the Eucharist by saying that the Eucharist is "at least" a memorial, a source of loving communion, and a source of the eschatological hope of his coming again.[69] As an expression of the strength of their common confession of faith, these two groups agreed that both Reformed and Catholic churches should give mutual recognition of baptism, provided that it was performed

66. Ibid., 798, par. 77.
67. Ibid., 317–18.
68. Ibid., 325, par. 32.
69. Meyer and Vischer, *Growth in Agreement*, 456, par. 91.

with water in the name of the Father, Son, and Holy Spirit. "Under no circumstances can there be a repetition of baptism which took place in the other church."[70]

Methodists and Catholics focused much of their energies on the church, particularly in dialogues four and five of their six-part series. Regarding church and sacraments, their agreement was substantial:

> Being a Christian has necessarily both a personal and a communal aspect. It is a vital relationship to God in and through Jesus Christ in which faith, conversion of life and membership in the church are essential. Individual believers are joined in a family of disciples, so that belonging to Christ means also belonging to the church which is his body. . . . Both the personal and communal aspects of the Christian life are present in the two sacraments that Methodists and Roman Catholics consider basic. Baptism initiates the individual into the koinonia of the church; in the eucharist, Christ is really present to the believer . . . , who is thus bound together in koinonia both with the Lord and with others who share the sacramental meal.[71]

Anglican-Catholic dialogue took up the subject of the Eucharist in more detail, since differing doctrine was a major hindrance to their stated goal of organic union. At the Reformation, rejection of the Catholic doctrine of transubstantiation (that the substance of the bread and wine are transformed into the body and blood of Christ) had been a prime factor leading to the emergence of a separate Anglican Church. Yet when speaking of the change taking place in the elements in the Catholic mass, this dialogue says of the Eucharist that "*becoming* does not here imply material change." It speaks of a "sacramental presence in which God uses realities of this world to convey the realities of new creation. Bread for this life becomes the bread of eternal life." These statements seem to represent a softening of traditional Catholic teaching on transubstantiation. With this explanation in place, both Catholics and Anglicans could affirm that after the Eucharistic prayer, the bread "is truly the body of Christ, the Bread of Life."[72]

Lutherans and Catholics agreed that the Eucharist is supernatural and spiritual, not merely spatial.[73] They agreed further that the Eucharist is far more than a memorial: "The Lord calls his people into his presence and confronts them with his salvation."[74] They also agreed to an eschatological aspect of the Eucharist: "The promised future begins

70. Gros, Meyer, and Rusch, *Growth in Agreement II*, 814, par. 152.
71. Ibid., 586, pars. 11–12.
72. Meyer and Vischer, *Growth in Agreement*, 75, par. 7.
73. Ibid., 196, par. 16.
74. Ibid., 200, par. 36.

in a mysterious way here and now in the Lord's Supper. . . . Everlasting life does not begin in the future, but is already present in anyone who is united with the Lord. The future world breaks into our present one even now."[75]

Because of differences among themselves on the sacraments, not all evangelicals would accept these statements of Protestant-Catholic agreement. But the fact that these agreements now exist is an invitation for evangelicals to rethink once-settled notions about permanent differences between what Catholics believe and what evangelicals believe.

MEMORIES

In their dialogue, Reformed Protestants and Catholics sensed that mutual hostilities at the time of the Reformation and since had thwarted attempts to find theological peace. Even more, the two churches retained differing perspectives on what had actually happened in the sixteenth century. At their second set of meetings (1984–90), therefore, they engaged in a "reconciliation of memories" in which each party reviewed events of the Reformation and subsequent years. This also provided an opportunity to confess sins, personal and corporate, present and past.

As a means to reconcile memories, Reformed and Catholics each put on paper their own perspectives about the sixteenth-century Reformation.[76] The Reformed delegates lamented that their Reformed ecclesiastical ancestors sometimes perpetrated the same faults they criticized in Catholics. They "became legitimators of sometimes oppressive political establishments, fell into clericalism, and grew intolerant of minority viewpoints. They were occasionally guilty of condemnations, burnings and banishment, for example in regard to the Anabaptists in Switzerland." The Reformed also confessed that their forbearers were sometimes guilty of chauvinism, colonialism, and racism.[77] As for the current era, they acknowledged appreciation for "the seriousness with which the Roman Catholic Church has placed the word of God at the centre of its life, not least in modern liturgical reforms."[78]

For their part, Catholics acknowledged that during the Reformation era their church had been characterized by "venality and political and military involvements of some of the popes and members of the curia; the absence of bishops from their dioceses; their often ostentatious wealth and neglect of pastoral duties; the ignorance of many of the lower clergy; the often scandalous lives of clergy, including bishops

75. Ibid., 203, par. 45.
76. Gros, Meyer, and Rusch, *Growth in Agreement II*, 782–95. The Reformed perspective appears in pars. 17–32; the Roman Catholic perspective follows in pars. 33–62.
77. Ibid., 784, par. 23.
78. Ibid., 786, par. 29.

and certain popes; the disedifying rivalry among the religious orders; pastoral malpractice through misleading teaching about the efficacy of certain rights and rituals," and more. Catholics pointed out that the church belatedly addressed these faults.[79] By the time the Council of Trent finally convened in 1545, a full generation had passed since Martin Luther had posted his Ninety-five Theses, time enough for positions to harden almost irreconcilably.[80] "Catholics agreed that there was need for reform in the church of the sixteenth century and acknowledged the fact that their church authorities did not undertake the reform which might have prevented the tragic divisions that took place."[81]

But to make sure that dialogue participants were acting realistically, the Catholics added an additional word: "At the same time the Roman Catholic Church has never agreed with some of the steps taken by the Reformers relating to their separation from the Roman Catholic communion, nor with certain theological positions that developed in the Reformed communities."[82]

Despite such recognition of continuing division, enough reconciliation took place for the group to create a common confession of faith. That confession included a citation from the Second Vatican Council's decree on ecumenism, *Unitatis Redintegratio*, and its definition of "separated brethren" who are "justified by their faith through baptism, who reverence the written word of God, share in the life of grace, receive the gifts of the Holy Spirit, celebrate Christ's death and resurrection when they gather for the Lord's supper, and witness to Christ through the moral uprightness of their lives, through their works of charity and their efforts for justice and peace in the world."[83]

In attempting to reconcile memories of the Reformation and to write a mutual confession of faith, these two Christian bodies acknowledged the need for further study and forgiveness. Quoting John Paul II, they affirmed that "remembrance of the events of the past must not restrict the freedom of our present efforts to eliminate the harm that has been triggered by these events."[84] They also announced the need for serious historical research to be undertaken jointly. They grieved that the mutual anathemas of the Reformation era were still in place and remained to be resolved. They also invited attention to the way that the historic divisions had infected mission work in the Americas, Africa, Asia, and Oceania.[85]

79. Ibid., 787, par. 34.
80. Ibid., 789, par. 40.
81. Ibid., 792, par. 53.
82. Ibid.
83. Ibid., 793, par. 59.
84. Ibid., 815, par. 154.
85. Ibid., 816, par. 156.

Agreements between Protestants and Catholics were hard won and carefully worded, yet the dialogues made progress in significant areas. Almost without exception, delegates expressed personal gratitude for the opportunity to work and worship together with those whom they recognized as spiritual family members from the other side of the Reformation divide.

Remaining Disagreements

Though the ecumenical dialogues found agreement on many important theological issues, inevitably they also highlighted differences—some of them apparently irreconcilable. On these matters, to which we now turn, Protestant-Catholic dialogue had to be content with striving for better understanding and mutual respect.

MARY

Most Protestant-Catholic disagreements about Mary concerned Protestant fears that Mary's position was so elevated in the Catholic Church that it usurped the place reserved for God alone. Devotion to Mary, prayers to Mary, the idea that Mary was sinless and was "assumed" into heaven all made Protestants nervous about the possibility that the Catholic attitude toward Mary crossed the line into idolatry. Most dialogues contained some discussion about Mary, even if only to admit that agreement was impossible. The dialogue between evangelicals and Catholics is one example.

Evangelicals saw the subject of Mary as a challenge to agreement on missions, in part because they feared that Catholics had elevated Mary almost to a place of co-redeemer with Christ. Much of this dialogue was thus spent interpreting Catholic documents such as Pope Paul VI's 1974 *Marialis Cultus* and the Second Vatican Council's *Lumen Gentium* in which Marian doctrine was prominent.

In response, Catholics explained that Mary herself needed to be redeemed, that "she was herself saved through her Son's death. In her case, however, 'salvation' did not signify the forgiveness of sins, but that because of her predestination to be the 'Mother of God,' she was preserved from original sin."[86] As for evangelical concerns about Mary intruding into the Trinity, Catholics explained that "the notion of Mary's 'immersion' in the Trinity means that she is the daughter of the Father, the mother of the Son, the temple of the Holy Spirit . . . but they strongly insist that, of course, she cannot be on a level with the three persons of the Trinity, let alone the fourth person."[87]

86. Ibid., 419.
87. Ibid., 420.

AUTHORITY

Protestants, even those who employ confessions and creeds, were troubled by what they saw as the three-legged stool of Catholic authority (Scripture, church, tradition). While many Protestants expressed appreciation for the wisdom of the church, including the creeds, and also a great debt to the lessons of tradition, they did not treat tradition as equal to Scripture. Instead, they stood ready in principle to reject any church decision or tradition that conflicted with Scripture—and they expected God to reveal the meaning of Scripture to individuals, not just to the authoritative church.

Baptists, with their strong individualistic bent, had particular difficulties with the Catholic view of authority: "Baptists rely on scriptures alone, as interpreted under the guidance of the Holy Spirit, the Reformation principle. Roman Catholics receive God's revelation from the scriptures interpreted in the light of the Tradition under the leadership of the magisterium, in a communal process guided by the Holy Spirit."[88] This expression of difference produced considerable anxiety on both sides. Catholics questioned whether Baptists subscribe to basic historical statements of Christian orthodoxy such as the creeds of Nicea and Constantinople or indeed to any standards of orthodoxy. Baptists, on the other hand, looked at Catholic dogmas such as the immaculate conception and the assumption of Mary into heaven and asked whether Catholics set any limits on what they allow tradition to define.[89]

Methodist-Catholic dialogue began with a striving for unity similar to that which motivated the Anglican-Catholic dialogue; they started by "seeking full unity in faith, mission and sacramental life."[90] Yet when in their fourth session together the issue of authority came into focus (Nairobi, 1986), the role of Peter and the Roman popes as his successor became a point of division. In the words of the dialogue, "For Roman Catholics reconciliation with the see of Rome is a necessary step towards the restoration of Christian unity."[91] Catholics were careful to point out that papal infallibility was, "properly speaking, not attributed to the pope, nor to the teaching, but rather to this particular act of teaching. It means that he has been prevented by God from teaching error on matters relating to salvation."[92] Even so, the report recorded that "Methodists have problems with this Roman Catholic understanding of infallibility, especially as it seems to imply a discernment of truth which exceeds the

88. Ibid., 382, par. 45.
89. Ibid., 383, par. 48.
90. Ibid., 590, par. 38.
91. Ibid., 593, par. 57.
92. Ibid., 595, par. 71.

capacity of sinful human beings."[93] Or, again, "Methodists have further difficulty with the idea that the bishop of Rome can act in this process on behalf of the whole church."[94]

Not to be deterred from their original goal, the representatives devoted their next series of meetings to "The Apostolic Tradition" (Paris, 1991). Although Methodists and Catholics discovered much about which to agree, they did not resolve their basic division over papal authority. By 1991, the Methodist practice of ordaining women to pastoral office underscored a deepening division on the subject of ecclesiastical authority.[95]

STRUCTURE OF THE CHURCH

Differing views of authority lead naturally to differing ideals for church structure. As the Baptists put it in their dialogue, for them "koinonia [fellowship] is expressed primarily in local congregations gathered voluntarily under the lordship of Jesus Christ for worship, fellowship, instruction, evangelism and mission." Baptists might join together in associations, conventions, or alliances, but they avoid structures that limit the freedom of individuals or the autonomy of local congregations. From the other side, church structure possessed a different form: "For Roman Catholics, the koinonia which the Spirit effects in the local congregation is simultaneously a koinonia with the other local congregations in the one universal church. Correspondingly, they recognize the Spirit's activity in the spiritual and institutional bonds which unite congregations into dioceses presided over by bishops and which unite dioceses into the whole church presided over by the bishop of Rome."[96]

The Methodist-Catholic dialogue touched on the nature of church in each of its six meetings, principally by highlighting questions of authority. At the end of the fifth meeting (on apostolic tradition), they acknowledged basic historic differences concerning who constitutes the church—and on what it is that constitutes the church.

> Catholic and Methodist formularies have differed over the concrete location of the church which they both confess. While Wesley and the early Methodists could recognize the presence of Christian faith in the lives of individual Roman Catholics, it is only more recently that Methodists have become willing to recognize the Roman Catholic Church as an institution that exists for the divine good of its members. For its part, the Roman Catholic Church since Vatican II certainly includes Methodists among those

93. Ibid., 595, par. 72.
94. Ibid., 596, par. 73.
95. Ibid., 616, pars. 95–97.
96. Ibid., 383, par. 48.

who, by baptism and faith in Christ, enjoy "a certain though imperfect communion with the Catholic Church"; and it has envisaged Methodism among the ecclesial communities that are "not devoid of meaning and importance in the mystery of salvation" (*Unitatis Redingratio*, no. 3). . . . A large measure of common faith has been brought to light, so that the increase in shared life that has begun may confidently be expected to continue.[97]

ACCEPTABLE PRACTICES

Anglicans, in contrast to other Protestants who joined these dialogues, announced the goal of unity with Catholics and therefore made major concessions on church structure. For them, the purpose of the dialogues was not simply better understanding and fellowship but structural unity: "the restoration of complete communion in faith and sacramental life."[98] It almost worked. The two bodies agreed on issues that had divided them for four hundred years, issues such as priesthood,[99] location of authority,[100] sacraments,[101] salvation,[102] even the practicality of using a common lectionary of Scripture to be read in public worship throughout the year.[103] But after two decades of dialogue, the goal of unity began to fade.[104] What finally sank the project was not the great theological divisions of the Reformation, although authority in the church did remain a contentious issue.[105] Rather, Anglicans and Catholics could not agree on populist practices in the day-to-day lives of their churches, in particular, divorce,[106] birth control,[107] and the ordination of women.[108] Had the dialogue continued, it would certainly have divided over the acceptance by some Anglicans of homosexual practice and abortion. In the end, the two bodies settled for mutual blessing and continued conversations but not a united church.[109]

Despite the lofty goal that Anglicans and Catholics set at the beginning of their dialogue, these practical differences emerged early on. The

97. Ibid., 616–17, pars. 100–101.

98. Meyer and Vischer, *Growth in Agreement*, 63.

99. Ibid., 80, par. 7; 81, par. 10; 85, par. 2.

100. Ibid., 97, par. 23; 91, par. 7. Compare with the later caution issued in 1990 as noted in Gros, Meyer, and Rusch, *Growth in Agreement II*, 342, par. 57.

101. Meyer and Vischer, *Growth in Agreement*, 74–75, par. 6.

102. Gros, Meyer, and Rusch, *Growth in Agreement II*, 325, par. 32.

103. Ibid., 341, par. 51.

104. Ibid., 327.

105. Ibid., 372.

106. Ibid., 359, par. 62; 361–63, pars. 68–70, 74–75, 77.

107. Ibid., 364–65, pars. 80–82.

108. Meyer and Vischer, *Growth in Agreement*, 87, par. 5; and Gros, Meyer, and Rusch, *Growth in Agreement II*, 327, 342, par. 57.

109. Gros, Meyer, and Rusch, *Growth in Agreement II*, 372.

Elucidation of 1979, for example, observed that "the Commission realizes that the ordination of women has created for the Roman Catholic Church a new and grave obstacle to the reconciliation of our communions." Even though the two sides agreed on the nature of priesthood, they admitted that "objections . . . to the ordination of women are of a different kind from objections raised in the past against the validity of Anglican Orders in general."[110]

Differences over these social practices and differing attitudes on how they could be sanctioned (or prohibited) within the structure of the church eventually doomed the search for unity. The final "Common Declaration" (1996) of George Carey, archbishop of Canterbury, and Pope John Paul II closed by expressing longing for a future day "when Anglicans and Catholics, with all their Christian brothers and sisters, have achieved that full, visible unity that corresponds to Christ's prayer 'that they may all be one . . . so that the world may believe.'"[111] But it was not going to happen soon.

BAPTISM

Among themselves, Protestants have almost as many views of baptism as there are different kinds of Protestants. But Baptists, in particular, differed sharply with Catholics on the mode and the purpose of this sacrament or ordinance (even what to call this rite reveals fundamental differences). Reports of the Baptist-Catholic dialogue on the subject showed improved understanding and mutual respect but also a firm commitment to retain their opposing views.

> Baptists, viewing faith primarily as the response of the individual to God's free gift of grace, insist that the faith response precede baptism. . . . Roman Catholics regard the sacraments, such as baptism, in a context of faith, as an exercise of the power of the risen Christ. . . . Emphasizing the corporate as well as the individual nature of faith, they baptize infants and catechize them through a process culminating in full participation in the church. . . . Catholics [concede] that there is little clear evidence in the scriptures for [infant baptism. It is] sustained principally by tradition and a more corporate understanding of faith.[112]

Although their differences remained sharp, Baptists and Catholics agreed to continue discussing other questions that could narrow the divide: "Is faith solely an individual's response to God's gift? Can the faith of the community supply for the personal faith of an infant?"

110. Meyer and Vischer, *Growth in Agreement*, 87, par. 5.
111. Gros, Meyer, and Rusch, *Growth in Agreement II*, 372.
112. Ibid., 383–84, pars. 49–50.

What is the meaning of the church as "community of faith" or "body of Christ" within which individual believers participate? Are sacraments/ ordinances "outward signs of a preceding inner commitment," or are they "the means through which Christ himself effects his healing and saving work?"[113]

Questions of Special Interest to Evangelicals

Evangelism

Two subjects featured in the ecumenical dialogues hold particular interest for evangelicals. Since evangelicals by definition are committed to proclaiming the good news, they are especially interested in missions and evangelism. When this subject came up in the dialogues, one problem became immediately apparent: The groups sitting across the table from each other had often tried to evangelize each other. With some trepidation, the dialogues took up issues such as proselytizing, unworthy witness, and the potential for common witness. Evangelical missiologists, Baptists, and Pentecostals made excellent—and perhaps surprising—progress on each of these subjects.

Evangelicals are also especially concerned about the doctrine of justification, both because of its intrinsic signification and because justification of sinners before God is what evangelicals proclaim as the good news. To evangelize is simply to offer the hope of justification before God. But what exactly is justification? What is its relationship to salvation more generally? How is it connected (or not connected) to the church? What (if anything) do humans do in the process of justification? What does God do? When? How is justification related to sanctification? On these questions, results from the Lutheran-Catholic dialogue were of supreme importance.

CATHOLICS AND BAPTISTS

When Baptists and Catholics began to discuss evangelism, they recognized that they sometimes found themselves in the same disadvantageous situations. Both Baptists and Catholics experienced and do experience—in different locales and under different conditions—some measure of discrimination. Ironically, the dialogue participants recognized that religious discrimination sometimes comes from Baptists against Catholics, sometimes from Catholics against Baptists. Some of the discrimination comes in the form of proselytizing, which is usually a term of negative connotation used to describe illegitimate means of religious persua-

113. Ibid., 384, par. 51.

sion.[114] In the dialogue, representatives tried to differentiate between legitimate evangelism and illegitimate proselytization. They agreed that it was improper to exploit situations of distress, weakness, or deficient education to bring about conversion. It was also improper to make explicit or implicit offers of temporal and material advantages or to exert moral compulsion and psychological pressure. It was proper to allow the one being addressed full freedom to make a personal decision.[115]

Each group also recognized that there were geographic trouble spots where one group bore down heavily against the other and for which each deserved reproof. In traditionally Catholic countries, such as in Latin America, Baptists sometimes did not have civil and religious freedom. But when Baptists held numerical majority, as in the American South, Catholics sometimes suffered discrimination and intolerance.[116] In their dialogue, Baptists and Catholics agreed to shun illegitimate proselytization and to practice legitimate evangelism, particularly in places where one or the other is a strong majority. They also identified important reasons for this kind of peace plan, both spiritual ("In an increasingly secularized world, division and religious strife between Christian bodies can be such a scandal that non-believers may not be attracted to the gospel")[117] and social ("Both groups need to exercise greater vigilance to assure respect for religious liberty").[118]

CATHOLICS AND EVANGELICALS DIALOGUING ON MISSION

Evangelicals dialogued with Catholics on the subject of missions over a period of seven years. During that time, they addressed the age-old conundrum, "What about those who have never heard?" On this question, they opened with the presupposition that the basis for discussion was human need. The discussion then proceeded to an agreement: "All of us are concerned to avoid an interpretation of the universal saving will of God, which makes salvation automatic without the free response of the person."[119] But from this point the dialogue participants disagreed substantially. "Roman Catholics would expect God's mercy to be exercised effectively in benevolent action of his grace for the majority of humankind, unless they specifically reject his offer. Such a position gives them cause for confidence."[120] This confidence was expressed in phrases from the Second Vatican Council:

114. Ibid., 380–82, pars. 31–44.
115. Ibid., 380–81, par. 35.
116. Ibid., 381, par. 38.
117. Ibid., 381, par. 37.
118. Ibid., 382, par. 43.
119. Ibid., 411.
120. Ibid., 412.

"Those also can attain everlasting salvation who through no fault of their own do not know the gospel of Christ or his church." On the one hand, there are those who "sincerely seek God and, moved by his grace, strive by their deeds to do his will." On the other, there are those who "have not yet arrived at an explicit knowledge of God, but who strive to live a good life, thanks to his grace." Both groups are prepared by God's grace to receive his salvation either when they hear the gospel or even if they do not. They can be saved by Christ, in a mysterious relation to his church."[121]

Evangelicals explained that, while they might entertain similar hopes deep in their merciful hearts, they could find no support for such conclusions in Scripture. They insisted that, according to the New Testament, "those outside Christ are 'perishing' and that they can receive salvation only in and through Christ. They are therefore deeply exercised about the eternal destiny of those who have never heard of Christ."[122] This difference caused Catholic and evangelical missiologists to consider larger frames of reference: "Roman Catholics think evangelicals overstress the corruption of human beings by affirming their 'total depravity' . . . while evangelicals think Roman Catholics underestimate it and are therefore unwisely optimistic about the capacity, ability, and desire of human beings to respond to the grace of God."[123] The discussion produced better understanding of the other's point of view but hardly agreement.

These same groups, both of them passionate about evangelism and evangelization in their own way, then took up the touchy subject of proselytizing, which remains a particularly volatile subject in any joint conference on mission. Yet as the discussion continued, the two groups grew more sympathetic to each other's motives and came to agree on what could be considered fair (and unfair) actions. Understandably, Catholics did not appreciate evangelical missionaries trying to convert resident Catholics. They did understand, however, that evangelicals sought to evangelize nominal members of even their own churches out of authentic concern for their need of the gospel. But they hoped evangelicals would avoid sheep stealing from Catholic ranks. By way of conciliation, the two groups agreed, "We recognize that conscientious conviction leads some people to change from Catholic to evangelical or evangelical to Catholic allegiance, and leads others to seek to persuade people to do so. If this happens in conscience and without coercion, we would not call it proselytism."[124]

121. Ibid., 416.
122. Ibid., 417.
123. Ibid., 413.
124. Ibid., 436.

The participants went on to agree that certain forms of witness are unworthy expressions of the cause of Christ. They agreed that Christian missionaries (both evangelical and Catholic) need to examine motive, method, and message in the following terms:

- Unworthy *motives* are those in which "real concern in witness is not the glory of God through the salvation of human beings but rather the prestige of our own Christian community or indeed our personal prestige."

- Unworthy *methods* are those that resort to any kind of "physical coercion, moral constraint or psychological pressure." Exploiting another person's needs, weakness, or lack of education is "an affront to the freedom and dignity of human beings and to the Holy Spirit whose witness is gentle and not coercive."

- Unworthy *messages* include "unjust or uncharitable reference to the beliefs or practices of other religious communities in the hope of winning adherents."[125]

Participants did not stop after they had condemned unworthy motive, method, and message. They went on to outline an encouraging number of ways that evangelicals and Catholics could work together in the business of missions. Specific suggestions included the following:

- We can develop and publish a common translation of the Bible. The RSV with Apocrypha (1973) could become a starting point. In deference to Protestant readers, the Apocrypha could be printed as a separate section between the testaments.

- We can publish and distribute common Bible study materials, including atlases, handbooks, dictionaries, commentaries, and films. We can (together) be aggressive about placing these items in locations where Christianity, of any form, is a minority.

- We can together meet basic human needs by providing disaster relief, shelter for refugees, urban and rural development, medical care, counseling services, rescue work for drug addicts and prostitutes.

- We can witness together with Christian thinking on worldwide social issues such as the arms race, North-South economic inequality, environmental issues, and sexual mores.

125. Ibid.

- We can demonstrate Christian unity by continued honest face-to-face dialogue with other Christian groups speaking the truth in love.

- We can worship together, though non-Catholics should not take communion in a Catholic service and "there is no ruling of the Roman Catholic Church which would permit its members to receive communion in a Protestant church service."[126]

CATHOLICS AND PENTECOSTALS

By the time Catholics and Pentecostals gave serious attention to missions and evangelization, they had been meeting for a quarter century. Earlier gatherings had canvassed such potentially volatile subjects as baptism in the Holy Spirit, speaking in tongues, faith and religious experience, and the role of Mary. On these issues, they had come to hard-won agreements, or they had agreed to disagree with mutual respect. They had worshiped and prayed and studied together. In their final session, they broached the subject of missions and evangelism, a subject of great interest to both sides.

The topic was taken up with a measure of trepidation. Would it damage the hard-won trust that had been so painstakingly built up between them? Would the dialogue itself suffer? Would they be able to endure subsequent fallout from their constituencies?[127] In the face of such challenges, the participants took heart from the mutual goodwill generated by their previous meetings. And they thought they could see some hope of convergence: "The Catholic Church is in a process of renewal in evangelization and pastoral formation, Pentecostals are growing in an awareness of their responsibilities in the matter of structures and social systems."[128] While the two bodies "do not have a common understanding of church,"[129] they had moved closer together on what it means to be a Christian and therefore had moved closer on the common goal of evangelism. "Catholics . . . hold that everyone who believes in the name of the Lord Jesus and is properly baptized . . . is joined in a certain manner to the body of Christ." For Pentecostals, "the foundation of unity is a common faith and experience of Jesus Christ as Lord and Savior through the Holy Spirit."[130] But "Pentecostals and Catholics affirm the presence and power of the gospel in Christian communities outside of their own traditions"—and were extending that grace to each other.[131]

126. Ibid., 431–35.
127. Ibid., 765, par. 68.
128. Ibid., 764, par. 65.
129. Ibid., 765, par. 69.
130. Ibid., 765, par. 69.
131. Ibid., 773, par. 112.

Together they defined proselytism as "a disrespectful, insensitive and uncharitable effort to transfer the allegiance of a Christian from one ecclesial body to another."[132] This definition drew them to consider religious freedom. They agreed that proselytism and evangelism were not synonyms and deplored "'anti-proselytism' laws which prohibited or greatly restricted any kind of Christian evangelism or missionary activity."[133] They agreed that

religious freedom affirms the right of all persons to pursue the truth and witness to the truth according to their conscience. It includes the freedom to acknowledge Jesus Christ as Lord and Saviour and the freedom of Christians to witness to their faith in him by word and deed. . . . Religious freedom includes the freedom to embrace a religion or to change one's religion without any coercion which would impair such freedom.[134]

They then confronted their own sins toward each other:

Catholics are well aware that attempts at Christianization have often been attached to political and economic expansion (e.g., Latin America) and that sometimes pressure and violence have been used. They also acknowledge that prior to Vatican II, Catholic doctrine has been reluctant to support full religious freedom in civil law. Today Catholics and Pentecostals condemn coercive and violent methods. Nevertheless, all too often aggressiveness still characterizes our interactions. Words have become the new weapons. Catholics are affronted when some Pentecostals assume that they are not even Christians, when they speak disrespectfully of the Catholic Church and its leaders or when Pentecostals lead Catholic members into newly established Pentecostal fellowships. Pentecostals are affronted when Catholics in some parts of the world view them as "rapacious wolves," when they are ridiculed . . . or when they are indiscriminately classified as "sects."[135]

The participants then agreed on certain methods that would allow them to do the work of evangelism while respecting each other. An evangelist coming into a new area should make courtesy calls on the established workers, sharing information and goals and respecting the long-term Christian work already embedded within the social structure of the culture.[136] "Instead of conflict, can we not converse with one another, pray with one another, try to cooperate with one another . . . ? In effect,

132. Ibid., 768, par. 83.
133. Ibid., 770, par. 97.
134. Ibid., 772, par. 104.
135. Ibid., 767, par. 82.
136. Ibid., 766, pars. 73, 76.

we need to look for ways in which Christians can seek the unity to which Christ calls his disciples . . . to love one another."[137] Both Pentecostals and Catholics spoke against evangelistic methods that treated people as objects rather than as individuals created with dignity in the image of God. They were troubled by strategies that limited congregations to one race, class, ethnic group, or other social grouping.[138] They insisted that this mutual respect need not limit evangelism. "All Christians have the right to bear witness to the gospel before all people, including other Christians. Such witness may legitimately involve the persuasive proclamation of the gospel in such a way as to bring people to faith in Jesus Christ to commit themselves more deeply to him within the context of their own church." Motive was important: "The legitimate proclamation of the gospel will bear the marks of Christian love . . . never seek its own selfish ends by using the opportunity to speak against or in any way denigrate another Christian community."

Participants cited Billy Graham as a prime example of this loving, respectful form of evangelism.[139] But they also admonished each other about the *purpose* of evangelism, that, even though divided, "Christ calls . . . Christians to unity 'so that the world may believe.'"[140] They agreed to build on their twenty-five years of dialogue to reduce future tensions in this area: "'Can it be,' Paul asks, 'there is no one among you wise enough to decide between one believer and another?'"[141]

The discussion then moved to the possibility of common witness. Here the agreement took a startling turn: the common witness of mutual forgiveness.

> Mutual forgiveness is itself an act of common witness. Here equity in the recognition of guilt is not the goal. One side may have offended more than the other. That determination is left to God. Rather, as Jesus himself has given us an example, each side takes on the sins of the other. In Christian forgiveness it is not a question of who threw the first stone (John 8:7), of who did what to whom first; rather it is the willingness to make the first step. Both sides should take the initiative according to gospel norms: Pentecostals should take the initiative for reconciliation because they feel themselves the most aggrieved; Catholics should take the initiative because they are the elder in interchurch relations. In both cases, if asked for our coat, we give also our cloak; if asked to go one mile, we go two.[142]

137. Ibid., 767, par. 79.
138. Ibid., 756, par. 16.
139. Ibid., 770, pars. 94–96.
140. Ibid., 772, par. 106.
141. Ibid., 773, par. 109.
142. Ibid., 775–76, par. 123.

These unusually frank and biblical words did not solve all problems, but they did provide a high goal for evangelistic efforts from both sides.

Justification

In their twenty-seven years of dialogue, Catholics and Lutherans discussed a variety of mutually important topics, but the subject that has gained the most attention was their work on justification. Of necessity, the dialogue first had to look at ecclesiology and address the question, What part does the church play in justification? Significant steps in addressing that issue and related matters included the nature of the church,[143] church as instrument and/or mediator of salvation,[144] Luther's statements on the church and salvation,[145] and Vatican II's vision of church as sacrament.[146] Eventually, they clarified an underlying tension by observing that "Catholics ask whether the Lutheran understanding of justification does not diminish the reality of the church; Lutherans ask whether the Catholic understanding of church does not obscure the gospel as the doctrine of justification explicates it."[147] They then elaborated on this tension as a subject for future discussion.[148]

The most visible fruit of this intensive discussion appeared in "The Joint Declaration on the Doctrine of Justification" (JDDJ), which was signed October 31, 1999: Reformation Day. But steps going back a quarter of a century paved the way for this joint declaration.[149] The Malta report (1972) set the challenge and sowed seeds for consensus:

> Out of the question about the center of the gospel arises the question of how the two sides understand justification—each side making concessions. Catholic theologians . . . emphasize . . . that God's gift for the believer is unconditional as far as human accomplishments are concerned. Lutheran

143. Ibid., 507, pars. 84–85; 508, pars. 91–92.
144. Ibid., 512, par. 108.
145. Ibid., 513, par. 111.
146. Ibid., 516, par. 120.
147. Ibid., 525, par. 166.
148. Ibid., 532, pars. 199–201.
149. Records documenting this dialogue include the Malta report titled *The Gospel and the Church* (1972), which worked on the relationship of Scripture and tradition; "The Eucharist" (1978), which eliminated several sacramental differences; *The Ministry in the Church* (1981), which examined a common priesthood, ordained ministry, ordination, and apostolic succession; *Confessio Augustana* (1980), which took up the Augsburg Confession of 1530; "Ways to Community" (1980); "Martin Luther—Witness to Jesus Christ" (1983); and *Facing Unity: Models, Forms, and Phases of Catholic-Lutheran Church Fellowship* (1984), which canvassed various forms of unity ranging from spiritual fellowship to organic union.

theologians emphasize that the event of justification is not limited to individual forgiveness of sins, and they do not see in it a purely external declaration of the justification of the sinner.[150]

Subsequent steps toward a joint declaration on justification took place throughout the dialogues, for example, during the work on the Augsburg Confession (1980)[151] and again in 1983 when the group looked at the work of Martin Luther on the five-hundredth anniversary of his birth.[152]

Along the way, dialogue in America between Catholics and Lutherans produced a most important interim report. In 1985, this local dialogue led to agreement on a statement that pointed the way to what came later in 1999:

> We believe that God's creative graciousness is offered to us and to everyone for healing and reconciliation so that through the Word made flesh, Jesus Christ, "who was put to death for our transgression and raised for our justification" (Rom. 4:25), we are called to pass from the alienation and oppression of sin to freedom and fellowship with God in the Holy Spirit. It is not through our own initiative that we respond to this call, but only through an undeserved gift which is granted and made known in faith, and which comes to fruition in our love of God and neighbor, as we are led by the Spirit in faith to bear witness to the divine gift in all aspects of our lives. This faith gives us hope for ourselves and for all humanity and gives us confidence that salvation in Christ will always be proclaimed as the gospel, the good news for which the world is searching.[153]

On October 31, 1999, exactly 482 years after Martin Luther nailed his Ninety-five Theses for debate on a Wittenberg church door, Cardinal Edward Cassidy of the Vatican and German Lutheran bishop Christian Krause, meeting in Augsburg, signed "The Joint Declaration on the Doctrine of Justification."[154] This concise document covered a mere eight pages containing forty-four paragraphs, but nearly every paragraph has been pondered deeply by a wide range of authorities.[155] Significantly, the "Joint Declaration" began with agreement on definition:

150. Meyer and Vischer, *Growth in Agreement*, 174, par. 26.
151. Ibid., 243, pars. 14–15.
152. Gros, Meyer, and Rusch, *Growth in Agreement II*, 439, pars. 9–10.
153. George H. Anderson, T. Austin Murphy, and Joseph A. Burgess, eds., *Justification by Faith: Lutherans and Catholics in Dialogue*, VII (Minneapolis: Fortress, 1985), 73–74.
154. Douglas Sweeney, "Taming the Reformation," *Christianity Today*, January 10, 2000, 63–65. This JDDJ statement represented official agreement between the Roman Catholic Church and the Lutheran World Federation.
155. As only a few of many examples, see ibid.; Anthony N. S. Lane, *Justification by Faith in Catholic-Protestant Dialogue: An Evangelical Assessment* (New York: T & T Clark, 2002); a multi-authored series of seven articles shaping a symposium on steps toward

Justification is the forgiveness of sins, liberation from the dominating power of sin and death, and from the curse of the law. It is acceptance into communion with God: already now, but then full in God's coming kingdom. It unites with Christ and with his death and resurrection. It occurs in the reception of the Holy Spirit in baptism and incorporation into the one body. All this is from God alone, for Christ's sake, by grace, through faith, in "the gospel of God's Son."[156]

With direct reference to the Reformation's insistence on *sola gratia*, the JDDJ stated in its key assertion:

Together we confess: by grace alone, in faith in Christ's saving work and not because of any merit on our part, we are accepted by God and receive the Holy Spirit, who renews our hearts while equipping and calling us to good works. . . . Faith is itself God's gift through the Holy Spirit who works through word and sacrament in the community of believers and who, at the same time, leads believers into that renewal of life which God will bring to completion in eternal life . . . Our new life is solely due to the forgiving and renewing mercy that God imparts as a gift and we receive in faith, and never can merit it in any way.[157]

By way of explication, the declaration then dipped into its familiar pattern of "Lutherans say, Catholics say."

When Catholics say that persons "cooperate" in preparing for and accepting justification by consenting to God's justifying action, they see such personal consent as itself an effect of grace, not as an action arising from innate human abilities. . . . According to Lutheran teaching, human beings are incapable of cooperating in their salvation, because as sinners they actively oppose God. . . . They mean thereby to exclude any possibility of contributing to one's own justification, but do not deny that believers are fully involved personally in their faith, which is effected by God's word. . . . Lutherans emphasize that the righteousness of Christ is our righteousness. . . . Catholics emphasize the renewal of the interior person through the reception of grace imparted as a gift to the believer.[158]

---

the Joint Declaration, *Pro Ecclesia* 7 (Fall 1998): 398–470; Michaël Root, "The Jubilee Indulgence and the Joint Declaration on the Doctrine of Justification," *Pro Ecclesia* 9 (Fall 2000): 460–75; and Mark Husbands and Daniel J. Treier, eds., *Justification: What's at Stake in the Current Debates?* (Downers Grove, IL: InterVarsity, 2004).

156. Gros, Meyer, and Rusch, *Growth in Agreement II*, 568, par. 11 (Scripture citations omitted).

157. Ibid., 568–69, pars. 15–17.

158. Ibid., 569, par. 20; 569, par. 21; 570, par. 23; 570, par. 24.

On the Reformation's critical insistence on *sola fide*, JDDJ spelled out differences of emphasis that remained within the broader consensus: "According to the Lutheran understanding, God justifies sinners in faith alone. . . . A distinction but not a separation is made between justification itself and the renewal of one's way of life that necessarily follows from justification and without which faith does not exist."[159] For Catholics, it was important to view "faith as fundamental in justification. For without faith, no justification can take place. Persons are justified through baptism as hearers of the word and believers in it. . . . This new personal relation to God is grounded totally on God's graciousness and remains constantly dependent on the salvific and creative working of this glorious God."[160]

In a similar manner, JDDJ addressed the subject of sin. It offered agreement that sin is a lifelong struggle for the Christian; the justified "ask God daily for forgiveness . . . are ever again called to conversion and penance, and are ever again granted forgiveness.[161] Lutherans then explained that Christians are "at the same time righteous and sinner" but that sin does not separate the Christian from God because they are "born anew by baptism."[162] Catholics, on the other hand, said that "when individuals voluntarily separate themselves from God . . . they must receive pardon and peace in the sacrament of reconciliation."[163]

Regarding the assurance of salvation, Lutherans and Catholics said together that "the faithful can rely on the mercy and promises of God . . . and so be sure of his grace."[164] Lutherans then added, "In the midst of temptation, believers should not look to themselves. . . . In God's promises they are assured of their salvation, but are never secure looking at themselves."[165] Catholics cautioned, "Every person, however, may be concerned about his salvation when he looks upon his own weakness and shortcoming. Recognizing his own failures, however, the believer may yet be certain that God intends his salvation."[166]

The joint statement on the role of works in justification was similarly nuanced. "We confess together that good works—a Christian life lived in faith, hope and love—follow justification and are its fruits."[167] Catholics added that a reward in heaven is promised for these good

---

159. Ibid., 570, par. 26.
160. Ibid., 570, par. 27.
161. Ibid., 571, par. 28.
162. Ibid., 569, par. 20; 571, par. 29.
163. Ibid., 571, par. 30.
164. Ibid., 572, par. 34.
165. Ibid., 572, par. 35.
166. Ibid., 572, par. 36.
167. Ibid., 572, par. 37.

works, though justification itself "always remains the unmerited gift of grace."[168] Meanwhile, Lutherans saw good works as the "fruits and signs of justification" but eternal life as "unmerited 'reward.'"[169]

Having come to satisfactory though guarded agreement on justification—the issue that was so critical for the divisions of the Reformation of the sixteenth century—both parties then removed the anathemas of that era: "The teaching of the Lutheran churches presented in this declaration does not fall under the condemnations from the council of Trent. The condemnations of the Lutheran confessions do not apply to the teaching of the Roman Catholic Church presented in this declaration."[170] They then outlined the need for future discussion, focusing, not surprisingly, on questions about the church.[171]

As might be expected, "The Joint Declaration on the Doctrine of Justification" has elicited a great deal of comment, both in popular journalism and serious scholarship, not all of it favorable. From evangelicals, solid examples of such journalism and scholarship have come respectively from Douglas Sweeney of Trinity Evangelical School of Divinity and Anthony N. S. Lane of London Bible College. Sweeney, writing in *Christianity Today,* admits that Catholics and Lutherans have come a long way since the divisive days of the sixteenth century but asks if JDDJ claims too much. "Well, yes," Sweeney responds. He goes on to opine that the real agreement here is "a very minimal core of common Christian language and . . . charitable renderings of one another's historic differences." He thinks that if these two bodies are to find genuine agreement on justification, they must also treat related issues such as indulgences, penance, and purgatory.[172]

From Lane has come a definitive book assessing fifty years of Protestant-Catholic dialogue set against five hundred years of doctrinal development since the Reformation.[173] Lane concludes that a significant number of Catholics have moved closer to the historic Protestant view of justification and that the "Joint Declaration" shows Rome at the highest level in accord with significant Reformation beliefs on the subject. He celebrates *sola fide* found in the Annex to JDDJ along with similar statements on sin, merit, and reward.

But Lane also cautions that "the myth of a monolithic Roman Catholic Church is long since dead," that many Catholics, including Catholic theologians, are subject to what Alister McGrath terms "Nicodemism,"

168. Ibid., 572, par. 38.
169. Ibid., 573, par. 39.
170. Ibid., 573, par. 41.
171. Ibid., 573, par. 43.
172. Sweeney, "Taming the Reformation," 63–65.
173. Lane, *Justification by Faith in Catholic-Protestant Dialogue,* 225–31.

selecting a la carte beliefs of their own choosing. He notes that Luther's perspective on justification is rarely heard in the classrooms of Catholic seminaries, universities, and colleges.

On the basis of wide-ranging analysis, Lane concludes that while Catholics agree in official dialogues with Protestants about important aspects of justification, they do not take the role of justification by faith as a touchstone for their theology. "The issue is not so much what Catholics teach about justification as their lack of interest in it." As confirmation, he quotes Cardinal Avery Dulles, who has worked long on the Protestant-Catholic dialogues: "Catholic theologians have felt more at home with the theology of grace . . . [but] have generally given only passing attention to justification as God's forensic deed on behalf of sinners. *Justification is rarely discussed at length except in polemics against, or dialogue with, Protestants.*"[174]

In sum, Lane asks the same question we ask as the title of this book: Is the Reformation over? His response: "By no means. There remain huge differences in other areas such as Mariology and the authority of the pope. The accord reached on the doctrine of justification is an important milestone on the path towards full agreement, but there remains a considerable distance still to be covered."[175]

Taking Stock

During the thirty-plus years of Protestant-Catholic dialogues, each paired group aimed for consensus of one kind or another. They frequently quoted Christ's prayer in John 17:21 "that all of them may be one . . . so that the world may believe." But unity comes in many forms. Only the Catholic-Anglican dialogue aimed self-consciously at organic unity, and this effort did not succeed. The Lutheran-Catholic dialogue considered alternative forms of unity within three general categories: partial union, comprehensive union, and fellowship.[176] Some form of partial union is available to all Christians and might include spiritual unity, fellowship in dialogue, fellowship in action, and intercommunion. Comprehensive union was more demanding and more carefully defined. Participants classified the possibilities of comprehensive union as organic or corporate union. Less ambitious than either partial union or comprehensive union were varieties of fellowship: church fellowship

---

174. Ibid., 230.
175. Ibid., 231.
176. Gros, Meyer, and Rusch, *Growth in Agreement II*, 446–50, pars. 8–34.

through agreement, conciliar fellowship, and (if all else failed) union in reconciled diversity.

Unreconciled Differences

Although each of the eight dialogues reviewed in this chapter strove for unity (of some kind) and although each made significant progress toward at least some doctrinal consensus, differences did not go away. A number of those differences showed up in almost every dialogue.

ECCLESIAL AUTHORITY OF THE CHURCH

The most serious differences were rooted in ecclesiology, contrasting versions of what the church is and how it functions. The dialogues covered much ground on the nature of Christian ministry, where significant agreement resulted. Even the practice of ordination found a measure of agreement in some of the dialogues. But the lines of authority that made ordination possible—for Catholics, pope to bishop to priest—yielded scant agreement. Only the Anglicans made major (and surprising) concessions on this issue. No other Protestant body would accept the infallibility of the pope, even after Catholics carefully qualified that papal infallibility is limited to when the pope speaks *ex cathedra*.

TRADITION AND SCRIPTURE AS AUTHORITY

On questions of authority, Protestants insisted on *sola scriptura*. Catholics held that the church has the authority to interpret Scripture and that interpretation is also authoritative. Private interpretation made Catholics nervous, as it did during the Reformation. Catholics are now invited to study Scripture privately but also to recognize the church's authority to interpret and apply its teachings. Catholics and Protestants agree that it was the church exercising its authority that defined the present canon of Scripture.

SACRAMENTS

What makes a sacrament valid? For Catholics, valid sacraments always retain a connection to ordination, which leads back eventually to the pope. Catholics currently observe seven sacraments, including ordination. Most Protestants observe only two sacraments (and some call them ordinances). These Protestant sacraments or ordinances are usually administered by an ordained pastor, but most Protestants do not see the need for connecting the administration of sacraments to higher church authority, such as the Catholic pope. For this reason, Protestants are often willing to have Catholics participate in their celebrations of the Lord's Supper. Informed Catholics, however, do not regard a Protestant

Communion or Eucharist as valid because it is not administered by an ordained priest in fellowship with their church and the pope. Catholics cannot welcome non-Catholics to their Eucharist because participating in the Catholic Eucharist entails recognition of papal authority, which Protestants by definition do not accept. Since only a Catholic priest ordained by a bishop can validly administer Catholic sacraments, mutual celebration of the sacraments remains a far distant possibility.

SMALL BUT PRACTICAL UNRESOLVED DIFFERENCES

A number of controversial issues popped up in the dialogues but did not receive significant treatment. Yet since many of these affect individuals in their day-to-day religious lives, they will continue to plague attempts at unity. They include devotion to Mary, celibacy of clergy, birth control, saints,[177] marriage and divorce,[178] and women in ordained ministry.

Common Agreements

No realistic reading of the reports of these dialogues can possibly miss the serious matters of doctrine and practice that continue to divide Catholic Christians and Protestant Christians. Yet no charitable reading can possibly miss the unexpectedly broad range of agreements that participants were able to reach. Even with many issues where agreement was impossible, participants did move closer in mutual understanding and respect. And with an atmosphere predisposed to maximize agreement and minimize difference, the results of these dialogues must give pause. Consensus between Catholics and at least some Protestants was reached on a remarkable number of long-standing contentious matters: baptism, justification, mission, social justice, the role of the laity, the functions of the clergy, the meaning of sacraments, the person of Jesus, the work of the Holy Spirit, the Trinity, the incarnation of Christ, and mutual forms of worship.

In almost every dialogue, the delegates met together for prayer, study of Scripture, and corporate worship with local congregations. They came to mutual respect and even affection. A number of the dialogues led to the cancellation of anathemas that had been issued during the Reformation. Even granting a certain artificiality to what the dialogues accomplished—even, that is, recognizing that goodwill may have occasionally triumphed over hardheaded realism—the cumulative results of these dialogues record a momentous shaking of once-settled ground. On the basis of the ecumenical dialogues, can it be said that the Reformation is over? Probably not. But a once-yawning chasm has certainly narrowed.

---

177. Ibid., 553, par. 294.
178. Meyer and Vischer, *Growth in Agreement,* 288, par. 28.

5

THE CATHOLIC *CATECHISM*

Comments such as the following are heard frequently when evangelical Protestants talk about Catholicism:

- "There is much that I admire about the Catholic faith. But Catholics think Mary is a god, and the pope is their dictator—and then there is the whole question of celibacy."
- "The people in my Baptist Sunday school class think that the Catholic Church is a cult. Should I argue about that?"
- "Do Catholics believe the Bible? Are they allowed to read it?"
- "Should we keep Ms. _____ in our employ? She is a Catholic, and we are an evangelical institution."
- "I wish that Catholics believed in grace. How can you be a Christian if you don't believe in salvation by grace through faith?"
- "I have good Catholic friends. They seem to pray to the same God I do. What do Catholics believe anyway?"

Behind such commentary lies a mixture of shrewd observation, mistaken inferences, partial understanding, and incomplete apprehension. What Catholics in fact believe, as a matter of official church policy, is found definitively stated in the complete and updated *Catechism of the Catholic Church* published in English in 1994 and filling 756 pages.[1]

1. United States Catholic Conference, *Catechism of the Catholic Church* (New York: Doubleday, 1994).

115

Unlike the various Protestant catechisms that have widely varying authority, this document is the official teaching of the Catholic Church, and it speaks for everyone within the church. If you are a Catholic, this is your doctrinal statement—whether or not you are fully aware of its contents. This point bears repeating. It is one thing to conclude that many Catholics do not live up to their church's official teaching or to argue that the Catholic hierarchy tolerates too much latitude in promoting official Catholic beliefs. It is an entirely different thing to make mistakes concerning the church's official standard of doctrine. The *Catechism*, as it was published in the mid-1990s, is the official teaching of the Roman Catholic Church. If something is not in the *Catechism*, it is not Catholic teaching. If something is in the *Catechism*, it is official Catholic doctrine. Therefore, this updated *Catechism* is the best place to look when seeking to understand what the Catholic Church teaches and what Catholics believe.

Evangelicals or confessional Protestants who pick up the *Catechism* will find themselves in for a treat. Sentences, paragraphs, whole pages sound as if they could come from evangelical pulpits, including passages on topics such as the nature of Scripture or the meaning of grace and faith. These readers will also notice the depth of scholarship, worn quite lightly, with hundreds of references to Scripture but also citations from early theologians of the Christian faith dating as far back as Ignatius of Antioch, who died in A.D. 110, and the *Didache*, an early document of worship and theology dated probably to the same decade. Readers familiar with standard statements of faith from the Reformation era—such as Luther's Small Catechism (1529), the Heidelberg Catechism (1536), and the Westminster Shorter Catechism (1647)—will quickly notice a different tone in this Catholic writing. While covering much of the same territory (the Apostles' Creed, the sacraments, the Ten Commandments, the Lord's Prayer), the Catholic *Catechism* is much more comprehensive. Moreover, it looks beyond the statement of doctrine to the care of souls.

The Catholic *Catechism* is strikingly pastoral in tone. It is in part a book of worship—focusing again and again on the majesty of God, inviting readers to reflect on God's character, to respond to his love, to live as he commands, and to devote themselves to his service. In spite of its length, the Catholic *Catechism* does not seek to solve all theological questions, though it does present some excellent sections of theological argumentation. Instead, it often rests contentedly within the mystery of God and invites its readers to do the same. Readers, both Catholic and Protestant, may come to the *Catechism* looking for information. Finding information, they may also find themselves (as we have done) stopping to pray.

But the Catholic *Catechism* is not an evangelical document. In the areas where Protestants and Catholics are likely to disagree (for example, the sacraments, the pope, Mary, purgatory), it expresses official Catholic teaching clearly. Protestant readers, though not likely to agree, will nonetheless come away with a better understanding of why Catholics think as they do on such subjects.

This chapter covers three major questions: Where can Catholics and many evangelicals find agreement in the words of the Catholic *Catechism*? In areas of disagreement, how does the *Catechism* help Protestants understand Catholic thinking? How does the Catholic understanding of the church, as expressed in the *Catechism*, shape the subjects on which evangelicals and Catholics agree or disagree? Although trying to answer these questions will take a number of pages, it is, of course, possible to say only a fraction of what needs to be said about such an important document. But for issues we do not address, the *Catechism* is a public document, with excellent indexes, and is open to the inspection of all. We begin with a word or two of background.

Background

In the sixteenth century, Protestant Reformers showered the countryside with tracts attacking Catholic doctrine and with their own catechisms intended to fill the void created by uneducated clergy leading a newly literate people. In response to the Reformation, Catholics clarified their own theology at the Council of Trent (1545–63). In 1562, that council ordered a catechism to be written and assigned four distinguished theologians to the task. Its purpose was to help priests in their care of souls. It was to be studied in home and church, discussed, memorized, and preached from—with an outline for a year of sermons based on its text. This Roman catechism, first published in 1566 (in Latin and Italian), eventually made its way into English.[2]

The *Baltimore Catechism*, familiar to many American Catholics, was descended from that sixteenth-century document. In 1884, when bishops of the United States gathered in Baltimore, they discussed the need for an English version of the Roman catechism—in language appropriate for American schoolchildren. This *Baltimore Catechism* was first published in 1891 with 100 questions and soon expanded to 421 questions

2. Charles G. Herberman et al., *Catholic Encyclopedia* (New York: Robert Appleton, 1912), s.v. "Roman Catechism."

(still pocket-sized). Later versions tripled that length and added notes for teachers.[3]

Just as the Council of Trent issued the Roman catechism to reinvigorate the spiritual health of clergy and laity, the Second Vatican Council (1962–65) also commissioned a catechism. In 1985, at a twenty-year celebration of Vatican II, the gathered Synod of Bishops expressed once again the need for such a teaching document. In 1986, Pope John Paul II commissioned twelve cardinals and bishops with the task. They were assisted by an editorial committee of seven diocesan bishops who were experts in theology. The commission prepared nine successive drafts as they consulted with Catholic bishops throughout the world; soon the document became "the result of the collaboration of the whole Episcopate of the Catholic Church." The stated purpose of this catechism was to "faithfully and systematically present the teaching of Sacred Scripture" and "to allow for a better knowledge of the Christian mystery and for enlivening the faith of the People of God." On October 11, 1992, Pope John Paul II signed his name to this new *Catechism of the Catholic Church,* declaring it "a statement of the Church's faith and of catholic doctrine, attested to or illumined by Sacred Scripture, the Apostolic Tradition, and the Church's Magisterium . . . a sure norm for teaching the faith."[4] Publication throughout the world, which often involved delicate questions of translation, soon followed. Catholics themselves greeted the *Catechism* with a mixture of gratitude and disquiet, but the mandate of the council was at last fulfilled.[5]

The *Catechism* opens with Scripture that reflects the priorities of Christ's high priestly prayer and other crucial passages from the New Testament: "Father, . . . this is eternal life, that they may know you, the only true God, and Jesus Christ whom you have sent" (John 17:3). "God our Savior desires all men to be saved and to come to the knowledge of the truth" (1 Tim. 2:3–4). "There is no other name under heaven given among men by which we must be saved" than the name of Jesus (Acts 4:12). The opening paragraph then invites readers to God: "He calls man to seek him, to know him, to love him with all his strength. . . . In his Son and through him, he invites men

3. Paul Boudreau, "What Is the Baltimore Catechism?" *U.S. Catholic* 68, no. 5 (May 2003): 26.

4. *Catechism of the Catholic Church,* 3–5.

5. See, as examples, Francis J. Buckley, "The Catechism of the Catholic Church: An Appraisal," *Horizons* 20 (1993): 301–10; Nathan Mitchell, "Eucharistic Theology in the New Catechism," *Worship* 68 (1994): 536–44; Avery Robert Dulles, "The Challenge of the Catechism," *First Things,* January 1995, 46–53; William S. Kurz, "The Use of Scripture in the Catechism of the Catholic Church," *Communio* 23 (1996): 480–507; and the entire winter issue of *Pro Ecclesia* 4 (1995).

to become, in the Holy Spirit, his adopted children and thus heirs of his blessed life."[6]

Areas of Agreement

Evangelical Protestants reading through the Catholic *Catechism* will be surprised by how much of it they can affirm. The *Catechism* is a book of doctrine, but its theology is presented in such a worshipful manner that Christians of all stripes will find paragraph after paragraph leading to worship and prayer. We estimate that evangelicals can embrace at least two-thirds of the *Catechism*. These parts of the *Catechism* contain a common orthodoxy, a common devotion to God (with numerous ways to express that devotion), and a common understanding of holy living.

Common Orthodoxy

A thoughtful Protestant attempting to create a brief outline of the Christian faith could do much worse than select quotations from the Catholic *Catechism*. Such an outline might look something like this:

- "The eternal God gave a beginning to all that exists outside of himself; he alone is Creator. . . . The totality of all that exists . . . depends on the One who gives it being."[7]
- "And so we see the Holy Spirit, the principal author of Sacred Scripture, often attributing actions to God without mentioning any secondary causes, . . . a profound way of recalling God's primacy and absolute Lordship over history and the world."[8]
- *"God is the author of Sacred Scripture.* . . . We must acknowledge that the books of Scripture firmly, faithfully, and without error teach that truth which God, for the sake of our salvation, wished to see confided to the Sacred Scriptures."[9]
- "The mystery of the Most Holy Trinity is the central mystery of Christian faith and life. It is the mystery of God himself. . . . *The Trinity is One.* We do not confess three Gods, but one God in three persons, the 'consubstantial Trinity.' . . . Everyone who glorifies

6. *Catechism of the Catholic Church*, 10, par. 1. The *Catechism* does not use gender inclusive language, which has been one of the most controversial decisions relating to its translation into English.

7. Ibid., 85, par. 290.

8. Ibid., 90, par. 304.

9. Ibid., 36–37, pars. 105, 107.

the Father does so through the Son in the Holy Spirit; everyone who follows Christ does so because the Father draws him and the Spirit moves him."[10]

- "God is not the property of any one people. But he acquired a people for himself from those who previously were not a people: 'a chosen race, a royal priesthood, a holy nation.'"[11]

- "Belief in the true Incarnation of the Son of God is the distinctive sign of Christian faith: 'by this you know the Spirit of God: every spirit which confesses that Jesus Christ has come in the flesh is of God.' . . . Because 'human nature was assumed, not absorbed,' in the mysterious union of the Incarnation, the Church was led over the course of centuries to confess the full reality of Christ's human soul, with its operations of intellect and will, and of his human body. . . . But at the same time, this truly human knowledge of God's Son expressed the divine life of his person. 'The human nature of God's Son, *not by itself but by its union with the Word,* knew and showed forth in itself everything that pertains to God.' . . . The Fathers see in the virginal conception the sign that it truly was the Son of God who came in a humanity like our own."[12]

- "By giving up his own Son for our sins, God manifests that his plan for us is one of benevolent love, prior to any merit on our part: 'In this is love, not that we loved God but that he loved us and sent his Son to be the expiation for our sins.' God 'shows his love for us in that while we were yet sinners Christ died for us.'"[13]

- "Apart from the cross there is no other ladder by which we may get to heaven."[14]

- "Our justification comes from the grace of God. Grace is *favor,* the *free and undeserved help* that God gives us to respond to his call to become children of God, adoptive sons, partakers of the divine nature and of eternal life."[15]

- "Believing in Jesus Christ and in the One who sent him for our salvation is necessary for obtaining that salvation. . . . Faith is an entirely free gift that God makes to man."[16]

- "Although the Resurrection was an historical event that could be verified by the sign of the empty tomb and by the reality of the

10. Ibid., 69, par. 234; 75, par. 253; 77, par. 259.
11. Ibid., 224, par. 782.
12. Ibid., 129, par. 463; 132, par. 470; 133, par. 473; 139, par. 496.
13. Ibid., 171, par. 604.
14. Ibid., 176, par. 618, quoting St. Rose of Lima.
15. Ibid., 538, par. 1996.
16. Ibid., 50, pars. 161–62.

apostles' encounters with the risen Christ, still it remains at the very heart of the mystery of faith as something that transcends and surpasses history. . . . The Paschal mystery has two aspects: by his death, Christ liberates us from sin; by his Resurrection, he opens for us the way to new life. . . . Finally, Christ's Resurrection—and the risen Christ himself—is the principle and source of our future resurrection: 'Christ has been raised from the dead, the first fruits of those who have fallen asleep. . . . For as in Adam all died, so also in Christ shall all be made alive.'"[17]

- "Since the Ascension Christ's coming in glory has been imminent, even though 'it is not for you to know times or season which the Father has fixed by his own authority.' This eschatological coming could be accomplished at any moment."[18]

- "Because of Christ, Christian death has a positive meaning: 'For to me to live is Christ, and to die is gain.' 'The saying is sure: if we have died with him, we will also live with him.'. . . In death, God calls man to himself."[19]

- "Every man receives his eternal recompense in his immortal soul from the moment of his death in a particular judgment of Christ, the judge of the living and the dead."[20]

- "The transmission of the Christian faith consists primarily in proclaiming Jesus Christ in order to lead others to faith in him. From the beginning, the first disciples burned with the desire to proclaim Christ: 'We cannot but speak of what we have seen and heard.' And they invite people of every era to enter into the joy of their communion with Christ."[21]

These and many similar passages reveal that the pages of the Catholic *Catechism* provide a substantial outline of Christian orthodoxy. These passages speak of God as Creator, as Lord and sustainer of the universe, as author of sacred Scripture "without error," as one who chooses a people and makes them his own. The *Catechism* upholds God as Trinity, Jesus as wholly human and wholly divine, born of a virgin, crucified for our salvation. It speaks of justification by grace through faith—and entirely as a gift from God. It speaks of Christ's physical resurrection from the dead and the new life (both temporal and eternal) this resurrection brings to his people. It promises Christ's return, anticipates a

17. Ibid., 185, par. 647; 187, par. 654; 188, par. 655.
18. Ibid., 193, par. 673.
19. Ibid., 285, pars. 1010–11.
20. Ibid., 297, par. 1051.
21. Ibid., 119, par. 425.

final judgment, and calls on the people of God to spread the good news of the Christian faith, as did those who first heard it. True, a Protestant reader will find woven throughout these straightforwardly orthodox statements a variety of teachings particular to the Catholic Church. But this realization need not negate the fact that the Catholic *Catechism* also announces loud and clear many, perhaps most, of the theological concepts dear to the hearts of evangelical Protestants. They are basic beliefs of these two branches of the Christian faith.

Common Devotion to God

Beyond recognizing an outline of basic Christian theology, evangelicals will also find much in the Catholic *Catechism* to nurture their faith. Because Catholics value the wisdom of ancient Christians, their *Catechism* is filled with quotations, prayers, and spiritual counsel that Protestants may also accept for the good of their souls. Along with theology, a thoroughgoing devotion to Christ and many practical examples of how to express that love come to prominent focus. For example, when praying for a pastor, a Protestant might gratefully borrow from the Byzantine prayer of ordination that the *Catechism* quotes:

> Lord, fill with the gift of the Holy Spirit
> him whom you have deigned to raise to the rank of the priesthood,
> that he may be worthy to stand without reproach before your altar,
> to proclaim the Gospel of your kingdom,
> to fulfill the ministry of your word of truth,
> to offer you spiritual gifts and sacrifices,
> to renew your people by the bath of rebirth;
> so that he may go out to meet
> our great God and Savior Jesus Christ, your only Son,
> on the day of his second coming,
> and may receive from your vast goodness
> the recompense for a faithful administration of his order.[22]

Part 4 of the *Catechism* offers more than eighty pages on Christian prayer, with the Lord's Prayer as an outline. Throughout this section, Protestants and Catholics alike will find ways to deepen their praying. All Christians longing to move prayer out of the rut of self-serving petitions will find much to reorient their hearts to the character and purposes of God.

22. Ibid., 442, par. 1587. This prayer comes from the Byzantine Liturgy, *Euchologion*, with prayers and service forms dating from at least the eighth century.

At the start of this section, the *Catechism* encourages readers with the reminder that prayer starts with God. "*God calls man first.* . . . The living and true God tirelessly calls each person to that mysterious encounter known as prayer. In prayer, the faithful God's initiative of love always comes first; our own first step is always a response."[23] Even after that invitation, the *Catechism* provides assurances that our efforts at prayer are not ours alone. It quotes Romans 8:26 about the help of God's Spirit in prayer, then adds, "The Holy Spirit, the artisan of God's works, is the master of prayer."[24] The *Catechism* admits that prayer is a battle and subject to all sorts of false notions: For example, prayer can be a psychological mind game, a mental void, or ritual words. It warns that if those who pray aim first at production, profit, and comfort, prayer may seem to fail. But it also affirms that prayer is "both a gift of grace and a determined response." Believers are to engage themselves in the spiritual battle of prayer and "be caught up in the glory of the living and true God."[25] According to Augustine (A.D. 354–430), Christ himself is involved in all aspects of prayer.

> He prays for us as our priest,
> prays in us as our Head,
> and is prayed to by us as our God.
> Therefore let us acknowledge our voice in him
> and his in us.[26]

For both Catholics and evangelicals who have discovered their hymnal as a source of prayer, Augustine, writing in his *Confessions*, has gone before: "He who sings prays twice."[27]

Besides engaging in prayer, Catholics express their devotion to Christ in a number of other ways that could help Protestants. One is in preparation to receive Communion. Putting aside for the moment differing views between evangelicals and Catholics regarding what the Eucharist is, all Christians may be encouraged by what the *Catechism* outlines as preparation for this sacrament.

It advises both minister and laity to approach Communion with humility. The spiritual power of Communion is not dependent on the humans who receive it, not even on the one who blesses and serves it. Christ himself is the host—as he was for his own disciples in the upper room.[28] The

---

23. Ibid., 675, par. 2567.
24. Ibid., 213, par. 741.
25. Ibid., 717–18, pars. 2725–27.
26. Ibid., 690, par. 2616.
27. Ibid., 327, par. 1156.
28. Ibid., 430, par. 1545.

Catechism draws from the words of Thomas Aquinas (1224/5–74): "The sacrament is not wrought by the righteousness of either the celebrant or the recipient but by the power of God." Yet believers may prepare for Communion by examining the conscience, as prescribed in 1 Corinthians 11, and may realize that the *fruits* of the sacrament depend "on the disposition of the one who receives them."[29] The *Catechism* recommends Scripture as the best guide for this process of preparation, including reading and meditating on the Ten Commandments, the Sermon on the Mount, and moral teachings in the letters of the New Testament. The Catholic liturgy specifies selections from these passages to be read aloud prior to the Eucharist section of the mass. The *Catechism* stresses that since Christians should shape their lives by God's standards, they should confess sins before receiving the sacrament.

For "grave sins," Catholicism requires the sacrament of reconciliation prior to receiving Communion. In this process, a priest guides an individual in admitting his or her sin and confessing it as an offense to God—thereby being reconciled to him. "Only God forgives sins," declares the *Catechism*, though it also states that God gives authority to priests of his church as "the sign and instrument of forgiveness and reconciliation."[30] "There is no offense, however serious, that the Church cannot forgive."[31] A certain leveling takes place at the foot of the cross—and at the Communion table. Protestants and Catholics (even though at separate tables) echo the thief on the cross, "Jesus, remember me when you come into your kingdom."[32]

Despite approval of such spiritual exercises, evangelicals will not be able to embrace all areas of Catholic devotion as outlined in the *Catechism*. Rosaries; relics; sacred places; pilgrimages; prayers to and through the saints; devotion to the elements of the Eucharist, to Mary, to a crucifix, and to Scripture itself—these and other practices make evangelicals squirm because they come too close to the prohibitions of the second commandment against idolatry.[33] Catholics deny that any of the above takes the place of God, that instead they are offerings of devotion to God through objects or people who are avenues to him.[34] Evangelicals will likely remain unconvinced.

29. Ibid., 319, par. 1128.
30. Ibid., 402, pars. 1441–42.
31. Ibid., 278, par. 982.
32. Ibid., 388, par. 1386, "Prayer of Chrysostom" (A.D. 347–407).
33. Ibid., 551. In their construal of the Ten Commandments, Catholics blend the commandment about graven images, which most Protestants call the second commandment, into the first commandment, which covers all forms of idolatry. The Catholic Decalogue then divides the Protestant tenth commandment against coveting into two parts: one regarding the coveting of people, the other material objects.
34. Ibid. See pars. 2111, 2113, 2141, 2502, 2168–75.

Common Understanding of Holy Living

Evangelical Protestants will also find much to approve of in the *Catechism's* admonitions to holy living. Such aspects of practical life involve the use of God's name, the Sabbath, abortion, suicide, respect for the dead, family devotions, sexual purity, modesty, marriage and divorce, social justice, gambling, care for the poor, Satan, and the nature of sin.

THE SABBATH AND GOD'S NAME

Regardless of how much both sides from the Reformation divide have fallen from biblical norms, the *Catechism* makes strong statements about how God's name should be used and how the Sabbath should be observed, with both kinds of statements rooted in the Decalogue. From the five pages given to the use of God's name, we read, "'The Lord's name is holy.' For this reason man must not abuse it. He must keep it in mind in silent, loving adoration. He will not introduce it into his own speech except to bless, praise, and glorify it."[35]

The section on the Sabbath begins with a thorough explanation about the transition from the Jewish seventh-day Sabbath to the Christian "eighth day" or "Lord's Day," which celebrates Christ's resurrection. To establish the Christian use of Sunday, the *Catechism* cites ancient texts, including writings from Jerome (A.D. 347–419/20).[36] When instructing Catholics on how to observe Sunday as the fulfillment of the Sabbath, the *Catechism* offers instructions familiar to many Protestants. Believers are to rest, join with others in Sunday worship (a "day of obligation for Catholics"), nurture family relationships, refrain from needless work, provide "humble service of the sick, the infirm, and the elderly." Moreover, they should engage in "reflection, silence, cultivation of the mind, and meditation which furthers the growth of the Christian interior life." Employers should provide time for their workers to rest and to worship.[37] Respect for God's name and his day is one way in which Catholics are urged to live out their faith.

RESPECT FOR HUMAN LIFE

A high valuation of human life is important to many evangelicals. This same commitment arises in dozens of ways throughout the Catholic *Catechism,* including statements on abortion, suicide, and respect for the dead. For both Catholics and Protestants, this value of individual persons originates in the *imago Dei* (image of God), in which God created humans and which the *Catechism* treats under the first article of

35. Ibid., 575, par. 2143.
36. Ibid., 330–31, pars. 1166–67.
37. Ibid., 583–86, pars. 2180–95.

the Apostles' Creed.[38] Drawn from the *imago Dei,* the *Catechism* presents strong statements against abortion and also certain kinds of fertility procedures. "Human life must be respected and protected absolutely from the moment of conception."[39] To emphasize that this injunction is not a recent reactionary reflex of modern social conservatives, the *Catechism* quotes *Didache* 2:2: "You shall not kill the embryo by abortion and shall not cause the newborn to perish."[40] As for suicide, the *Catechism* provides both warning and comfort. "We are stewards, not owners, of the life God has entrusted to us. It is not ours to dispose of."[41] And for grieving families, "We should not despair of the eternal salvation of persons who have taken their own lives. By ways known to him alone, God can provide the opportunity for salutary repentance. The Church prays for persons who have taken their own lives."[42] Even after death the *Catechism* remembers the *imago.* Though allowing organ donation and cremation, it says, "The bodies of the dead must be treated with respect and charity, in faith and hope of the Resurrection."[43] Of necessity, a high valuation of human life also spills over to many other global concerns, including war, famine, health care, euthanasia, murder, and the death penalty. All of these issues are addressed in the *Catechism* under the command "You shall not kill."[44]

SEXUAL ETHICS

As for sexual purity, the *Catechism* stresses much the same teaching that evangelical youth pastors present to their charges or that evangelical pastors spell out in private counseling. In explaining the Decalogue's command against adultery, the *Catechism* condemns fornication (sex between an unmarried man and woman), pornography, rape, homosexual acts (but counsels respect, compassion, and sensitivity toward the homosexually inclined), lust, trial marriage, adultery (sex of a married person with someone other than the spouse), prostitution, sex between those engaged to be married, incest, sexual abuse of children, even masturbation. In other words, the *Catechism,* like other conservative Christian documents, reserves sex for a man and a woman married to each other. It does so without embarrassment or apology.[45] It does, however, admit

---

38. Ibid., 101–8, pars. 356–84.

39. Ibid., 606, par. 2270.

40. Ibid., 606, par. 2271. As noted above, the *Didache* is a document of the early church dated most likely to the early second century. It reveals patterns of worship, early theology, and moral principles expected of Christians during that era.

41. Ibid., 609, par. 2280.

42. Ibid., 609, par. 2283.

43. Ibid., 613, par. 2300.

44. Ibid., 602–19.

45. Ibid., 623–26, 632, 634–35, pars. 2348–59, 2380, 2388–89, 2391.

that purity is a battle in a world full of permissiveness and erotica. Therefore, the *Catechism* counsels modesty, not merely modesty in clothing (though it does that) but also a modesty in feelings and in words so as to preserve human dignity, "the intimate center of the person."[46] The closing paragraph of this section offers supernatural help:

> The Good News of Christ continually renews the life and culture of fallen man; it combats and removes the error and evil which flow from the everpresent attraction of sin. It never ceases to purify and elevate the morality of peoples. It takes the spiritual qualities and endowments of every age and nation, and with supernatural riches it causes them to blossom, as it were, from within; it fortifies, completes, and restores them in Christ.[47]

FAMILY, MARRIAGE, AND DIVORCE

Evangelicals can join Catholics in affirming the *Catechism*'s high valuation of the family. Catholic teaching about family devotions, marriage, and divorce will sound familiar to evangelicals and other conservative Protestants. Devout Protestants working to maintain the habit of daily "quiet time" may be startled to find that their Catholic brothers and sisters are admonished to do the same. "The Christian begins his day, his prayers, and his activities with the Sign of the Cross: 'in the name of the Father and of the Son and of the Holy Spirit.' . . . Daily prayer and the reading of the Word of God strengthen [the family] in charity. . . . For young children in particular, daily family prayer is the first witness of the Church's living memory as awakened patiently by the Holy Spirit."[48]

Catholic views of marriage and divorce are often confusing to Protestants. Why don't Catholics allow divorce—at all? But why do they occasionally allow annulments instead? In spite of this confusion, Catholics and evangelicals share a high view of marriage and a strong resistance to divorce. Understanding the Catholic view of divorce must begin with the Catholic view of marriage—and of the church. For Catholics, marriage is a sacrament of the church. As a sacrament, it is understood as taking place between a man and a woman who have both been baptized in the Catholic Church. The marriage ceremony happens within the church, it is an action of the church, and it is blessed by God himself. It also reflects Ephesians 5, which speaks of the unbreakable unity between Christ and his church. According to Catholic teaching, mere humans may not dissolve this God-given union. To be sure, there are exceptions, which is why provisions for annulment exist. But annulment is a state-

---

46. Ibid., 664–66, pars. 2520–27.
47. Ibid., 666, par. 2527.
48. Ibid., 578, par. 2157; 589, par. 2205; 708, par. 2685.

ment that true marriage never took place. In Catholic teaching, many marriages (those not meeting the criteria for a sacramental marriage) are not the indissoluble kind described above. Such marriages are those in which one of the parties is not a baptized Catholic or the marriage was not solemnized by the Catholic Church. The church recognizes these marriages in a civil sense but not in the unbreakable sacramental mode.[49] Even so, love and faithfulness within marriage is a high priority for both evangelicals and Catholics. Evangelical Protestants may want to borrow a statement that John Chrysostom (A.D. 347–407) suggested young husbands say to their brides:

> I have taken you in my arms, and I love you, and I prefer you to my life itself. For the present life is nothing, and my most ardent dream is to spend it with you in such a way that we may be assured of not being separated in the life reserved for us. . . . I place your love above all things, and nothing would be more bitter or painful to me than to be of a different mind than you.[50]

Social Justice

Themes of social justice thread throughout the Catholic *Catechism*, many of them resonating with principles that evangelicals can also affirm as they seek to live within a pluralistic society. When speaking of "common good," the *Catechism* admonishes those in authority to "put themselves in the service of others."[51] On an international scale, social justice requires that "the more prosperous nations are obliged, to the extent they are able, to welcome the *foreigner* in search of the security and the means of livelihood which he cannot find in his own country."[52] On civil questions, Catholic social justice requires the church "to pass moral judgments even in matters related to politics whenever the fundamental rights of man or the salvation of souls requires it." But it also urges methods of peace: "The means, the only means, she may use are those which are in accord with the Gospel and the welfare of all men according to the diversity of times and circumstances."[53]

When addressing the command not to steal, the *Catechism* takes up the subject of gambling. Is gambling a form of stealing? The *Catechism* warns of potential "enslavement," then becomes more lenient. As long as no one is deprived "of what is necessary to provide for his needs and those of others," friendly wagers may be all right. Crooked play and cheating, however, are grave matters "unless the damage inflicted

49. Ibid., 452–60, pars. 1621–51; 462, par. 1659; 632–33, pars. 2382–86.
50. Ibid., 628, par. 2365.
51. Ibid., 520, par. 1917.
52. Ibid., 599, par. 2241.
53. Ibid., 600, par. 2246.

is so slight that the one who suffers it cannot reasonably consider it significant."[54] Hence, the stereotypical bingo in the church basement is viewed as good clean fun. But no high stakes!

On care for the poor, a more significant concern of social justice, the *Catechism* is firm, weaving quotations from James 2:15–16; 5:1–6 with the words of Gregory the Great (A.D. 540–605) and Chrysostom to make its points. From Chrysostom: "Not to enable the poor to share in our goods is to steal from them and deprive them of life." From James: "He who has two coats, let him share with him who has none; and he who has food must do likewise." From Gregory: "When we attend to the needs of those in want, we give them what is theirs, not ours. More than performing works of mercy, we are paying a debt of justice."[55] In its social teaching as a whole, the *Catechism* offers many ways for Christians of all sorts to cooperate in living out the civil meaning of the gospel.

SIN AND THE SUPERNATURAL

What are the challenges to holy Christian living? Here too the Catholic *Catechism* expresses a view held by many evangelical Christians. It accepts sin as a reality, however unpopular the word is in today's relativistic world, and it accepts a supernatural source of evil: Satan. The *Catechism* speaks of Satan as a fallen angel, "a seductive voice opposed to God, which made . . . [our first parents] fall into death out of envy." He is the one who "throws himself across God's plan and his work of salvation accomplished in Christ." He is a "murderer from the beginning, . . . a liar and the father of lies, . . . the deceiver of the whole world."[56] Yet the power of Satan is not infinite. God limits what Satan can do, and God will win in the end. The *Catechism* then touches briefly on the problem of evil by saying that Satan can cause "grave injuries—of a spiritual nature and, indirectly, even of a physical nature—to each man and to society." This harm "is permitted by divine providence which with strength and gentleness guides human and cosmic history. It is a great mystery that providence should permit diabolical activity, but 'we know that in everything God works for good with those who love him.'"[57]

Like many Protestant documents, the Catholic *Catechism* defines sin as "an offense against God." It is a "failure in genuine love for God and neighbor caused by a perverse attachment to certain goods." As was the first sin, so is all later sin: "It is disobedience, a revolt against God through

54. Ibid., 639, par. 2413.
55. Ibid., 647–48, pars. 2446–47.
56. Ibid., 111, par. 391; 753, par. 2852.
57. Ibid., 111, par. 395.

the will to become 'like gods.'"[58] In a distinction that is uniquely Catholic, the *Catechism* distinguishes between mortal and venal sins. Mortal sin has three qualities simultaneously: It is (1) a "grave matter" (2) "committed with full knowledge" and (3) "deliberate consent." Mortal sin requires "a new initiative of God's mercy" normally accomplished through the sacrament of reconciliation. All other sins are venal. They weaken our spiritual progress and may cause us to fall into mortal sin, but they "do not break the covenant with God."[59] Even with this distinction, the *Catechism*, quoting Augustine, warns Christians not to become casual about even small sins:

> Do not despise these sins which we call "light":
> if you take them for light when you weigh them,
> tremble when you count them.
> A number of light objects makes a great mass,
> a number of drops fills a river;
> a number of grains makes a heap.
> What then is our hope?
> Above all, confession.[60]

Yet it is not confession itself that removes sin. When describing the dark violent sins surrounding the death of Christ, the *Catechism* specifies the divine antidote: "The sacrifice of Christ secretly becomes the source from which the forgiveness of our sins will pour forth inexhaustibly."[61]

In summary, how Christians live out the life of faith is as varied as the people gathered into God's family. Yet the Catholic *Catechism* provides many themes for holy living that devout Protestants also hold: respect for the person of God expressed by giving his name and his day a place of honor, a high valuation of human life because God created all people in his own image, a protectiveness toward marriage and family that includes sexual purity, a God-given sense of responsibility for social justice, and a consciousness of the destructive power of sin along with trust in God's redeeming grace.

Understanding Differences

Yet in spite of many important matters taught in the *Catechism* that offer a bridge between Catholics and evangelical Protestants, a great deal of teaching is found in this official document that evangelicals will

58. Ibid., 505, pars. 1849–50.
59. Ibid., 506–9, pars. 1854–64.
60. Ibid., 509, par. 1863.
61. Ibid., 506, par. 1851.

not accept. Some differences from the era of the Reformation remain important, and some of these appear irreconcilable. The Catholic *Catechism* does not hide those differences or even acknowledge them as problematic for other Christians. It is, after all, a document for those within the Catholic fold. What the *Catechism* does provide for the Catholic faithful, as well as for all others, is a clear statement of what Catholics believe. Because it is such a comprehensive statement of Catholic faith, Protestant readers are able to see how specific teachings, with which they may disagree, fit into the broader pattern of Catholic theology.

Authority

As noted above, Catholics believe that the Scriptures were inspired by the Holy Spirit, that they are without error, and that they should be regularly read by all believers as a guide for faith and practice. Catholics do, however, add several books to the biblical canon that are not found in Protestant Bibles, although most experts on both sides agree that these additional books do not significantly alter major theological teachings. Catholics and Protestants also agree that the exact, authoritative list of biblical books (the canon) was not finalized until the fourth century A.D. Where they differ is in attitudes toward the standards by which Christians lived prior to the final fixing of Holy Scripture.

How did the canon take shape? The Catholic *Catechism* speaks of *oral* apostolic teaching prompted by the Holy Spirit and handed down through the generations from mouth to mouth, as well as of *written* apostolic teaching penned by the original apostles, who were also guided in that work by the Holy Spirit. These writings were protected by the Spirit until they could be compiled into a single book of sacred Scripture.[62] By whose authority was Scripture determined to be God's written word? The answer provided by the *Catechism* is that the gathered leaders of the church, led by God's Spirit, adjudicated the question of the canon. How early did this authority of church leaders begin? The *Catechism* quotes the well-attested words of Ignatius of Antioch, who died in A.D. 110: "Let all follow the bishop, as Jesus Christ follows his Father, and the college of presbyters as the apostles; respect the deacons as you do God's law. Let no one do anything concerning the Church in separation from the bishop."[63] In other words, the church, acting through its bishops, *determined* what should be considered the Bible. Most Protestants, by contrast, think that inherent authority existed in the apostolic writings that the church in due time came to *recognize.*

62. Ibid., 30, par. 76.
63. Ibid., 258, par. 896.

As the question of Scripture indicates, Catholics have a three-legged conception of the authority on which their faith rests: Scripture, tradition, and the magisterium (or teaching office of the church). The *Catechism* both describes this authority structure and is itself a product of the same authority structure. A quick survey of the *Catechism*'s footnotes reveals numerous citations from all three sources. It links them seamlessly in statements such as the following:

- "'*Sacred Scripture* is the speech of God as it is put down in writing under the breath of the Holy Spirit.' And *Tradition* transmits in its entirety the Word of God which has been entrusted to the apostles by Christ the Lord and the Holy Spirit. . . . As a result the Church, to whom the transmission and interpretation of Revelation is entrusted, 'does not derive her certainty about all revealed truths from the holy Scriptures alone. Both Scripture and Tradition must be acepted and honored with equal sentiments of devotion and reverence.'"[64]

- "'The task of giving an authentic interpretation of the Word of God, whether in its written form or in the form of Tradition, has been entrusted to the living, teaching office of the Church alone. Its authority in this matter is exercised in the name of Jesus Christ. . . . Yet this Magisterium is not superior to the Word of God, but is its servant.'"[65]

- "'It is clear therefore that, in the supremely wise arrangement of God, sacred Tradition, Sacred Scripture, and the Magisterium of the Church are so connected and associated that one of them cannot stand without the others. Working together, each in its own way, under the action of the one Holy Spirit, they all contribute effectively to the salvation of souls.'"[66]

- "The task of interpreting the Word of God authentically has been entrusted solely to the Magisterium of the Church, that is, to the Pope and to the bishops in communion with him."[67]

Evangelical Protestants do not accept such formulas, since for them Scripture is the supreme authority for doctrine and practice. Although some evangelicals treasure their own traditions, and many even respect the traditions of the Catholic fathers (often adopting them as their own), they do not view tradition as paired with Scripture in authority. In prin-

64. Ibid., 31, pars. 81–82.
65. Ibid., 32, pars. 85–86.
66. Ibid., 34, par. 95.
67. Ibid., 35, par. 100.

ciple, all extrabiblical authority, no matter how important or revered, must be subject to correction by Scripture. Catholics also read and study the Bible individually, but they are wary of "private interpretation," since they look to the corporate wisdom of the church for the definitive interpretation of the Bible. Protestants, by contrast, have a more individualistic sense of how biblical authority works. However helpful tradition is (and many evangelicals hold great respect for tradition), the ruling principle is that Scripture interprets tradition rather than that tradition interprets Scripture. The decisive break of the Reformation era over Protestant insistence on *sola scriptura* (the Bible as supreme authority) may not be as decisive as it once seemed, since so much of contemporary Catholic doctrine is obviously conforming to the main teachings of Scripture. Yet the principle of Scripture over all other authorities still constitutes a major divide between official Catholic teaching and what most evangelicals believe.

Mary, the Mother of God

When evangelicals and Catholics think of their differences, the subject of Mary quickly comes to the top of the list. Besides bearing theological weight, Mary also stirs deep emotions, particularly for Catholics who have loved her as their spiritual mother from earliest memories. Brides lay flowers on her altar, mothers call on her during pains of childbirth (she too gave birth), and the dying ask her to welcome them and lead them to her Son. Protestants see little ground for such practices in Scripture, and they worry about making Mary into an idol. "God is Trinity, not four persons," they warn. In response, Catholics insist that, as the *Catechism* frequently repeats, they are careful to distinguish between devotion to Mary and worship of God.[68] For evangelicals, however, this discrimination does not seem careful enough.

What do Catholics believe about Mary? According to the *Catechism*, Mary was predestined from the beginning of time to be the new Eve who would undo the impact of Eve's sin on the human race.[69] She was conceived free of original sin and remained sinless throughout her life.[70] At the annunciation, she made a choice to obey God's plan for her.[71] She was impregnated by the Holy Spirit and gave birth to Jesus Christ yet remained a virgin all her life.[72] When her life was finished, she was taken body and soul directly into heaven, where she is "exalted by the

68. Ibid., 275, par. 971.
69. Ibid., 137–38, pars. 488, 494.
70. Ibid., 116, par. 411; 138, par. 491.
71. Ibid., 138, par. 494.
72. Ibid., 139–40, pars. 496, 499.

Lord as Queen over all things."[73] Because she gave birth to Jesus, she is rightly called the mother of God.[74] And because Christ is the head of the church, Mary is the mother of the church and therefore also the mother of all true believers within that church.[75] Mary is not the Redeemer, since she herself is redeemed by "the merits of her Son."[76] But she brings to God's people the "gifts of eternal salvation."[77] It is appropriate to pray to Mary.[78] She is rightly honored as Blessed Virgin, Advocate, Helper, Benefactress, Mediatrix, and Mother of God.[79]

The terse tone of such a paragraph above cannot capture the respect, honor, and joy with which Catholics speak of Mary. For that we need the words of the *Catechism* itself. In linking Mary with Eve, for example, it quotes Irenaeus (A.D. 130–200) and then Epiphanius (d. 403):

> "Being obedient she became the cause of salvation for herself and for the whole human race." Hence not a few of the early Fathers gladly assert . . . : "The knot of Eve's disobedience was untied by Mary's obedience: what the virgin Eve bound through her disbelief, Mary loosened by her faith." Comparing her with Eve, they call Mary "the Mother of the living" and frequently claim: "Death through Eve, life through Mary."[80]

Again, regarding Mary's immaculate conception, the *Catechism* quotes the proclamation of Pope Pius IX in 1854:

> The most Blessed Virgin Mary was, from the first moment of her conception, by singular grace and privilege of almighty God and by virtue of the merits of Jesus Christ, Savior of the human race, preserved immune for all stain of original sin.[81]

To be sure, the *Catechism* specifies that Mary's lack of sin was not the cause of her redemption (though Protestants might ask why a sinless Mary would need redemption). The *Catechism* is careful to note that even Mary's redemption came through her Son, the Son of God:

> "The splendor of an entirely unique holiness" by which Mary is "enriched from the first instant of her conception" comes wholly from Christ: she is

73. Ibid., 274, par. 966.
74. Ibid., 706, par. 2677.
75. Ibid., 273, par. 963.
76. Ibid., 138, par. 492.
77. Ibid., 274, par. 969.
78. Ibid., 704–5, pars. 2675–77.
79. Ibid., 139, par. 495; 274, par. 969.
80. Ibid., 138, par. 494.
81. Ibid., 138, par. 491.

"redeemed, in a more exalted fashion, by reason of the merits of her Son." The Father . . . chose her "in Christ before the foundation of the world to be holy and blameless before him in love. . . . At the announcement that she would give birth to the "Son of the Most High" without knowing man, by the power of the Holy Spirit, Mary responded with the obedience of faith. . . . She gave herself entirely to the person and to the work of her Son; she did so in order to serve the mystery of redemption with him and [is] dependent on him, by God's grace.[82]

What, then, is Mary's place in the redemption of others? To evangelical ears, the *Catechism* seems to come close to describing her as a co-redeemer:

By her complete adherence to the Father's will, to his Son's redemptive work, and to every prompting of the Holy Spirit, the Virgin Mary is the Church's model of faith and charity. . . . "In a wholly singular way she cooperated by her obedience, faith, hope, and burning charity in the Savior's work of restoring supernatural life to souls. For this reason she is a mother to us in the order of grace." . . . "Taken up to heaven she did not lay aside this saving office but by her manifold intercession continues to bring us the gifts of eternal salvation."[83]

Yet as if responding to Protestant nervousness, the *Catechism* goes on to issue a caution:

Mary's function as mother of men in no way obscures or diminishes this unique mediation of Christ, but rather shows its power. But the Blessed Virgin's salutary influences on men . . . flows forth from the superabundance of the merits of Christ, rests on his mediation, depends entirely on it, and draws all its power from it. . . . The unique mediation of the Redeemer does not exclude but rather gives rise to a manifold cooperation which is but a sharing in this one source.[84]

The close relationship that the *Catechism* describes between Mary and the church can help evangelicals understand why she is so important to Catholics. In a word, the *Catechism* shows Mary as a symbol of the church. Because she is the mother of Jesus, she is also the mother of those who become a part of his body, the church, and therefore is an appropriate recipient of prayer.

82. Ibid., 138–39, pars. 492–94.
83. Ibid., 274–75, pars. 967–69.
84. Ibid., 275, par. 970.

- "At once virgin and mother, Mary is the symbol and the most perfect realization of the Church: 'the Church indeed . . . by receiving the word of God in faith becomes herself a mother. By preaching and Baptism she brings forth sons, who are conceived by the Holy Spirit and born of God, to a new and immortal life.'"[85]

- "Mary gave her consent in faith at the Annunciation and maintained it without hesitation at the foot of the Cross. Ever since, her motherhood has extended to the brothers and sisters of her Son 'who still journey on earth surrounded by dangers and difficulties.' Jesus, the only mediator, is the way of our prayer; Mary, his mother and ours, is wholly transparent to him: she 'shows the way.'"[86]

- "Beginning with Mary's unique cooperation with the working of the Holy Spirit, the Churches developed their prayer to the holy Mother of God, centering it on the person of Christ."[87]

- "Because she gives us Jesus, her son, Mary is Mother of God and our mother; we can entrust all our cares and petitions to her: she prays for us as she prayed for herself: 'Let it be to me according to your word.'"[88]

- "Mary is the perfect *Orans* (pray-er), a figure of the Church. When we pray to her, we are adhering with her to the plan of the Father, who sends his Son to save all men. Like the beloved disciple we welcome Jesus' mother into our homes, for she has become the mother of all the living. We can pray with and to her. The prayer of the Church is sustained by the prayer of Mary and united with it in hope."[89]

Evangelicals reading this section of the *Catechism* may ask whether too much is given to Mary. Despite recognizing the *Catechism*'s many references to Jesus, evangelicals will insist that addressing prayer to anyone other than the Triune God is a violation of the second command, an offense to God, and dangerous to the soul. They might also wonder about the perceived humanity of Mary. If she were born sinless, remained sinless, and then was assumed directly into heaven, is Mary truly human (Christ having been portrayed in Scripture as the only sinless human)? And if her humanity is in doubt, what does that say about the nature of her Son, who (according to the creeds) is fully human and fully divine? In general, while evangelicals might tolerate

85. Ibid., 142, par. 507.
86. Ibid., 704, par. 2674.
87. Ibid., 704–5, par. 2675.
88. Ibid., 706, par. 2677.
89. Ibid., 706, par. 2679.

Catholic reliance on extrabiblical sources, as long as such sources parallel Scripture, they fret that much of what the Catholic Church teaches about Mary seems to have little biblical support. When evangelicals in their hotter moments describe the Catholic Church as a cult, they are usually thinking of doctrines and practices related to Mary. The emotion of such evangelical objections juxtaposed with the emotional ties Catholics feel in devotion to Mary suggests that agreement on this subject is not likely in the near future.

Baptism

Among Christians, the sacrament of baptism is taught and practiced with almost as much variation as there are Christian traditions. It is no surprise, therefore, that evangelicals and Catholics differ on this subject. How much they disagree depends on which variety of evangelical Christianity is being compared. Even the ancient churches differed between East and West on the subject—though this difference had more to do with mode than with theology.[90] What does the Catholic *Catechism* teach about baptism?

Baptism is a joyful event for Catholics, one that calls for spiritual preparation and family celebration. It is an event that the baptized Catholic will look back on with confidence throughout his or her life. This confidence is based not on oneself but on God. Baptism, according to the *Catechism*, is a work of God's grace, and God alone is responsible for its merit. This is why Catholics see it as appropriate for babies. (How

90. Almost from the beginning, slightly different forms of Christianity emerged in the East (centered in Constantinople) and the West (centered in Rome). The East was guided by philosophers who looked at the spirit, the West by lawyers who looked at the mind. The East spoke and read Greek; the West spoke and read Latin. Three events around the end of the first millennium solidified the division for much of the next thousand years. First, in A.D. 589, the West added the phrase "and from the Son" (*filoque*) to the Nicene Creed, indicating that the Holy Spirit proceeds from the Father and the Son. The Eastern Church disagreed. Second, in 1054, a half millennia of feuding became official schism when the Western church excommunicated the Eastern patriarch and the Eastern church excommunicated the pope. The schism was cemented during the Fourth Crusade (1202–4), when Western Crusaders sacked Constantinople, destroying icons, burning churches, and murdering women and children in the streets. Only in the past fifty years has this breach begun to be repaired through various ecumenical dialogues as well as direct meetings of the Roman pope and the Orthodox patriarch. Regarding the specific practice of baptism, Roman Catholics (West) baptize infants and new converts by pouring water on their heads in the name of the Triune God. The Orthodox (East) baptize infants and new converts by triple immersion and anointing with oil, accompanied by a number of ancient rites and prayers. A more detailed account of the schism between Eastern and Western Christianity is found in Mark A. Noll, *Turning Points: Decisive Moments in the History of Christianity*, 2nd ed. (Grand Rapids: Baker, 2000), 129–50.

better to illustrate that God's grace is totally unmerited than to apply baptism to a helpless infant?)[91] It is also why anyone (in an emergency) may baptize a child in the name of the Triune God. That person does not even need to be a baptized Catholic for God to do his work through the sacrament of baptism.[92] Regardless of the human instrument, it is Christ, spiritually present at the baptism, who hosts the sacrament.[93]

The joy the *Catechism* describes in its picture of baptism is commended by Gregory of Nazianzus (A.D. 330–90) as he attempted to depict and define the sacrament:

> Baptism is God's most beautiful and magnificent gift. . . . We call it gift, grace, anointing, enlightenment, garment of immortality, bath of rebirth, seal, the most precious gift. It is called *gift* because it is conferred on those who bring nothing of their own; *grace* since it is given even to the guilty; *Baptism* because sin is buried in the water; *anointing* for it is priestly and royal as are those who are anointed; *enlightenment* because it radiates light; *clothing* since it veils our shame; *bath* because it washes; and *seal* as it is our guard and the sign of God's Lordship.[94]

Furthermore, the *Catechism* goes on, baptism lasts for eternity. No sin can erase it. It never needs to be repeated.[95] Moreover, a person is baptized into the church; baptism is never a solo symbol. When an adult convert is baptized, he or she is asked, "What do you ask of God's Church?" The response is: "Faith!" Catholics expect faith to grow *after* baptism and that the church will nourish that faith: "The whole ecclesial community bears some responsibility for the development and safeguarding of the grace given at Baptism."[96]

Most of this teaching is not troubling to Protestants who follow directly in the line of Reformers such as Martin Luther, John Calvin, and Thomas Cranmer or to modern evangelicals who baptize infants. Yet for evangelicals who baptize only those able to make an informed profession of faith, such teaching seems amiss. For such ones, the ordinance of baptism is more a testimony to a convert's faith in God's saving grace than a sacrament of that grace. Many evangelicals also hold that the proper mode of baptism is immersion, a mode that Catholics admit was practiced by the early church and that is still practiced in the Eastern Church, where believers are immersed three times, once for each person

---

91. *Catechism of the Catholic Church*, 350, par. 1250; 357, par. 1282.
92. Ibid., 362, par. 1257.
93. Ibid., 308, par. 1088.
94. Ibid., 343, par. 1216.
95. Ibid., 356, par. 1272.
96. Ibid., 351, pars. 1253–55.

of the Trinity.[97] Regarding infant baptism, the *Catechism* refers to historical records showing that Christians baptized infants as early as the second century—and perhaps as part of the "households" of Acts 16:15, 33; 18:8.[98] Catholics assume that biblical and early historical accounts of adult baptisms were the result of a rapidly expanding church, which meant that many people first learned of the Christian faith as adults and were then baptized. On such matters, some evangelicals agree and some do not.

More consistently troubling to evangelicals is the *Catechism*'s teaching that baptism confers justification, in fact, that baptism is uniquely necessary for salvation.[99] With respect to the sacrament, the *Catechism* proclaims that it removes original sin, puts sin to death, imparts forgiveness of sin, and makes recipients into children of God:

> Baptism, by imparting the life of Christ's grace, erases original sin and turns a man back toward God, but the consequences for nature, weakened and inclined to evil, persist in man and summon him to spiritual battle. . . . [Baptism] signifies and actually brings about death to sin and entry into the life of the Most Holy Trinity. . . . By Baptism *all sins* are forgiven, original sin and all personal sins, as well as all punishment for sin. In those who have been reborn nothing remains that would impede their entry into the Kingdom of God. . . . Baptism not only purifies from all sin, but also makes the neophyte "a new creature," an adopted son of God, who has become a "partaker of the divine nature," member of Christ and co-heir with him, and a temple of the Holy Spirit. . . . The Most Holy Trinity gives the baptized sanctifying grace, the grace of *justification*.[100]

Custom has made such an important rite rich with symbols: "The white garment symbolizes that the person baptized has 'put on Christ,' has risen with Christ. The *candle*, lit from the Easter candle, signifies that Christ has enlightened the neophyte. In him the baptized are 'the light of the world.'"[101]

With so much spiritual significance attached to baptism, it should not surprise Protestants when Catholic grandmothers worry about delayed baptism of their infant grandchildren or maybe even carry out their own private ceremony at the kitchen sink. As the *Catechism* does for those who died of suicide, it also offers comfort to families of children who die without baptism. Such children are entrusted to the mercy of God,

97. Ibid., 348, pars. 1239–40.
98. Ibid., 351, par. 1252.
99. Ibid., 536, par. 1992; 352, par. 1257.
100. Ibid., 114, par. 405; 348, par. 1239; 354, par. 1264; 354, par. 1265; 354, par. 1266.
101. Ibid., 349, par. 1243.

which "allows us to hope that there is a way for salvation for children who have died without Baptism." But it warns recalcitrant parents about "the Church's call not to prevent little children coming to Christ through the gift of holy Baptism."[102]

While most evangelicals cannot link baptism so directly to salvation, the *Catechism* aids them in understanding how important baptism is to Catholics and why they practice it as they do. At the same time, the tremendous Catholic emphasis on baptism as the sacrament of justification also accounts for a great deal of evangelical suspicion that Catholicism is a religion of form that (by its emphasis on the rite of initiation) unduly neglects the practice of religion (and therefore winks casually at the unfaithfulness of the baptized).

Salvation by Works or Grace

Salvation by grace through faith is a, if not *the,* pivotal doctrine for evangelical Protestants. Those five words are the nub of the gospel evangelicals proclaim from pulpits and on mission fields. Is this also the faith of Catholics according to their *Catechism?* The answer is both yes and no. Largely, it is yes. As many statements already quoted have shown, Catholics believe that God justifies his people by grace alone, through faith, and that God himself initiates that action. Augustinian evangelicals—whether Baptists, Calvinists, or Lutherans—could hardly say more.

It is confusing, however, that Catholics seem to blend what evangelicals regard as two steps in the way of salvation, namely, justification (the start) and sanctification (the continuation). In defense of how they use the terminology, Catholics appeal to Augustine (A.D. 354–430). For Catholics, justification is conferred at baptism,[103] continues with faith personally proclaimed at confirmation,[104] develops as the Christian grows in knowledge and faithfulness[105] in the context of the church and through being nourished by the sacraments,[106] and continues even after death, when God cleans away remaining sin during purgatory.[107] In a particularly fair-minded but also searching review of the *Catechism,*

102. Ibid., 353, par. 1261.
103. Ibid., 536, par. 1992.
104. Ibid., 398, par. 1428–29.
105. Ibid., 400, par. 1435.
106. Ibid., 302, par. 1068.
107. Ibid., 411, par. 1472. The *Catechism* uses the terms *salvation, justification,* and *conversion* throughout these paragraphs with nuances similar to but not exactly the same as Protestant understandings.

evangelical theologian Alister McGrath wrote about this Catholic order of salvation:

> For the Roman Catholic . . . justification means both the event by which the Christian life is initiated and the process by which the believer is regenerated. In other words, the Catholic understands by justification what the Protestant understands by justification and sanctification taken together. Thus, theologically, Protestants and Roman Catholics, more or less, believe the same things regarding God's active role in both initiating and sustaining the Christian life; however, this convergence is obscured by the different understandings of the word justification.[108]

Since Catholics view salvation as a process, not a single event, there is a possibility of interruption (through choice or mortal sin) anywhere along the continuum. That interruption can lead to a departure from God's kingdom, even to eternity in hell.[109] Catholics, therefore, find it presumptuous to announce assurance that salvation is complete and heaven is certain. They take seriously the biblical admonition, "He who stands firm to the end will be saved" (Matt. 10:22). Against standard evangelical teaching on the assurance of salvation, they ask if any of us knows for certain the limitations of our endurance.

Such a question is more uncomfortable for some Protestants than for others. Arminians, including various followers of Wesley, find this view of salvation quite similar to their own. They too believe that God initiates salvation by offering prevenient grace to all. They also believe that personal choice plays a part in deciding whether salvation is received and, if received, whether a Christian will remain faithful until the end. They see an inner assurance of salvation as a part of justification, but they also believe that their own sins may remove them from God's family. For Arminian evangelicals, assurance of salvation may exist for the present but not for the future. Since many Arminians, however, are staunch individualists, particularly in matters of faith, they are uncomfortable with the high place of the church in the Catholic view of salvation. For Protestant Arminians, salvation is a one-on-one transaction with God. God grants salvation when individuals choose Christ. For Catholics, God saves *through* the church—beginning with the sacrament of baptism and continuing throughout a lifetime of growth within its fold.

Reformed or Calvinistic Protestants, on the other hand, can agree with Catholics, at least to some extent, that the church participates in salvation, since God's covenant with his people in the Old Testament has

108. Alister E. McGrath, "A Review of the New Catholic Catechism," *Christianity Today,* December 12, 1994, 28–32.

109. *Catechism of the Catholic Church,* 403, par. 1446; 509, par. 1461.

been extended to the body of Christ, the church in the New Testament. Covenant children grow up in the church and so are raised within the context of faith, which God eventually makes (individually) their own. But Reformed Protestants strongly object to any human contribution to salvation or to the idea that merit can be gained through good works. For Reformed Protestants, God does the inviting, God saves his people by imputing his own righteousness to them, and God keeps them to the end by taking them to the eternal home he has prepared for his chosen from the beginning of time. To say less, in their view, is to elevate humans to the place of God.

Therefore, while Catholics and Protestants agree on many areas related to salvation, disagreements remain and will likely continue, though the nature of disagreement varies from one Protestant tradition to another. Because questions of salvation are so intimately related to what it means to be Christian, differences on these issues remain particularly crucial. If, however, both groups can agree (as they appear to) that salvation is by grace through faith in Jesus Christ, evangelicals and Catholics can welcome each other as brothers and sisters of the family created by God's grace, regardless of whatever else either may want to say.

Celibacy and Saints

In spite of the importance of celibacy in the Catholic Church, the *Catechism* gives it surprisingly little attention—a mere two or three pages in total, spread over several subtopics. When speaking of Mary's virginal conception, it adds almost as an afterthought, "The spousal character of the human vocation in relation to God is fulfilled perfectly in Mary's virginal motherhood."[110] Under the sacrament of holy orders, it says that ordained ministers are chosen from among men of faith "who live a celibate life and intend to remain *celibate* 'for the sake of the kingdom of heaven,'" adding that they are able to serve with an "undivided heart to the Lord."[111] A section on monasticism says that virgins [nuns] "'are betrothed mystically to Christ, the Son of God and are dedicated to the service of the Church . . . a transcendent sign of the Church's love for Christ, and an eschatological image of this heavenly Bride of Christ and of the life to come.'"[112] For Protestants wondering why the Catholic Church has held so persistently to celibacy in the face of clergy shortages and infamous accounts of sexual abuse, the *Catechism* offers little explanation other than the idea that Mary was a virgin and that those who follow her Son in leadership of the church will live

110. Ibid., 142, par. 505.
111. Ibid., 440, par. 1579.
112. Ibid., 264, par. 923.

the same way. Not stated explicitly is the investment that the exercise of papal authority has made in defining and maintaining celibacy for Catholic priests and members of religious orders; to back away from that teaching now could look like a backing away from a high view of papal wisdom as well.

Since evangelicals speak of saints as all true believers in Christ, they are mystified as to why Catholics set apart certain people for this designation. The *Catechism* speaks briefly of how and why Catholics canonize saints.[113] Saints, of course, are dead and with Christ. The *Catechism* says that because they are more closely united to Christ than those on earth, they "do not cease to intercede with the Father for us," that they "proffer the merits which they acquired on earth through the one mediator between God and men, Christ Jesus," that through them "our weakness [is] greatly helped," and that "our communion with saints joins us to Christ."[114] Protestants, their ears tuned to Scripture, notice that much of what the *Catechism* ascribes to saints is usually given by Scripture to Christ himself. They become more alarmed when the *Catechism* moves to prayer and says that saints "constantly care for those whom they have left on earth" and that in our praying "we can and should ask them to intercede for us and for the whole world."[115] Here, as in similar statements about Mary, evangelicals worry that prerogatives are being passed around that belong to God alone.

Sacraments and Worship

Catholics observe seven sacraments; it is a *sacramental* church.[116] As such, the Eucharist is the high point of the mass that all other aspects of worship point toward or flow from. By contrast, evangelical tradition has given the sermon preeminence in worship. Seminarians are regularly instructed to spend twenty hours each week preparing for their major responsibility, preaching the Word of God. In the Catholic order of service, the sermon is usually only a homily—intentionally short, aimed more at informal pastoral advice. In the mass, a homily points toward the real purpose of coming together, which is to encounter Christ in the sacrament of Communion.[117] Catholic worship does not disregard Scripture. Indeed, long passages of biblical text are read aloud in each service, covering much of the Bible every year—resulting in far more public hearing of Scripture than in almost any Protestant

113. Ibid., 239, par. 828.
114. Ibid., 271, pars. 956–57.
115. Ibid., 707, par. 2683.
116. Ibid., 315, par. 1113.
117. Ibid., 308, par. 1088.

denomination.[118] But Catholics see the focus of their worship as God himself, not a human explanation of what the Bible says about him. Many Catholics see Protestant worship services, when Communion is not celebrated, as little more than light religious entertainment accompanied by a motivational speaker. By contrast, evangelicals see Catholic worship as prescribed ritual devoid of a personal response to God and lacking adequate teaching from Scripture.[119] This difference in worship expresses an underlying difference in the importance (and number) of sacraments.

The Catholic *Catechism* describes seven sacraments, providing in its more than 150 pages of teaching some of the most eloquent reading of the book. The sacraments are baptism, confirmation, the Eucharist, penance, anointing of the sick, holy orders, and matrimony.[120] According to Catholics, these seven sacraments draw the presence of Christ and his church into every major event of a Christian's life.[121] Most Protestants practice only the Eucharist/Communion and baptism, pointing to biblical texts where Jesus specifically instituted these rites.[122] (It is, in fact, for partially anti-Catholic reasons that some Protestant churches call them ordinances rather than sacraments.) Many Protestant traditions observe the remaining five rites with official church-recognized exercises, though they do not think of them as sacraments.

Regarding the sacrament of Communion (the Eucharist), Catholics believe that at the priestly blessing, the bread and wine truly change into the body and blood of Christ, not because of what the priest says but because of God's action in making that change. The *Catechism* refers to John Chrysostom (A.D. 347–407) for explanation:

> It is not man that causes the things offered to become the Body and Blood of Christ, but he who was crucified for us, Christ himself. The priest in the role of Christ pronounces these words, but their power and grace are God's. This is my body, he says. This word transforms the things offered.[123]

As with other distinctly Catholic practices, evangelicals should be able to appreciate the depth of reasoning, along with the seriousness of biblical exposition, that the *Catechism* uses to set out its teaching. At

118. Ibid., 309, par. 1093; 312, par. 1100.

119. In contrast to some Protestant misconceptions, the Catholic *Catechism* defines liturgy as "'public work' or a 'service in the name of/on behalf of the people'" (302, par. 1069). It describes liturgy as the "work of Christ" "involving the 'conscious, active, and fruitful participation' of everyone" (302–3, par. 1071).

120. Ibid., 315, par. 1113.

121. Ibid., 316, par. 1116.

122. Catholics believe that Christ instituted all seven sacraments (315, par. 1115).

123. Ibid., 384, par. 1375.

the same time, the weight of tradition and the exercise of magisterial teaching authority push the *Catechism* to affirm practices and beliefs that most evangelicals consider mistakes or irrelevancies.

In summary, Catholics and Protestants do indeed differ, and the Catholic *Catechism* reveals those differences. On a theological level, questions of authority and salvation carry the most weight, but it is possible to recognize a remarkable degree of agreement between official Catholic teaching and the beliefs of many evangelicals. At the emotional level, devotion to Mary remains important to Catholics, while it remains foreign to most evangelicals. On the practical level, habits of worship, attitudes toward saints, and standards for celibacy make lived Catholicism different from the lived religion of evangelicals, but differences on these issues do not appear as profound as they once seemed. Baptism and the other sacraments hint at differing conceptions of the church, however, and since these differences are foundational, they require further elucidation.

Catholics and the Church

At various Catholic-evangelical discussions that have taken place in recent years, irreverent evangelicals have grown accustomed to repeating the same witticism: "The main difference between us and the Catholics is ecclesiology. They have one and we don't." While the joke is not entirely true (evangelicals do in fact have strong views, however informal, concerning the church), like many jokes, it is funny because it is at least partially true.

The Catholic *Catechism* expresses a high view of the church on virtually every page. Indeed, the book itself is a document of the church, speaking the voice of the church. What, then, do Catholics believe the church is? How do other doctrines within the *Catechism* connect to Catholic ecclesiology? In working through the Apostles' Creed, the *Catechism* explains the creed line by line, coming eventually to the statement "I believe in the holy catholic church." It then describes the church with biblical images familiar to Protestants and held in common by both groups. The church is the people of God, the body of Christ, and the temple of the Holy Spirit.[124]

The body of Christ is a favorite image for many evangelicals as well, particularly those with a congregational bent. Based on Romans 12, 1 Corinthians 12, and Ephesians 4, this image expresses the interdepen-

124. Ibid., 224–32, pars. 781–810.

dence of God's people—each member using unique God-given gifts for the benefit of the entire body, each individual important, and all linked to the others because all are joined by God's mercy to the Head, which is Jesus Christ. Evangelicals, to the extent that they live up to their ideals, conduct their church business, ministries, and relationships in an atmosphere of grace and mercy inspired by the image of the church as the body of Christ. How can they disrespect one another if each person is linked by God's love to the Head? How can they jockey for position, lord it over one another, or cut a less desirable person out of their circle if they all make up a single body and if Christ (who modeled servant leadership) is their Head?

Catholics also value the biblical image of the church as the body of Christ. But in drawing insights from great thinkers of the Christian past, the *Catechism* takes the image one step beyond a Protestant understanding. In doing so, a long list of ecclesiological differences falls into place. An unusually clear statement of the Catholic position is found in the *Catechism*'s 795th paragraph:

> Christ and his church thus together make up the "whole Christ" *Christus totus.* The Church is one with Christ. The saints are acutely aware of this unity:
>
> "Let us rejoice then and give thanks that we have become not only Christians, but Christ himself. Do you understand and grasp, brethren, God's grace toward us? Marvel and rejoice: we have become Christ. For if he is the head, we are the members; he and we together are the whole man. . . . The fullness of Christ then is the head and the members. But what does 'head and members' mean? Christ and the Church." (Augustine, *In Jo. Ev.* 21, 8:PL 35, 1568) [date: 396–430]
>
> "Our redeemer has shown himself to be one person with the holy Church whom he has taken to himself." (Pope St. Gregory the Great, *Moralia in Job, praef.*, 14:PL 75, 525A) [date: 540–604]
>
> "Head and members form as it were one and the same mystical person." (St. Thomas Aquinas, *STh* III, 48, 2) [date: 1224/5–74]
>
> A reply of St. Joan of Arc to her judges sums up the faith of the holy doctors and the good sense of the believer: "About Jesus Christ and the Church, I simply know they're just one thing, and we shouldn't complicate the matter." [date: 1412–31][125]

Christ and his church are one! This basic confession explains why Catholics can offer salvation through baptism into the church.[126] It is why the pope (as the vicar of Christ) can speak without error in matters

---

125. Ibid., 228, par. 795.
126. Ibid., 354, par. 1266. The *Catechism* says repeatedly that salvation comes from God alone (not baptism itself). See pars. 169, 846, 1584.

of faith and morals.[127] It is why Ignatius, who died in 110, could say that only priests in connection with a bishop, in connection with the pope, can offer valid sacraments.[128] It is why Protestants may not share a Catholic Eucharist. To do so would acknowledge the authority of the pope as representing Christ through his church.[129] It is why a church marriage is unbreakable.[130] It is why Cyprian, who died in 258, could say, "No one can have God as Father who does not have the Church as Mother."[131] It is why Mary is called the mother of the church; she is the mother of Christ.[132] It is why the church can interpret the keys given to Peter as authority to forgive sins.[133] This is why the church is self-correcting (the whole body cannot err in matters of belief).[134] It is why the word of the church is higher than individual conscience and reason.[135] It is why sin against God is also sin against the church and requires reconciliation to both.[136] It is why Catholics view the Protestant Reformation as such a drastic mistake—a splintering of the church is an attack on Christ himself.

If Christ and his church are one, then a great deal of Catholic doctrine simply follows naturally. In a word, ecclesiology represents the crucial difference between evangelicals and Catholics.

Protestants are accustomed to thinking that the Reformation restored the church to its early purity. This Protestant commonplace is undoubtedly true in some ways: The Reformation did exercise a corrective force against the corruption of the clergy, human-centered theologies of salvation, the neglect of lay education, and other problems common in the late medieval era. But arguments for Catholic ecclesiology also appeal to standards from the early church. The *Catechism*, for example, repeatedly cites the words of Ignatius of Antioch, who died in roughly A.D. 110:

- "Let all follow the bishop, as Jesus Christ follows his Father, and the college of presbyters as the apostles; respect the deacons as you do God's law. Let no one do anything concerning the Church in separation from the bishop."[137]

127. Ibid., 256, pars. 890–91.
128. Ibid., 382, par. 1369; 258, par. 896; 316, par. 1118.
129. Ibid., 381, par. 1369; 391, par. 1396.
130. Ibid., 462, par. 1659; 633, par. 2384.
131. Ibid., 54, par. 181.
132. Ibid., 273, pars. 963–64.
133. Ibid., 155–56, pars. 552–53.
134. Ibid., 33, par. 92.
135. Ibid., 548, par. 2039.
136. Ibid., 401–2, pars. 1440–42.
137. Ibid., 258, par. 896.

- "Let only that Eucharist be regarded as legitimate, which is celebrated under [the presidency of] the bishop or him to whom he has entrusted it."[138]
- "Let everyone revere the deacons as Jesus Christ, the bishop as the image of the Father, and the presbyters as the senate of God and the assembly of the apostles. For without them one cannot speak of the Church."[139]

The principles taught by Ignatius in (or before) the early second century continue to ground current Catholic ecclesiology. In explaining the sacrament of holy orders, for example, the *Catechism* points back to Christ and the apostles as a precedent:

Christ himself chose the apostles and gave them a share in his mission and authority. Raised to the Father's right hand, he has not forsaken his flock but he keeps it under his constant protection through the apostles, and guides it still through those same pastors who continue his work today. Thus, it is Christ whose gift it is that some be apostles, others pastors. He continues to act through the bishops.[140]

Likewise, when discussing teachings of what constitutes a moral life, the *Catechism* points to the ecclesiastical descendents of Christ and the apostles:

The Roman Pontiff and the bishops are the "authentic teachers, that is, teachers endowed with the authority of Christ, who preach the faith to the people entrusted to them, the faith to be believed and put into practice." The *ordinary* and universal *Magisterium* of the Pope and the bishops in communion with him teach the faithful the truth to believe, the charity to practice, and the beatitude to hope for.[141]

Through this line of succession from Christ, and because Christ, the Head, is entwined with his body, the church, Catholic ecclesiology sees Christ as present and at work whenever the church gathers to worship. Through and behind the visible human figures, Christ himself presides at the sacraments:

Christ is always present in his Church, especially in her liturgical celebrations. He is present in the Sacrifice of the Mass, . . . when anybody baptizes, it is really Christ himself who baptizes. He is present in the word since it

138. Ibid., 382, par. 1369.
139. Ibid., 433, par. 1554.
140. Ibid., 439, par. 1575.
141. Ibid., 546, par. 2034.

is he himself who speaks when the holy Scriptures are read in the Church. Lastly, he is present when the Church prays and sings.[142]

Salvation itself comes from Christ through the church:

All salvation comes from Christ the Head through the Church which is his Body. "Basing itself on Scripture and Tradition, the Council teaches that the Church, a pilgrim now on earth, is necessary for salvation: the one Christ is the mediator and the way of salvation; he is present to us in his body which is the Church."[143]

The church that participates in the spiritual birth of a child through the sacrament of baptism also follows that child to the end of human existence. In discussing the Christian funeral, the *Catechism* calls it "the Christian's Last Passover." Prior to death, the church makes every effort to provide an opportunity for confession and reconciliation with God and his church. Just as in extreme circumstances anyone can baptize a child into faith and into the church, so at death "any priest, even if deprived of faculties for hearing confessions, can absolve from every sin and excommunication."[144] The Christian funeral celebrates hope—in the context of the church. No mere memorial service, the Catholic funeral is about God, it is held in the church, and it is a ministry of the church:

The Church who, as Mother, has borne the Christian sacramentally in her womb during his earthly pilgrimage, accompanies him at his journey's end, in order to surrender him "into the Father's hands." She offers to the Father, in Christ, the child of his grace, and she commits to the earth, in hope, the seed of the body that will rise in glory. This offering is fully celebrated in the Eucharistic service; the blessings before and after Mass are sacramentals.[145]

Evangelicals may well wonder whether the Catholic Church has made too much of the identity between Christ as Head of the church and the church as his body. Have Catholics confused one with the other, ascribing to the church those powers and qualities that ought to belong to Jesus Christ alone? Is this another area where the Catholic Church has (according to Protestant understanding) slipped into idolatry? Perhaps so. The numerous ways in which the *Catechism* interweaves Christ and his church cause Protestants, even those who view their own ecclesiology as inadequate, to wonder if the Catholic Church has raised the power, authority, and role of the church too high as it strives toward the high goals set out by Augustine, Gregory the Great, Thomas Aquinas, and Joan of Arc in the *Catechism*'s 795th paragraph.

142. Ibid., 308, par. 1088.
143. Ibid., 244, par. 846.
144. Ibid., 408, par. 1463.
145. Ibid., 468, par. 1683.

Yet no matter how closely entwined Christ is with his body, the *Catechism* does not view head and body as one and the same. In explaining the opening lines of its *Dogmatic Constitution of the Church,* the Second Vatican Council insisted that the article of faith about the church depends entirely on the articles concerning Christ: "The Church has no other light than Christ's; according to a favorite image of the Church Fathers, the Church is like the moon, all its light reflected from the sun."[146]

For Catholics, the church is central, an axis on which all of life pivots. Evangelicals, with our love of independence and our emphasis on "personal faith," would do well to ponder the high ideals for the church set forth in the *Catechism.* Since those ideals state so well the hope that evangelicals also entertain for their life in God, we might borrow selected pages from the Catholic *Catechism* to strengthen our evangelical spiritual health:

> It is in the Church, in communion with all the baptized, that the Christian fulfills his vocation. From the Church he receives the Word of God containing the teachings of "the law of Christ." From the Church he receives the grace of the sacraments that sustains him on the "way." From the Church he learns the *example* of *holiness* and recognizes its model and source in the all-holy Mary; he discerns it in the authentic witness of those who live it; he discovers it in the spiritual tradition and long history of the saints who have gone before him and whom the liturgy celebrates in the rhythms of the sanctoral cycle.[147]

And so once again, after reading the *Catechism,* it is pertinent to ask, Is the Reformation over? The *Catechism* proclaims a deeply Christian faith, and it does so with grace. It is not intended as a conciliatory document but simply a statement of what Catholics believe and how they are to live out that belief. Undergirding all is a verbal picture of the majesty and mystery of God. Protestant readers will find much in the *Catechism* that leads them to worship. They will also discover a better connection with early fathers and mothers of the faith, a clearer picture of their brothers and sisters from the other side of the Reformation, and much that they can make their own. Where that is impossible, the *Catechism* leads to a better understanding of what Catholics believe and why.

Is the Reformation over? Maybe a better question we evangelicals should ask ourselves is, Why do we not possess such a thorough, clear, and God-centered account of our faith as the *Catechism* offers to Roman Catholics?

146. Ibid., 214, par. 748.
147. Ibid., 546, par. 2030.

6

EVANGELICALS AND CATHOLICS TOGETHER

B y the early 1990s, ecumenical dialogues between Catholics and various Protestant groups had been under way for a quarter of a century. Most of these dialogues were official in the sense that a Protestant denomination sent delegates representing its body to dialogue with official Catholic delegates approved by the Secretariat for Promoting Christian Unity and therefore linked to the Vatican. The delegates spoke *for* their represented bodies, and the resulting documents spoke *to* the people of both groups. But evangelicals are an individualistic lot. Because of the decentralized nature of evangelicalism, evangelicals were represented in these ecumenical conversations only indirectly. And many evangelicals, because of their historical aversion to official ecumenism, whether from the World Council of Churches or the Vatican, did not take seriously the content of these dialogues.

Yet on a personal level, some evangelical Protestants and some Catholics were coming together. With the admonition of the Second Vatican Council that Catholics make study of Scripture a personal practice, neighborhood Bible study groups sprang up nationwide—particularly among women. During the 1970s and the 1980s, thousands of evangelical and Catholic women sat across from each other at kitchen tables and pored over biblical texts together. This interest grew, and by 1991, researcher Judy Hamlin could create a resource guide listing more than one thousand small group Bible study books designed to guide precisely this kind of joint exploration.[1] Most of this curriculum came from evangelical publishing companies. Yet many Catholic women, at first somewhat unfamiliar with personal study of Scripture, soon joined their evangelical neighbors on a biblical journey.

But not all evangelical-Catholic connections were of the kitchen table variety. In 1992, Catholic Richard John Neuhaus and evangelical Charles Colson, commiserating with each other over mutual pain caused by Protestant-Catholic tensions in Central and South America, expressed together the hope that Latin America would not become the next Northern Ireland. Sometime during their conversation it occurred to them that evangelical and Catholic leaders could create an unofficial joint statement that might soften those tensions. Hence, Evangelicals and Catholics Together (ECT) I: "The Christian Mission in the Third Millennium" was published in the spring of 1994.[2]

Both Neuhaus and Colson had undergone significant spiritual change as adults. Neuhaus, editor-in-chief of *First Things*, was a Lutheran pastor who in the 1980s became a Roman Catholic priest. His Catholic and neoconservative conscience guides *First Things* as it speaks to thoughtful readers on issues at the intersection of religion and public life. Charles Colson first came to public attention when he served as special counsel to President Nixon during the Watergate Crisis. Then after an experience of Christian conversion and after serving a prison term for his role in Watergate, Colson became a leading "public evangelical" through publishing, speaking, and serving as chair of Prison Fellowship Ministries. Both men are effective communicators; both exert strong influence in their respective bodies.[3]

This chapter describes what Neuhaus, Colson, and a substantial body of their Catholic and evangelical colleagues have tried to accomplish through the ECT process.[4] It examines the four joint statements that to date have come out of this informal effort, sometimes pausing to examine at considerable length how Catholic and evangelical participants wrote about issues of historic disagreement between the two communions. Along the way, we also pause briefly to canvass reactions to the documents, though analysis of that sort is mostly reserved for the next

1. Judy Hamlin, *Curriculum and Small Group Resource Guide: Over 1,000 Topical and Bible Study Resources Listed and Evaluated* (Colorado Springs: NavPress, 1991).

2. *First Things*, May 1994, 15–22.

3. For useful background, see Donald W. Sweeting, "From Conflict to Cooperation? Changing American Evangelical Attitudes towards Roman Catholics: 1960–1998" (Ph.D. diss., Trinity Evangelical Divinity School, 1998), 290–91.

4. In the interests of full disclosure, we note that Mark Noll signed the first two documents, ECT I and ECT II.

chapter, which tries to lay out the spectrum of evangelical responses to contemporary Roman Catholicism. In this chapter, as in the previous two, the emphasis is on exposition in order to explain as fully as possible the nature and extent of agreements (as well as continuing disagreements) that have been expressed in this significant effort at Catholic-evangelical engagement.

ECT I: "The Christian Mission in the Third Millennium"

ECT I is an eight-thousand-word document with an introduction and a conclusion bracketing five "together" statements: We affirm together, we hope together, we search together, we contend together, and we witness together.

As part of what "we affirm together," the document declares, "We affirm together that we are justified by grace through faith because of Christ."[5] This common affirmation results in a strong statement of relationship: "All who accept Christ as Lord and Savior are brothers and sisters in Christ. Evangelicals and Catholics are brothers and sisters in Christ."[6] The section on affirmation ends by jointly affirming the Apostles' Creed.

Under "we search together," the document acknowledges ten areas that continue to divide evangelicals and Catholics, each stated as two opposing possibilities separated by the word *or*. These issues include the following:

- "The church as an integral part of the Gospel or the church as a communal consequence of the Gospel."
- "The sole authority of Scripture (*sola scriptura*) or Scripture as authoritatively interpreted in the church."
- "Sacraments and ordinances as symbols of grace or means of grace."
- "Remembrance of Mary and the saints or devotion to Mary and the saints."
- "Baptism as sacrament of regeneration or testimony of regeneration."[7]

5. "Evangelicals and Catholics Together: The Christian Mission in the Third Millennium," *First Things*, May 1994, 16.
6. Ibid., 16.
7. Ibid., 17–18.

This extensive acknowledgment of differences reflects an overarching purpose: "We reject any appearance of harmony that is purchased at the price of truth."[8]

Under "we contend together," ECT I affirms a common principle of cobelligerency: "Christians individually and the church corporately also have a responsibility for the right ordering of civil society."[9] The final section on common witness presents a measure of agreement on evangelism and proselytizing by affirming that the true Christian faith is present in both churches: "Evangelicals and Catholics affirm that opportunity and means for growth in Christian discipleship are available in our several communities. . . . It is neither theologically legitimate nor a prudent use of resources for one Christian community to proselytize among active adherents of another Christian community."[10]

Though not an official ecumenical dialogue, ECT I reflects the influence of previous dialogues in its statements. For example, the document's definition of conversion comes (appropriately) from the Baptist-Roman Catholic conversation of 1988, where tensions between individual and corporate salvation were addressed: "Conversion is personal but not private. Individuals respond in faith to God's call but faith comes from hearing and proclamation of the word of God and is to be expressed in the life together in Christ that is the church."[11]

Since conflict in Latin America over evangelism (usually evangelicals evangelizing Catholics) inspired Colson and Neuhaus to take up this joint effort, ECT I lays special stress on the knotty problem of proselytizing but only after affirming a strong joint statement on respect for personal freedom in religious decisions. Here again the influence of the official dialogues is evident, this time in the dialogue titled "The Evangelical–Roman Catholic Dialogue on Mission" (1977–84). ECT I also anticipates what would come soon thereafter in the dialogue between Catholics and Pentecostals (1990–97), with its powerful argument on this same subject. Thus, ECT I states, "It is understandable that Christians who bear witness to the Gospel try to persuade others that their communities and traditions are more fully in accord with the Gospel. There is a necessary distinction between evangelizing and what is today commonly called proselytizing or 'sheep stealing.'"[12]

The shapers of ECT I recognized that one major cause of proselytizing between the two groups is a differing view of baptism and the role that baptism plays in salvation. This differing view of baptism both

8. Ibid., 16.
9. Ibid., 18.
10. Ibid., 21.
11. Ibid.
12. Ibid.

stems from and leads to a differing view of the church. They acknowledged this difference, described it, and decided that they could inform new converts of these differing views, then respect converts' choices of church affiliation:

> For Catholics, all who are validly baptized are born again and are truly, however imperfectly, in communion with Christ. That baptismal grace is to be continuingly reawakened and revivified through conversion. For most Evangelicals, but not all, the experience of conversion is to be followed by baptism as a sign of new birth. For Catholics, all the baptized are already members of the church, however dormant their faith and life; for many Evangelicals, the new birth requires baptismal initiation into the community of the born again. These differing beliefs about the relationship between baptism, new birth, and membership in the church should be honestly presented to the Christian who has undergone conversion. But again, his decision regarding communal allegiance and participation must be assiduously respected.[13]

Fifteen evangelicals and Catholics participated in creating this first ECT document, and another twenty-five signed it. All signatories emphasized that this was an unofficial, nonecclesiastical statement shaped by individuals. Even so their belief that the ancient Catholic-Protestant standoff needed to be overcome was unmistakable from the document's opening lines:

> We are Evangelical Protestants and Roman Catholics who have been led through prayer, study, and discussion to common convictions about Christian faith and mission. . . . The love of Christ compels us and we are therefore resolved to avoid such conflict between our communities and, where such conflict exists, to do what we can to reduce and eliminate it. Beyond that, we are called and we are therefore resolved to explore patterns of working and witnessing together in order to advance the one mission of Christ.[14]

The document does not pretend that all historic differences are now passé, differences, for example, concerning the nature of baptism or the structure of authority. But the list of common affirmations is extensive: They include belief in the lordship of Christ, the divine inspiration of Scripture, the enduring validity of the Apostles' Creed, and the reality of salvation through justification by faith. The signers also pledged themselves to work together for morality in public life, the free exercise

13. Ibid., 22.
14. Ibid., 15.

of religion at home and abroad, legal protection of the unborn, and parental choice in education.

Firestorm

The publication of ECT I was greeted by both jeers and cheers. Jeers came from some evangelicals who felt that their leaders had betrayed Reformation faith. Jeers also came from those who felt that modern Roman Catholics could not maintain their faith's heritage and at the same time affirm the document. The cheers, though often expressed with caution, came from evangelicals who found substantial areas of doctrinal and practical solidarity with at least some Catholics. Again, it was indicative of how much attention the two groups typically paid to each other that commentary, pro and con, was much more extensive from evangelicals than from Catholics.

Evangelical critics accepted, for the most part, the concept of moral cobelligerency, which had become familiar through the writings of Francis Schaeffer.[15] A few evangelicals with political leanings to the left felt uneasy about what they perceived as the document's hawkish nationalistic tone, but for the most part they appreciated its intent as a whole and settled for quiet dissent. Conservative evangelicals, by contrast, were anything but quiet. First, these critics objected to the claim of ECT I that evangelicals and Catholics were spiritual brothers and sisters. Second, they perceived ambiguity on whether justification was by grace *alone* through faith *alone*. Third, they protested the moratorium on evangelistic outreach to adherents of the Catholic Church.[16]

Several evangelicals who signed ECT I paid heavily in the resulting conflagration. Signer Bill Bright, head of Campus Crusade for Christ, saw a dangerous drop in donations. Charles Colson experienced the same thing with Prison Fellowship.[17] When Larry Lewis, a Southern Baptist ECT participant, was invited to speak to a mission conference in Bayou DuLarge, Louisiana, a predominately Catholic community with a number of converts to the Baptist faith, the local pastor, Jerry Moser, declared Lewis a heretic and refused to allow him into the pulpit. Then Moser subjected Lewis to a thirty-minute parade of critics who insisted that Lewis publicly repent for signing the document. In the fallout, Moser

15. For example, Francis A. Schaeffer, *The Church at the End of the Twentieth Century* (Downers Grove, IL: InterVarsity, 1970), 36–37.

16. For extensive documentation of these reactions, see Jennifer V. Suvada, "A Study of the Evangelical Protestant Reception to Evangelicals and Catholics Together, from Its Release in March 1994 through December 1996, Including a Case Study of the Southern Baptist Convention" (M.A. thesis, Trinity Evangelical Divinity School, 1997).

17. Ibid., 77.

lost his job, and Lewis removed his name from the ECT document.[18] Another Southern Baptist denominational figure, Richard Land, heard similar criticism at the 137th annual Southern Baptist Convention and at subsequent meetings. After a year of denominational pressure, Land also withdrew his name from the document he had helped to write.[19]

Two organizations, mostly from the Reformed wing of evangelicalism, mobilized to oppose ECT I, eventually joining their forces: Christians United for Reformation (CURE), headed by Michael Horton (a scholar and writer from California), and the Alliance of Confessing Evangelicals (ACE), chaired by the late James Montgomery Boice, pastor of Philadelphia's Tenth Presbyterian Church. Just two months after ECT I appeared in *First Things*, Michael Horton published a critical riposte in his magazine, *Modern Reformation*, titled "Resolutions for Roman Catholic and Evangelical Dialogue." Thirty evangelical leaders signed these resolutions, including three who had also signed ECT I. J. I. Packer, an ECT signatory, assisted in drafting these resolutions. Packer explained that he saw Horton's resolutions as an agenda for future ECT dialogues and that he hoped to prevent schism within evangelical ranks.[20]

But critics of the critics could also dish it out. One of the statements in Horton's "Resolutions" to which Catholic ECT signers reacted most strongly was this judgment of the Catholic Church: "We perceive that the Roman Catholic Church contains many [genuine] believers. We deny, however, that in its present confession it is an acceptable Christian communion."[21] An exercised Richard John Neuhaus replied sharply:

> I take note also of your opinion that the Church sanctified by the martyr blood of the Apostles Peter and Paul, the Church in continuity with the Petrine ministry established by Christ, the Church that has sustained the Scriptural, patristic, conciliar, and the theological traditions that define Christian orthodoxy (also for Protestants), the Church that has claimed the allegiance of the great majority of Christians over two millennia is not "an acceptable Christian communion." Really.[22]

With the hope of creating a measure of unity among divergent responses, a group of evangelical conservatives critical of ECT met in

18. Ibid., 65–68.

19. Ibid., 63–65.

20. J. I. Packer, "Why I Signed It," *Christianity Today,* December 12, 1994, 37. Additional information is from a conversation between Packer and Carolyn Nystrom in the spring of 2004.

21. Paragraph 6 from a document titled "Resolutions for Roman Catholic and Evangelical Dialogue" attached to a letter from Michael S. Horton to Richard John Neuhaus, July 5, 1994.

22. Letter from Richard John Neuhaus to Michael S. Horton, July 7, 1994.

Fort Lauderdale on January 19, 1995, with several who had signed the document. John Ankerberg (host of a syndicated television program), D. James Kennedy (author and pastor of Coral Ridge Presbyterian, PCA, in Fort Lauderdale, Florida), John MacArthur (author and pastor of Grace Community Church in Sun Valley, California), and R. C. Sproul (Reformed author and preacher) composed the team of ECT critics. Bill Bright, Charles Colson, and J. I. Packer represented evangelicals with the ECT perspective. Joe Stowell, president of Moody Bible Institute, and John Woodbridge, professor of church history at Trinity Evangelical Divinity School, moderated the meeting. The critics' first goal was to have ECT signers recant. They refused. The next option was to ask endorsers to have ECT I amended. This was not possible. Evangelical signers of ECT did, however, issue a clarification statement (published by *Christianity Today* on March 6, 1995), but fewer than half of the evangelicals who had signed the original document put their names on this clarification.[23]

After the Fort Lauderdale meeting of January 1995, four of those who opposed ECT I participated in a six-part series on the *John Ankerberg Show* that was highly critical of the document and the evangelicals who had signed it. Clearly, ECT I had touched a nerve.

J. I. Packer received so much criticism for his part in ECT I that he mused in a later article, "Some people have concluded that I have gone theologically soft, and others think I must be ignorant of Roman Catholic beliefs, and others guess that I signed ECT without reading it."[24] In response, Packer stated emphatically that he could not become a Roman Catholic (and he explained reasons for not taking that route), but he also defended his signature on three grounds. First, good Catholics and good evangelicals are Christians together and ought to behave toward each other as such. Second, in view of tremendous social needs surrounding all Christians, evangelicals and Catholics ought to combine their resources to meet those needs. Third, in view of deep spiritual needs throughout the world, evangelicals and Catholics should not compete with each other but should evangelize side by side wherever possible.[25]

ECT II: "The Gift of Salvation"

Despite—or perhaps because of—a high volume of criticism, the ECT process went on. Picking up the challenge of conservative evangelicals,

23. Suvada, "Study of the Evangelical Protestant Reception," 42–44.
24. Packer, "Why I Signed It," 35.
25. Ibid., 35–36.

ECT participants began to discuss the nature of justification. The resulting statement, "The Gift of Salvation," was, like all other ECT documents, preceded by a number of meetings, discussions, papers, drafts, and debates, including one gathering in New York City on September 16–17, 1996. Even though evangelical participants spoke as individuals and not as official representatives of any group, it was apparent to some that a genuine shift was taking place as influential thinkers from both sides of the Reformation divide listened and spoke together. For example, evangelical Timothy Phillips, a theology professor at Wheaton College, was startled to hear Catholic theologian Avery Dulles say that he had moved closer to the evangelical understanding of salvation in the past decade and that Dulles's position was "now very near my own." Of his experience at this meeting, Phillips later wrote, "I was stunned! Here the dean of Roman Catholic theology in America was affirming that he had become more conservative in the last decade!" As Phillips listened to other Catholic voices around the table, interjecting his own comments from time to time, he began to see one previously unseen motive for ECT. "Rome wants to renew its church and it realizes that Evangelicalism's piety and lay activism is crucial to this goal."[26] As if in confirmation, at this same meeting, Cardinal Edward Cassidy, president of the Pontifical Council for Promoting Christian Unity, spoke in support of evangelicals and Catholics sharing the gospel with each other, especially with those who were nominal in either camp, because, "It is far more important for one truly to know Jesus and find salvation in him than to belong without conviction to any particular community."[27]

Much of the evangelical criticism of the first ECT document hung on the absence of one word. It had affirmed that salvation was by grace through faith but not by grace *alone* through faith *alone*. The ECT initiative therefore addressed this concern in "The Gift of Salvation" (December 1997). Among other things, ECT II responded to criticism that questioned the sincerity of the signers in affirming a common picture of Christian salvation. A central paragraph of the new document expanded on the core theological agreement that the ECT process had defined:

> Justification is central to the scriptural account of salvation, and its meaning has been much debated between Protestants and Catholics. We agree that justification is not earned by any good works or merits of our own; it is entirely God's gift, conferred through the Father's sheer graciousness, out of the love that he bears us in his Son, who suffered on our behalf and

26. Timothy Phillips, "Report on the Second Evangelical-Catholic Theological Conference, September 16–17, 1996," unpublished summary of event, 5.

27. Timothy George, "Evangelicals and Catholics Together: A New Initiative (An Evangelical Assessment)," *Christianity Today*, December 8, 1997, 35.

rose from the dead for our justification. Jesus was "put to death for our trespasses and raised for our justification" (Romans 4:25). In justification, God, on the basis of Christ's righteousness alone, declares us to be no longer his rebellious enemies but his forgiven friends, and by virtue of his declaration it is so.[28]

Thus, having treated the Reformation principle of *sola gratia*, ECT II moved on to the place of faith in salvation:

By faith, which is also the gift of God, we repent of our sins and freely adhere to the gospel, the good news of God's saving work for us in Christ. By our response of faith to Christ, we enter into the blessings promised by the gospel. Faith is not merely intellectual assent but an act of the whole person, involving the mind, the will, and the affections, issuing in a changed life. We understand that what we here affirm is in agreement with what the Reformation traditions have meant by justification by faith alone (*sola fide*).[29]

Because evangelicals tend to see salvation as an event and Catholics tend to see it as a process, ECT II addressed the subject of growth in grace over a lifetime, or sanctification:

Sanctification is not fully accomplished at the beginning of our life in Christ, but is progressively furthered as we struggle, with God's grace and help, against adversity and temptation. In this struggle we are assured that Christ's grace will be sufficient for us, enabling us to persevere to the end. . . . We may therefore have assured hope for the eternal life promised to us in Christ. . . . Thus it is that as justified sinners we have been saved, we are being saved, and we will be saved. All this is the gift of God.[30]

Six years later, when ECT IV summarized previous agreements, it said of ECT II, "We together affirmed the way we understand justification by faith alone as a gift received by God's grace alone because of Christ alone."[31] Again, the authors and signers of the second ECT document went out of their way to underscore its informal character, and again there was an outcry from a few Protestant quarters. But the salient fact of the ECT process certainly was that, however imperfect its promulgations and however limited the number of evangelicals and

28. Evangelicals and Catholics Together, "The Gift of Salvation," *Christianity Today,* December 8, 1997, 36.

29. Ibid., 36.

30. Ibid.

31. Evangelicals and Catholics Together, "The Communion of Saints," *First Things,* March 2003, 26.

Catholics it was speaking for, such cooperation on questions of doctrine and social practice would have been simply unimaginable less than a generation ago.

ECT III: "Your Word Is Truth"

The third major document of the ECT process, which was published in January 2002, took up the Bible, a subject of particular interest to evangelicals.[32] *Sola scriptura* had been a rallying cry of the Reformers. Of the three Reformation *soli* (*sola gratia, sola fide, sola scriptura*), ECT participants saw "Scripture alone" as the remaining major stumbling block between evangelicals and Catholics. Scripture had long functioned for Catholics alongside the authority of tradition and the authority of the church's own role as teacher (or magisterium). Though Catholics read and recommend the Bible, they are wary of private interpretation. Many evangelicals, on the other hand, regard Scripture as a personal letter from God. They are wary of creeds, confessions, and councils purporting to interpret Scripture for them. Both traditions can cite outrageous failures of authority on the other side: Evangelicals complain that Catholics have accepted unwarranted additions to Scripture; Catholics complain that evangelicals have accepted unlicensed confusion in interpreting Scripture.

Current evangelical-Catholic differences on the subject of Scripture relate to historic issues descending from the era of the Reformation but also current differences regarding the nature of the church. Does God's Word speak to the church as a whole, to individuals, or to both, and to what extent? ECT III produced a summary statement of thirty-five hundred words signed by nineteen participants. This document highlighted evangelical-Catholic agreement but also outlined several subjects on which disagreement continued. Following the initial statement, participants contributed several essays that expanded on disagreements. Because debates over Scripture remain central, this section examines several of the participants' statements at length after summarizing the positive agreements of the joint declaration.

ECT III admitted at the outset that evangelicals and Catholics work with different views of the church, but it also highlighted several matters of agreement on the connections between Scripture, tradition, and truth.[33]

32. Charles Colson and Richard John Neuhaus, eds., *Your Word Is Truth* (Grand Rapids: Eerdmans, 2002), 1–8.
33. The following points are from ibid., 3–5.

- The signers affirmed together that "the entire teaching, worship, ministry, life, and mission of Christ's church is to be held accountable to the final authority of Holy Scripture which, for Evangelicals and Catholics alike, constitutes the word of God in written form."
- They agreed that the phrase Word of God "refers preeminently to Jesus Christ."
- They agreed that "Scripture is the divinely inspired and uniquely authoritative written revelation of God."
- They affirmed together "the coinherence of Scripture and tradition: Tradition is not a second source of revelation alongside the Bible, but must ever be corrected and informed by it, and Scripture itself is not understood in a vacuum apart from the historical existence and life of the community of faith."
- They jointly held to "a firm commitment to the intense devotional, disciplined, and prayerful engagement with Scripture," including "joint study involving people from both communities."
- They agreed that God's Spirit had worked in elucidating Scripture through church decisions including "the Apostles', Nicene, and Athanasian creeds, and in the conciliar resolution of disputes regarding the two natures of Christ and the triune life of God. . . . In this way, the Lord has enabled faithful believers both to counter error and to make explicit what is implicit in the written word of God."
- They agreed that "Scripture is to be read in company with the community of faith past and present. Individual ideas of what the Bible means must be brought to the bar of discussion and assessment by the wider fellowship."

To reach these agreements, an obvious process of negotiation took place in which each side adjusted to the other. Thus, evangelicals acknowledged the importance of creeds, confessions, and the wisdom of corporate interpretation of Scripture. Catholics, for their part, placed tradition under (not alongside) the Bible.

ECT III could not, however, arrive at unity on other important issues surrounding tradition, Scripture, and truth. The authors, therefore, specified these concerns. Evangelicals held to the formal principle of the Reformation reiterated in the Amsterdam Declaration, which came from a conference in 2000 sponsored by the Billy Graham Evangelistic Association: Scripture is "the inspired revelation of God . . . totally true and trustworthy, and the only infallible rule of faith and practice."[34] To

---

34. Ibid., 4.

be sure, the evangelicals did admonish their constituencies that *sola scriptura* does not mean *nuda scriptura* or that a principle concerning the final authority of Scripture does not equal a disregarding of all authorities except the Bible. The evangelicals also conceded that Bible study should not be isolated from the believing community of faith because that would disregard "the Holy Spirit's work in guiding the witness of the people of God . . . [leaving] the interpretation of that truth vulnerable to unfettered subjectivism."[35] Yet they insisted that all Christians should have free access to Scripture because in it "all that is necessary for salvation is set forth."[36] Furthermore, the evangelicals did not agree with the Catholic view of a "teaching authority in the life of Christ's church." They felt that the Catholic understanding of "magisterium, including infallibility, results in the Church standing in judgment over Scripture."[37] Evangelicals also disagreed with certain Catholic teachings that had grown out of Catholic traditions, including the Eucharistic sacrifice of the mass, the transubstantiation of bread and wine into the body and blood of Christ, purgatory, the immaculate conception and assumption of Mary, and magisterial authority, including papal authority.[38] While they admonished their evangelical constituency that tradition was not an addition to Scripture or an independent source of authoritative teaching, they insisted that the combination of Scripture and tradition was entirely proper; it was "the ministry of faithful interpreters guided by the Holy Spirit in discerning and explicating the revealed truth contained in the written word of God, namely, Holy Scripture."[39]

On the other side, Catholics believed that Scripture gives authority to the church to interpret Scripture through "the bishop of Rome, who is the successor of Peter, and the bishops in communion with him." They insisted that the Holy Spirit "enables the church to explicate the truth of Holy Scripture obediently and accurately."[40] In addition, Catholics viewed evangelicalism as "an ecclesially deficient community that needs to be strengthened by the full complement of gifts that they believe Christ intends for his church." Specifically, Catholics held that "evangelicals are deficient in their understanding of apostolically ordered ministry, the number and nature of the sacraments, the company and intercession of the saints, the Spirit-guided development of doctrine, and the continuing ministry of the Peterine office in the life of the church."[41]

35. Ibid., 4.
36. Ibid., 5.
37. Ibid., 6.
38. Ibid., 7.
39. Ibid., 5.
40. Ibid., 6.
41. Ibid., 7.

In spite of these differences, the signatories of ECT III expressed confidence that the Lord was watching over his gospel. They vowed to continue their dialogue with mutual respect and to anticipate together the return of Christ.

Since Scripture is such an important matter to evangelicals, the following sections examine in detail four of the essays accompanying the ECT III statement. The writers of these essays agreed (at least) on the premise of the title: "Your Word Is Truth." But what God's Word is and what truth is—and to what extent tradition, interpretation, ecclesial authority, and historical-cultural context shape the finding of truth—continue as areas of dispute. Notably, however, in discussing these contentious matters, the authors quoted one another with respect and even affection.

Timothy George: "An Evangelical Reflection on Scripture and Tradition"

Timothy George, a Baptist and the dean of Beeson Divinity School in Birmingham, Alabama, is a teacher of church history and theology whose book *Theology of the Reformation* has become a standard text in many institutions. In his commentary on ECT III, George casts a self-deprecating eye on his theological progenitors by quoting Billy Sunday (1862–1935)—"I know no more about theology than a jackrabbit knows about ping-pong!"—and also Huldrych Zwingli (1484–1521), who called Catholic tradition "this 'whole rubbish-heap of ceremonials' and 'hodgepodge of human ordinances' which amounted to nothing but 'tom-foolery.'"[42] George then takes up serious work on the subject at hand: "Because evangelicals are, as John Stott says, a Gospel people and Bible people, the importance of the lay appropriation of Holy Scripture can hardly be exaggerated."[43]

Since the relationship between Scripture and tradition (in its various forms) is part of the unresolved conflict between evangelicals and Catholics, George carefully differentiates among three forms of tradition: Tradition (with a capital T) is "the Gospel itself, transmitted from generation to generation in and by the church, Christ himself present in the life of the Church." Scripture is Tradition in written form. The second tradition (with a small t) represents the means by which Tradition is conveyed. It includes creeds, sacraments, preaching, theological exposition, and church doctrine. Third, traditions (plural) are the diverse forms of expression, confessional families, and cultural settings in which the Christian faith

42. Timothy George, "An Evangelical Reflection on Scripture and Tradition," in ibid., 13, 16.
43. Ibid., 20.

has come to expression—for example, the Anglican tradition.[44] When evangelicals and Catholics compare ways of relating Scripture and tradition, it is helpful to clarify which form of tradition is under consideration.

George observes that evangelicals have learned to appreciate Catholic tradition and also that many Catholics now have a heightened awareness of Scripture: "One need only look at syllabi from courses on spiritual formation in Evangelical seminaries, or read works of spiritual theology by Evangelical writers such as Richard Foster, Dallas Willard, and James Houston, to realize the way in which 'the Catholic tradition' is being mined and appropriated for Evangelical purposes."[45] Likewise, "Many Catholics are learning that the liturgy of the Word, including the sermon, is more than a dispensable preliminary to the eucharist."[46]

Yet despite such confluences, George spotlights the critical disagreements that remain concerning the church. He quotes the Catholic theologian Yves Congar: "Protestants want a Church ceaselessly renewing herself by a dramatic and precarious confrontation with the Word of God. Together with the Fathers [Catholics] see the Church as the continuous communication, through space and time, of the mystical community born from the Lord's institution and Pentecost."[47] With reference to agreement over the way the church formed ancient creeds, George observes, "Evangelicals and Catholics differ on the scope and locus of the Magisterium but not on whether it exists as a necessary component in the ongoing life of the church.[48]

George is not overly optimistic that evangelicals and Catholics can come together on this subject. Differences about Scripture and tradition have hardened. On the one side is the Catholic view, summarized by *Dei Verbum* from the Second Vatican Council: "Therefore both sacred tradition and sacred Scripture are to be accepted and venerated with the same sense of loyalty and reverence." On the other side, in George's summary, "Evangelicals can affirm the coinherence of sacred Scripture and sacred Tradition, but not their coequality."[49]

Avery Cardinal Dulles, S.J.: "Revelation, Scripture, and Tradition"

Avery Dulles, son of Secretary of State John Foster Dulles, is the first U.S. theologian named to the College of Cardinals. He is professor

44. Ibid., 22.
45. Ibid., 26.
46. Ibid., 30.
47. Ibid., 29.
48. Ibid., 33.
49. Ibid., 34.

of religion and society at Fordham University, has written more than twenty-five books, including the well-known *Models of the Church,* and is widely respected by both Protestants and Catholics.

The focus of Dulles's contribution to ECT III is the question, Why and how does God reveal himself? His answer is straightforward: "God, out of sheer love, emerges from his silence, and enters into conversation with human beings in order to bring them into fellowship with himself and make them sharers in his divine life (DV 2). . . . By his words and deeds in history God enables us to know him and his salvific intentions for his people."[50]

In an effort to soften contention over Scripture, Dulles first points to Christ himself. The primary revelation of God is his Son, also named the Word: "As the eternal Word of God, Christ is identified with God the revealer. God reveals by means of his Word, the Logos, the reflection of his glory."[51] Quoting John of the Cross (1542–91), Dulles underscores the main priority: "Fasten your eyes in Him alone, because in Him I have spoken and revealed all, and in Him you shall discover even more than you ask for and desire."[52] Dulles then refers to "the perspectives of Vatican II," in which "there is only one economy of revelation. Every element in the economy finds its true revelatory meaning in relation to Christ, the center, who stands first in the order of the divine intention."[53]

Dulles speaks of both oral and written revelation, noting that before the establishment of the agreed upon list of biblical books (the canon), oral revelation was predominant. Indeed, in Dulles's view, oral tradition established the canon:

> The apostles handed on, by their oral preaching, exemplary actions, and ordinances, what they had received from Christ's lips, his way of life or his works, or had learned by the prompting of the Holy Spirit (DV 7). . . . Although the church did not yet have a fixed collection of canonical Scriptures, it was not a totally fluid community. Tradition, without being crystallized in rigid formulas, was a stabilizing force. . . . [According to the writings of Tertullian (160–220+) and Irenaeus (140–202)], bishops became the guardians of the apostolic tradition (LG 20).[54]

How was Scripture revealed? How did God inspire Scripture? What does divine inspiration mean? Here Dulles uses phrases that are familiar

---

50. Avery Cardinal Dulles, S.J., "Revelation, Scripture, and Tradition," in ibid., 38–39. DV is a reference to the Second Vatican Council's document on revelation, *Dei Verbum.*

51. Ibid., 39.

52. Ibid.

53. Ibid., 40.

54. Ibid., 44–46. LG is the Vatican Council's *Lumen Gentium.*

to most evangelicals, yet he also expresses a degree of comfort with God's mystery, which is not as widely shared among evangelicals. He also distinguishes between revelation and inspiration: "God . . . brought about composition of the sacred books by employing human agents, using their own powers and faculties, so that they wrote as authors in a true sense, and yet in such a way that they set down all that God intended, and nothing else (DV 11)."[55] For Dulles, it is important to make fine distinctions: "When he reveals, God communicates new knowledge of himself. When he inspires, God moves a human being to communicate and directs the process so that it achieves the divinely intended end. . . . It is quite possible for God to make a revelation through oral or written inspiration."[56] The end point is a very high doctrine of Scripture: "Since everything asserted by the inspired authors or sacred writers must be held as asserted by the Holy Spirit, it follows that the books of Scripture must be acknowledged as teaching firmly, faithfully, and without error that truth which God wanted put into the sacred writings for the sake of our salvation (DV 11)."[57]

How was revelation preserved after the apostolic era? Here Dulles speaks of the more than three hundred years between the death of Christ and the formation of the canon of Scripture and looks (not surprisingly) to the other two legs of the Catholic three-legged stool of authority. "In the first few generations the apostolic churches, under the direction of their bishops, were accepted as authoritative witnesses." Then, quoting from the Vatican II document *Dei Verbum*, Dulles defines tradition as "a dynamic process of transmission under the guidance of the Holy Spirit . . . continuously handing down the faith received from the apostles."[58] This document also "speaks of the power of discernment of the ecclesiastical Magisterium, which has received what Irenaeus called the 'sure charism of truth' (DV 8)."[59]

Dulles summarizes the Catholic view of revelation as it relates to Scripture and tradition:

> While revering Scripture as containing the word of God in unalterable form, [the church] denies that Scripture is sufficient in the sense that the whole of revelation could be known without tradition. . . . Although particular traditions are subject to critical scrutiny, tradition as a Spirit-governed transmission of the gospel in the church is to be revered, like Holy Scripture, as a form of the word of God. Tradition hands on the

55. Ibid., 46.
56. Ibid., 47.
57. Ibid., 48.
58. Ibid., 51.
59. Ibid., 55.

word of God in such a way that it can be grasped by the faithful of every time and place.[60]

J. I. Packer: "The Bible in Use: Evangelicals Seeking Truth from Holy Scripture"

James I. Packer, an Anglican and the Board of Governors Professor Emeritus of Theology at Regent College in Vancouver, Canada, is also senior editor and visiting scholar for *Christianity Today*. His well-received articles and books, including *Knowing God*, have earned him wide respect in the evangelical world. He has been the key figure explaining the ECT process to evangelicals and responding to those who oppose ECT's work. Packer opens his chapter with a paragraph lauding the evangelical use of Scripture—a description cited by several subsequent writers:

> Evangelicals maintain that as God has enthroned his Son, the living Word, as Lord of the universe, so he has enthroned the Bible, his writ-ten word, as the means of Christ's rule over the consciences of his disciples. The 66-book Protestant canon is held to be divinely inspired and authoritative, true and trustworthy, informative and imperative, life-imparting and strength-supplying to the human heart, and to be given to the church to be preached, taught, expounded, applied, absorbed, digested and appealed to as arbiter whenever questions of faith and life, belief and behavior, spiritual wisdom and spiritual welfare, break surface among the saints. Of the unifying bonds of evangelicalism, this view and use of Scripture is the strongest of all. . . . Evangelicals do not see themselves as in full unity with any who do not live in this overtly Bible-based way.[61]

In subsequent sections of his chapter, Packer describes evangelical expectations of the Bible, evangelical elucidations of the Bible, immer-sion in the Bible as an evangelical discipline, and (with some regret) isolation of the Bible as an evangelical failing.

When he treats evangelical expectations of the Bible, Packer draws from the leaders of the Protestant Reformation:

- Luther: "Scripture is God's writing and God's word. . . . Whoever would know God and have eternal life should read this book with diligence and search its testimony of Christ God's Son."[62]

60. Ibid., 57–58.
61. J. I. Packer, "The Bible in Use: Evangelicals Seeking Truth from Holy Scripture," in ibid., 62–63.
62. Ibid., 64.

- Calvin: "The Bible was not given to us to satisfy our foolish curiosity and pride. Yet Paul says it is useful. For what? To instruct us in sound doctrine, to comfort us, to inspire us, and to make us able to perform every good work. . . . Through it we learn to place our trust in God and to walk in fear of him."[63]
- Thomas Cranmer: "Every man that cometh to reading of this holy book ought to bring with him first and foremost this fear of Almighty God; and then next, a firm and stable purpose to reform his own self according thereunto."[64]

Packer supplements these testimonies with the contemporary voice of Thomas Howard (evangelical turned Catholic), who has written, "Evangelical spirituality stands or falls with private Bible reading. . . . There is an agile immediacy about an evangelical's attitude towards Scripture."[65]

Under elucidations, Packer looks to the Renaissance rule of trying to find the meaning that was expressed and therefore presumably intended by the human writer: "This was what they called the *literal* sense, as distinct from various time-honored ways of allegorizing the text. They quoted texts as proofs, but were not proof-texting. . . . The flow of thought running through the book was what they were after, as Calvin's classic commentaries and recorded sermons working through whole books in the pulpit, as was his habit, clearly show."[66] In Packer's phrase, evangelical biblical interpretation is "characteristically christocentric, covenantal, doxological, and devotional."[67]

In regard to evangelical immersion in Scripture, Packer refers to the at-homeness that evangelicals feel with their Bibles:

> Evangelicals see their Bible as the primary means of God's grace to their minds and hearts, and have therefore labored to immerse themselves in it by constantly reading it, memorizing it, meditating on its promises and encouragements, displaying texts in their homes, and generally doing all they can to ensure that Bible truths will always be before their minds. . . . Out of the cultural matrix between the mid-nineteenth and mid-twentieth centuries, there grew a home-, church-, and parachurch-based family style spirituality—intimate, cozy, gossipy, Sabbatarian, conscientiously cheerful, somewhat simplistic, somewhat exhibitionist.[68]

63. Ibid.
64. Ibid., 65.
65. Ibid., 67–68.
66. Ibid., 68–69.
67. Ibid., 71.
68. Ibid., 74.

To Packer, it is only to be expected that more recently, given this Scripture-infused way of life, "evangelicals should be found going on retreats, consulting spiritual directors (often Roman Catholic), experimenting with fasts, and trying out modes of meditation and contemplation that they never knew before, in order to center their souls more directly on God and his word."[69]

When he treats evangelical biblical isolation, Packer turns to the negative implications of evangelical fervor over Scripture. To him, it is a sad thing that

> evangelical emphasis on the Bible has often led to the neglect of other important elements of Christian thought. It has meant evangelical isolation from the mainstream Christian heritage of Bible-based theology and wisdom over two millennia, which evangelicals should claim but which few seem to know or care about; from evangelicalism's own heritage of theology and exposition, which most simply ignore; and from the searchings and findings of the physical, historical, and human sciences, with their never-ending quests to push out further the walls of human knowledge.[70]

Of these excesses, Packer is frankly critical: "But *sola scriptura* was never meant to imply that what is not mentioned in the Bible is not real, or is unimportant and not worth our attention, or that the history of biblical exegesis and exposition, and of theological construction and confession, over two millennia, need not concern us today, or that we should restrict our interest in God's world and in the arts, sciences, products, and dreams of our fellow-human beings."[71] In summary, *sola scriptura* does not mean Bible-without-science: "The Bible has been given us, not to define for us the realities of the created order, nor to restrain our interests in them, but to enable us to diagnose, understand, appreciate, and handle them as we meet them, so that we may use and enjoy them to the Creator's praise."[72]

Francis Martin: "Reading Scripture in the Catholic Tradition"

Francis Martin received his licentiate in sacred theology from St. Thomas University in Rome and later a doctorate in sacred Scripture from the Pontifical Biblical Institute, also in Rome. As a professor of biblical studies at the John Paul II Institute for Studies on Marriage and

69. Ibid., 75.
70. Ibid., 76–77.
71. Ibid., 77.
72. Ibid., 78.

Family and a chaplain to the Mother of God Community in Washington, D.C., he writes often on the subject of Scripture and spirituality.

Martin sets out two goals for his essay. First, he wants to establish that "the Catholic manner of reading Scripture is basically a contact with the Sacred Text as it mediates divine realities." Catholics thus view revelation "as an act of God by which he manifests and communicates *himself* and a knowledge of his plan of salvation (see *Dei Verbum* #2, 6)." Second, Martin wants to work on "an authentic retrieval of this way of reading Scripture," which would mean drawing on "other Christian Communions, particularly in regard to the personal, Spirit-guided reading of Scripture and the need for preaching the word."[73]

For evangelicals who doubt the reality of Catholic engagement of Scripture, Martin's own fifteen years of experience with monastic life should clear the air. The rhythms of the monastic day and the church's liturgical year breathe Scripture:

> The day, which began at 2:00 am and ended at 7:00 pm, was structured around eight periods of common prayer, all in Latin, the backbone of which was the Psalter sung or recited in such a way that the whole of the 150 psalms were prayed in the period of a week, with many of these being repeated several times in a week. The psalms were sung in the context of antiphons, readings from Scripture, and prayers which were composed in such a way that the ordinary days repeated themselves and the great feast days had special components. In addition there was a daily Eucharist Liturgy, also sung in its entirety. The church and monastery in which this prayer took place, after we had helped to build it, was a place of beauty and spiritual peace. The music, the Gregorian chant, sung by a group of monks considered to be among the most skilled in the country, was a constant education in the interpretation of Scripture. Let me explain.
>
> The basic principle of Gregorian chant is that it should be "a carpet for the words of Scripture to walk upon and thus enter your soul"; it is a musical exegesis of the sacred text composed in an atmosphere of prayer and fasting. . . .
>
> Our song makes us one with those who sang this song before us. We are bound together by the living Christ who sings his song in us on earth and in them in heaven. It is because of this mystery, the Christ in us, the hope and fulfillment of glory, that time is no longer a neutral reality but rather something that, once caught up in the life of the Body—the Christ—becomes eternal. . . .
>
> In the monastic liturgy the Books of Samuel and Kings are read throughout the summer, the time "after Pentecost" which symbolizes the life of the church. . . . Foremost among these, of course, is David since Jesus the new David is the one Shepherd who feeds the flock of God (Ezek. 34:23–24).

73. Francis Martin, "Reading Scripture in the Catholic Tradition," in ibid., 168.

. . . The melody even carries the sound of David's weeping—Christ weeping over us—and teaches us what it means to continue on earth the prayer of forgiveness of Christ himself. Finally, on a Sunday, as we approach the Lord at Communion, we sing the dialogue between Jesus and the woman taken in adultery, the confrontation of *Misericordia* and *miseria*, to quote Augustine's memorable phrase: "Has no one condemned you woman? No one Lord. Nor do I condemn you—go in peace and do not sin anymore." . . .

Even the monastic practice of *lectio divina* (private contact with the Sacred Text for several hours a day) is a continuation of the communal prayer which is basically the singing of the biblical text in a setting that repeated itself year after year drawing the cyclic time of the cosmos into the eternal dimension of the Resurrection.[74]

Martin's mystical entering into the text of Scripture mirrors a similar relationship between God's Spirit and Scripture. Quoting Henri de Lubac, Martin writes, "Scripture is not only divinely guaranteed, it is divinely true. The Spirit did not only dictate it; he is, as it were, contained in it. He inhabits it. His breath perpetually animates it. The Scripture is 'made fruitful by a miracle of the Holy Spirit.' It is 'full of the Spirit.'"[75]

Martin reminds those who consider study of Scripture primarily a scientific analysis of word meanings and sentence structure of the four ways in which ancient Christians viewed Scripture: "It is important to realize that, for the ancients, these four senses—the literal, the allegorical/spiritual, the tropological, and the anagogical—are not four meanings of the words, but four dimensions of the *event* which is being mediated by the words: the words are important because they are a privileged means of mediating the realities." Martin uses St. Augustine's caution when speaking to evangelicals who occasionally fret that an overemphasis on the text might become its own form of idolatry: "It is in the event itself, and not only in the text, that we must seek the mystery."[76] Martin further emphasizes a God-focused approach to Scripture: "It is upon this basis for the spiritual sense of Scripture that we can point to one characteristic of reading Scripture in the Catholic tradition, namely that it concentrated on the *acts* of God rather than on the words of Scripture which bear these acts to us."[77]

How then is a devout Christian (Catholic or evangelical) to approach Scripture? Martin contrasts a hermeneutic of trust, as exemplified by the evangelical biblical scholar Anthony Thiselton, with a hermeneutic of suspicion: "A hermeneutic of trust is founded in faith and operates on

74. Ibid., 148–50.
75. Ibid., 151.
76. Ibid., 152.
77. Ibid., 154.

the implicit epistemological presupposition that the mind of the reader can participate in the mind of the author by sharing his intention."[78] Martin thinks that the Renaissance and then the Protestant Reformation, especially with its conflicts over the exercise of biblical authority, began to move consideration of Scripture toward a hermeneutic of suspicion. What had been a "cultural world which had borne the Sacred Text" was transformed from an accepted "atmosphere" into an object that observers thought they could study objectively.[79] The result was movement toward a hermeneutic of suspicion, movement that has been accelerated by the postmodern view of language: "The ultimate stage in the journey is arrived at in the postmodern suspicion of language itself which, rather than being an instrument of intersubjective communication, becomes the tool of power."[80]

Martin challenges both evangelicals and Catholics to deepen their souls by attending to each other's way of reading Scripture: "It is time for Catholics, under the aegis of the Evangelical example (and of the Protestant example in general), to retrieve the monastic practice of *lectio divina* and make it once again, and in a much more widespread way, one of the backbones of lay piety." Martin urges Catholics to embrace what he calls "a *personal* reading of Scripture, with its concomitant experience of the presence of God and the efficacy of the mysteries of Christ as they are mediated by the Sacred Text." He thinks Catholics have only begun to benefit from the traditional Protestant way of a personal appropriation of Scripture, but he also concludes that "the thirst of Catholics for this type of reading is evidenced by the number of ecumenical Bible studies taking place all over the world and the way in which Catholics are profiting by the Evangelical charism for the simple and direct teaching of the Scriptures."[81]

In regard to Protestants, Martin recognizes that Catholic approaches to Scripture are event-oriented—are close to liturgy—and therefore are disconcerting. Especially disconcerted are those Protestants "whose epistemology is still tinged with the hermeneutic of suspicion (this holds as well for Catholics), when there is a question of the relation between Scripture and Tradition, particularly in the matter of the development of doctrine." Retrieving what Martin calls "this Catholic instinct" for the substance of divine action manifest in Scripture requires dialogue with Protestants, who manifest the "evangelical . . . instinct for the uniqueness of the scriptural expression of the divine truth." Martin's

78. Ibid., 159.
79. Ibid., 162.
80. Ibid., 163.
81. Ibid., 166.

hope is that, for Catholics and evangelicals, "the meeting point will be found in a mutual deepening of the understanding of the interpersonal nature of truth, and in a common experience of the Trinitarian source of revelation which is communicated by Jesus Christ as the revealer of the Father and thus, in Johannine terms, is himself the way, the Truth, and the Life."[82]

George, Dulles, Packer, and Martin represent varied expressions of "Evangelicals and Catholics Together" as participants struggled to find common ground on Scripture, truth, and authority. In their examination of Scripture, the participants were not always able to reach agreement, but they did discover deepened understanding of the theological systems that undergird Catholic and evangelical habits of faith. In that discovery, they could recognize the integrity of the other's system, and they could see the value of enriching their own stance toward Scripture with elements from the other's position. If Scripture is better read and better lived as a result, then the ECT process has already succeeded.

ECT IV: "The Communion of Saints"

The fourth ECT statement, which appeared in March 2003, took up the subject of the communion of saints.[83] The subject was difficult because, for one thing, evangelicals and Catholics define the term *saints* differently. For another, the nature of communion and the basis for that communion are also understood differently. After an initial summary of the previous three ECT statements, this latest joint document of some fifty-five hundred words treats the subject in a four-part outline: God's holiness as the basis for communion, communion between believers, sacraments/ordinances as ways of fostering communion, and communion with believers who have died (including the "saints").

The first section states briefly that any genuine communion among God's people must grow out of holiness, first, God's holiness, and then his people's sanctification (or commitment to a life of holiness). But this is no mere bootstraps self-purification: "To be holy is to participate in the holiness of Jesus who is 'the way, the truth, and the life.' . . . The communion of saints signifies, first of all, communion, through Christ and in the power of the Spirit with God the all-holy."[84]

82. Ibid., 167–68.
83. "The Communion of Saints," *First Things,* March 2003, 26–33.
84. Ibid., 28.

The second section of ECT IV admits that "we Evangelicals and Catholics do not now live out together the fullness of the unity for which Christ prayed. Yet we do not lack blessings of unity in the body of Christ, which includes the vast company of believers of all times and places." While conceding that full unity cannot occur in this life, the signatories describe their task as not to create unity but to "give full and faithful expression to the unity that is . . . [Christ's] present gift."[85]

In pursuit of that gift, the document then lists a number of challenges that evangelicals and Catholics can take up together: listen to the Word of God, pray, worship, give thanks, intercede for one another, study Scripture together, serve the poor and needy, work for public recognition of moral truths, protect the sanctity of human life at all stages, secure the integrity of marriage, protect the disabled and vulnerable, care for the marginalized and imprisoned, express solidarity with persecuted Christians, protect non-Christians who are denied rights of conscience, defend one another against unfair attacks, and share worship space in time of need.[86]

As it acknowledges Christ's command to "make disciples of all nations," the document quotes mission statements from both Amsterdam 2000 and John Paul II's 1990 encyclical *Redemptoris Missio* (The Mission of the Redeemer) to contend that "as we are sent by the same Lord, as we go forth in the name of the same Lord, as we proclaim the same Lord, so we ought to evangelize with one another rather than against one another."[87] In this section, the authors also rejoice in the ways that evangelicals and Catholics are already enriched by each others' strengths:

> In communal worship, Evangelicals and other Protestants have helped Catholics to value more highly the effective proclamation of the word of God. At the same time, Evangelicals have learned from Catholics and Orthodox to appreciate more fully the importance of ordered liturgy, including a lectionary based on the seasons of the Christian year. Noteworthy also is the greater use of one another's legacy of hymnody. Patristic and medieval hymns are finding greater currency among some Evangelicals, while Catholics today praise God in the songs of Isaac Watts, Charles Wesley, and others in the Evangelical tradition. In seminaries and programs of ministerial formation, leaders are increasingly being educated in both the unity and diversity of the one Christian movement in world history.[88]

85. Ibid.
86. Ibid., 29–30.
87. Ibid., 29.
88. Ibid.

After this recognition of communion already taking place, the third section of ECT IV takes up the question of communion as expressed in sacraments or ordinances. With sadness, the document admits to irreconcilable differences on the number and meaning of sacraments and also records the painful impossibility of sharing together in the Eucharist or the Lord's Supper.

Since the authors agreed that differences concerning sacraments arise in large part from differing views of the church, they worked hard to make a unified statement about the church. Because ecclesiology seems to be the direction of several current and future conversations between evangelicals and Catholics, it is worth expanding on what this document says about the church. Signers of ECT IV quote in agreement a definition of the church from Amsterdam 2000 and also a definition of the church from the Second Vatican Council. They also agree that one expression of the church is her sacramental nature. From Amsterdam 2000:

> The Church is the people of God, the body and bride of Christ, the temple of the Holy Spirit. The one, universal Church is a transnational, transcultural, transdenominational, and multi-ethnic family, the household of faith. In the widest sense, the Church includes all the redeemed of all the ages, being the one body of Christ extended throughout time as well as space. Here in the world, the Church becomes visible in all local congregations that meet to do together the things that according to the Scripture the Church does. Christ is the head of the Church. Everyone who is personally united to Christ by faith belongs to his body and by the Spirit is united with every other true believer in Jesus.[89]

From the Second Vatican Council:

> All are called to belong to the new People of God. Wherefore this People, while remaining one and unique, is to be spread throughout the whole world and must exist in all ages, so that the purpose of God's will may be fulfilled. . . . It follows that among all the nations of earth there is but one People of God, which takes its citizens from every race, making them citizens of a kingdom which is of a heavenly and not an earthly nature. For all the faithful scattered throughout the world are in communion with each other in the Holy Spirit. (*Lumen Gentium* II.13)[90]

After affirming both statements, ECT IV adds its own summary:

> The church itself can be understood as a sign and instrument of grace instituted by the one mediator between God and man, Jesus Christ, and,

89. Ibid., 30.
90. Ibid.

through the gospel, mediating his grace to the world. While the ancient formula "outside the Church no salvation" may lend itself to misunderstanding, we agree that there is no salvation apart from the Church, since to be related to Christ is necessarily to be related, in however full or tenuous a manner, to the Church which is his body.[91]

This third section of ECT IV is notable more for what it does not say than for what it says. Clearly, Protestants and Catholics are not going to agree soon on the number of sacraments, the meaning of the two that both groups employ, or on the precise nature of Christian communion. Since sacraments relate so closely to the nature of the church, this document's progress consists in the common acceptance of minimal definitions of the church, and it points toward a future when those minimal definitions might be enlarged: "We Evangelicals and Catholics gratefully acknowledge our unity in being reconciled to God through Christ, and pray for the day when that unity can be expressed and strengthened by agreement on all the means of grace that Christ intends for his Church."[92]

The fourth part of ECT IV addresses the subject of saints. It acknowledges both the evangelical sense of all believers (past and present) and the more restricted Catholic use of the term. As might be expected, in this document, "The Communion of the Saints," the subject of "saints" manifests less agreement than the subject of "communion." Here ECT IV settles for a clarification of what each body believes rather than an agreement on the subject. It also outlines areas for future discussion by pointing occasionally to likely points of connection. For example:

> The *communion sanctorum* [communion of the saints] embraces all Christians, including those whose lives are not notably marked by holiness. In the New Testament, the term "saints" generally refers to all who are baptized and confess Christ as Lord. The Christian tradition, following the New Testament, also lifts up some persons for special respect and veneration. The Letter to the Hebrews, for instance, proposes an honor roll of those in the history of salvation who are exemplars of heroic faith.[93]

The statement goes on to describe Christian history of the second century in which believers gathered for worship at the tombs of martyrs, expressing *communion sanctorum* with "the faithful who had gone before," especially those martyred for their faith. This historical obser-

91. Ibid.
92. Ibid., 31.
93. Ibid.

vation then leads to an outline of evangelical-Catholic differences on the subject:

- Catholics believe in a "lively interaction" with believers who have died—including intercession on their behalf. They are careful to point out that prayers *to* the saints are also prayers *with* the saints ultimately directed to Christ and to the Father and that God (not the saints) gives all blessings.
- By the same principle, Catholics also pray to/through Mary.
- Evangelicals do not find biblical warrant for this practice. They are "puzzled, if not repelled" by it. They caution Catholics against abuse and superstition based on saints and relics.
- Evangelicals express concern about Catholic teaching on the "merits" of saints, because this emphasis detracts from Christ as the "sole Redeemer."
- Catholics hold that believers who die will be cleansed by the spiritual fire of purgatory, basing their belief in part on 1 Corinthians 3:14–15.
- Evangelicals agree that "our lives will be reviewed before the judgment seat of Christ, and that all that is unworthy will be burned away," but they see no biblical warrant for purgatory.

The document leaves further contentious subjects for later discussion, including suffrages for the dead, indulgences, the role of Mary in Christian piety, and sins of denominations against one another. Yet at the end, participants affirm that "no true Christian living or dead, can be outside the *communion sanctorum*, the fellowship of all who live in the crucified, risen, reigning, and returning Lord."[94] They close with words of challenge and hope: "In a world where many believe that this life is all there is, Christians are called to bear bold witness to the solidarity of the *communion sanctorum*, a solidarity secured by our communion with Jesus Christ—crucified, risen, and coming again—and with all, both the living and the dead, who are alive in Christ."[95]

ECT I through IV and Beyond

The ECT process has been only one of many signs of Catholic-evangelical engagement in recent decades. But because of its bold assertions,

94. Ibid., 32.
95. Ibid., 31.

because of the renown of some of its sponsors, and because of the controversy it has generated, the ECT initiative deserves special consideration in any effort to ask if the Reformation is over. On several critical questions, ECT has made progress toward unity; on other questions, it has highlighted already existing unity; on still others, it has defined continued differences. Throughout, it has conducted its business in an atmosphere of kindness and respect.

Justification by Faith

A main goal of ECT has been to advance consideration of the meaning of Christian salvation. Debates over evangelism, and hence also over proselytization, arise out of a concern for a correct understanding of salvation. If evangelicals or Catholics view the other as not redeemed, then the biblical Great Commission mandates evangelism. But are active, wholehearted practitioners of the other faith tradition actually lost or simply viewing salvation from a different angle? ECT II supplies the fullest answer to such questions. It defines salvation as *sola fide*—by faith alone—and affirms (as does the Catholic *Catechism* and many of the ecumenical dialogues) that this is Catholic as well as evangelical doctrine. ECT II does not employ the term *sola gratia*—by grace alone—but it does define saving grace in a way acceptable to many evangelicals.

Reformed or Calvinistic evangelicals, as well as a few Lutherans, who want to see an explicit statement of forensic justification (or salvation defined strictly as God's act of imputing Christ's righteousness to the repentant sinner) will remain disappointed. By contrast, Arminian and other evangelicals who do not stress imputation as strongly find little difficulty with the theology of salvation expressed in the ECT documents. This reality points to a basic though subtle difference between Reformed and Catholic teachings on salvation. Catholics emphasize justification as a heart change that gradually shapes a believer into the image of Christ. Reformed Protestants see justification as an external legal (forensic) declaration of God that pardons a sinner and then leads to growth in holiness.[96]

Some Reformed theologians think that anything other than a forensic view of justification endangers humans by suggesting that in some way they can earn the gift of salvation. Even so, they would agree that genuine justification results in movement toward practical godliness. In return, Catholics affirm that while redemption means God makes his people righteous, part of the change worked by God is his declara-

---

96. This difference is set out with special clarity in Alister E. McGrath, "The New Catholic Catechism," *Christianity Today*, December 12, 1994, 28–33.

tion that sinners are righteous in Christ. It is unlikely that any group of Catholics and evangelicals will come up with a united statement of forensic justification. Disagreement, however, lies not so much in contradictory affirmations as in affirmations that look at the course of salvation differently. But this kind of disagreement is also widespread among evangelicals.

Debate on the exact definition of justification may not be as important as it seems. J. I. Packer explains why when he contrasts the shape of dogma with the essence of belief: "The Tridentine assertion of merit and the Reformational assertion of imputed righteousness can hardly be harmonized." But evangelicals and Catholics have "sufficient account of the gospel of salvation for shared evangelistic ministry." As Packer puts it, "What brings salvation, after all, is not any theory about faith in Christ, justification, and the church, but faith itself in Christ himself."[97] Moreover, as we have seen repeatedly, older theories of merit have receded in official statements of Catholic belief since the Second Vatican Council.

In summary, what the ECT initiative has developed are general statements on justification by faith that reveal more unity between the Catholics and evangelicals who embrace these statements than among evangelicals at large.

For Catholics, the situation is somewhat different, since it is possible for Catholics to say what the official teaching of their church is with a clarity not possible for evangelicals. Positions on salvation that are held by Catholics around the world do, in fact, reveal a spectrum of belief just as wide as that found among Protestants. In situations that evangelicals always find disconcerting, the Catholic Church seems to tolerate many forms of syncretism—amalgamations of Catholic and pagan practice—in many parts of the globe. Similarly, the church seems to act only fitfully in restraining the modernistic beliefs expressed by some academic Catholics in the Western world. Yet in its official teachings, which are found most recently in the documents of the Second Vatican Council and the Catholic *Catechism*, the Roman Catholic Church now articulates positions on salvation—even on justification by faith—that are closer to the main teachings of the sixteenth-century Protestant Reformation than are the beliefs of many Protestants, indeed, of many evangelical Protestants. Strange as it may seem to put it this way, the ECT documents present what can only be called a classically orthodox depiction of Christian salvation, primarily *because* they emphasize and build upon these official Catholic teachings.

97. Packer, "Why I Signed It," 37.

Cobelligerence

When ECT I first appeared, its emphasis on the moral failures of modern American society was obvious to all. Even those evangelicals most critical of how the document resolved theological differences did not usually object to that emphasis. With Charles Colson and Richard Neuhaus both active as leaders of conservative moral causes, it was apparent that they were working toward doctrinal consensus out of a background of shared social-political conviction. Only a few evangelicals who otherwise approved the doctrinal rapprochement worried about the social-political context in which doctrine was being addressed. Yet these evangelicals, as well as the secular observers who reacted to ECT I as if it were a transparently political statement merely garnished with theological rhetoric, raised a valid question. If cobelligerency on the moral issues of modern American politics paved the way for ECT, is ECT captive to the partisanship of modern American politics? Or to put such questions more crassly, Is ECT more than an arm of the American religious Right with an add-on of theology? Does ECT's cobelligerency equate to American conservative Republicanism?

If ECT I had appeared under the chairmanship of Charles Colchild and Richard Althaus, these questions may not have seemed so pertinent. In point of fact, ECT I was less partisan and more generic in its social, cultural, and political injunctions than sometimes credited. Yet because it was Colson and Neuhaus who chaired the effort, attention was naturally drawn to the tone and emphases of the document as well as to what, paragraph by paragraph, it actually said. Thus, critics noticed that ECT I inveighed full-out against "relativism, anti-intellectualism, and nihilism" but not nearly so directly against racism, greed, and egoism. They observed that the document was strong in denouncing pornography and defending "parental choice in education" but silent on the treatment of immigrants and the availability of affordable health care to all citizens.

In addition, there were friends of the document who agreed with much in its section on "contending together" in "public responsibilities" but who wondered if the cause of expanding doctrinal agreement should be organically linked to specific ideological causes. Taken by themselves, such statements as the following certainly deserve serious consideration: "We affirm the importance of a free economy not only because it is more efficient but because it accords with a Christian understanding of human freedom. . . . The American experiment has been, all in all, a blessing to the world and a blessing to us as Evangelical and Catholic Christians." But inserted in a statement of what Catholic Christians and evangelical Christians share in belief, and especially in light of how strife between evangelicals and Catholics in Latin America had sparked the document in the first place, such sentences were a distraction.[98]

Whether in response to such challenges or not, subsequent ECT statements concentrated more narrowly on doctrine and ventured toward partisan social-political commentary gingerly, if at all. In addition, leaders of the initiative, such as Neuhaus, have always insisted that the main purpose of the process was theological and that ECT statements concerning moral values grew out of basic theological concerns, not the reverse: "The main intention and, God willing, lasting importance is the affirmation of Christian faith and mutual recognition of one another as brothers and sisters in Christ."[99]

By the time ECT IV appeared, cobelligerence was being phrased in more general terms: "Evangelicals and Catholics together share, and must together contend for, the Christian world view. . . . Such solidarity in opposition to the forces of unbelief is aptly called cobelligerency, and such cobelligerency is the more solid as it is more firmly grounded in the Bible, the creeds, and our confessions and worship of Jesus Christ as Lord."[100] The theme of cobelligerency was critical for the rise of the entire ECT project. Yet especially in a world in which the majority of both evangelicals and Catholics now live outside the Western world—and often with pressing needs vastly different from the discontents of American society—cobelligerency will make the most sense when it rises unambiguously from shared Christian commitment rather than from the cultural contingencies, national aspirations, or political agendas of particular places on the globe.

Ecclesiology

As in the ecumenical dialogues and the Catholic *Catechism*, so also in the ECT documents, issues concerning the church define the most serious continued differences between evangelicals and Catholics. In his justification for signing ECT I, J. I. Packer cited the nature of the church as the key remaining difference and the one most likely to impede future unity.

> Rome's claim to be the only institution that can without qualification be called the church of Christ is theologically flawed, for it misconceives the nature of the church as the New Testament explains it. . . . The infallibility claimed for all conciliar and some papal pronouncements, and the insistence that the faithful should take their beliefs from the church as such

98. Quotations from "Evangelicals and Catholics Together," 18–20.
99. Richard John Neuhaus, letter to Michael S. Horton, July 7, 1994.
100. "The Communion of Saints," *First Things*, March 2003, 27.

rather than from the Bible as such, make self-correction, as ordinarily understood, impossible.[101]

ECT IV touched on ecclesiology as it studied communion of the saints, but it did not take up the larger subject of the church's nature. Evangelicals vary in their theology of the church almost as widely as their dozens of denominations suggest. But the Protestant-Catholic divide over ecclesiology will continue to affect any future ECT discussions. It may simply become a subject where the difference is assumed and accepted rather than overcome. As evangelicals and Catholics approach non-Christian religions, Islam for example, these ongoing differences in ecclesiology may shrink in importance.

Taking Stock

The four existing ECT documents to date have examined critical areas and have found common ground on important issues such as co-belligerency, evangelism, justification by faith, and Scripture. The ECT process has helped both to clarify differences and to enhance mutual respect. Criticism from evangelical conservatives seems to have abated. Each ECT statement has emphasized that those who signed the document did so as individuals, not as representatives of any organization: "We speak from and to the communities of which we are part, but we do not presume to speak for them."[102] Participants have been personally enriched by the process of exploring each other's understanding of the Christian faith and have gained a sense that their combined efforts were more than any could have accomplished alone—indeed, that they are not alone: "In each statement we carefully note that we have not resolved all our differences on the subjects addressed, and it should be evident that we resolutely reject any thought of evading such differences. . . . We understand Evangelicals and Catholics Together as a work in progress. We are convinced that this is a work of the Holy Spirit. This work was underway long before ECT was begun."[103] That work will doubtless go on.

101. Packer, "Why I Signed It," 35.
102. "Communion of Saints," 27.
103. Ibid.

7

REACTIONS FROM ANTAGONISM
TO CONVERSION

Where once evangelicals had been united in a consistent critique of Roman Catholicism, today evangelical attitudes have become diverse in the extreme. These attitudes range from unilateral rejection through intense theological criticism to varieties of cautious acceptance and partnership. Some evangelicals have even responded to the contemporary Roman Catholic Church by converting. These positions—as antagonists, critics, partners, and converts—define a broad spectrum, yet each one also reveals something significant about strengths and weaknesses within evangelicalism itself.

Antagonists

Evangelicals who continue to reject Catholicism in toto feel that they have history on their side. They may not be fully informed about the details, but they are troubled about Catholic domination over civil affairs (as claimed, for example, in *Unam Sanctam* [1302], when Pope Boniface VIII asserted ultimate papal authority over both spiritual and temporal realms). They often know about the anathemas of the Council of Trent (1545–63), when Rome directly attacked key Reformation doctrines such as justification by faith alone through grace alone.[1] They invariably know about the Catholic claim of papal infallibility from 1870, though they may not understand how that declaration was qualified.

In addition, all-out antagonists enjoy an immense reservoir of voices from the history of Protestantism on which they can draw for warnings about the dangers of Catholicism. The twenty-fifth chapter of the 1647 edition of the Westminster Confession, for example, describes the Roman pontiff as "that antichrist, that man of sin, and son of perdition."[2] A. J. Gordon (1836–95), a devout Baptist who founded institutions that became Gordon College and Gordon-Conwell Theological Seminary, declared, "It is Satan who is the real Pope and his subordinate demons who are the real cardinals."[3] Though sometimes less vitriolic, evangelicals who espoused J. N. Darby's premillennial dispensationalism regularly saw the Roman Catholic Church as the ten-horned beast of Revelation 17. Harry Ironside, who became pastor of Chicago's Moody Church in 1930, assured his audience that the papacy would be revived and would once again clothe itself with royal purple and ecclesiastical scarlet, "riding the Beast."[4] Bible teacher Donald Grey Barnhouse (1895–1960), in his commentary on Revelation (first published serially 1934–42), wrote that "in the seventeenth chapter of Revelation God speaks of religious Babylon and identifies it with the Roman ecclesiastical system."[5] A few decades later, as already shown, evangelicals registered their concern at the prospect of electing Catholics to American national office. Thus, evangelicals today who reject the Roman Catholic Church without qualification as a minion of Satan carry on a long tradition.

1. For example, "The Decree Concerning Justification" from the sixth session of the Council of Trent (1547). This decree is reprinted in many places, including Mark A. Noll, ed., *Confessions and Catechisms of the Reformation* (Grand Rapids: Baker, 1991), 173–88.

2. Quoted in Donald W. Sweeting, "From Conflict to Cooperation? Changing American Evangelical Attitudes towards Roman Catholics: 1960–1998" (Ph.D. diss., Trinity Evangelical Divinity School, 1998), 7. Sweeting's dissertation is an excellent source of information on its subject. Also helpful are Jennifer V. Suvada, "A Study of the Evangelical Protestant Reception of the Document, *Evangelicals and Catholics Together,* from Its Release in March 1994 through December 1996, Including a Case Study of the Southern Baptist Convention" (M.A. thesis, Trinity Evangelical Divinity School, 1997); and Nathan Andrew Baxter, "Toward a Decorous Rhetoric of Public Theology: Evangelicals and Catholics Together—Betrayal, Alliance, or Good Beginning" (Ph.D. diss., Indiana University, 1999).

3. A. J. Gordon, "Modern Delusions," a speech given at the International Prophetic Conference, Chicago, November 1886, in *Prophetic Studies of the International Prophetic Conference* (New York: Revell, 1886), 67.

4. Harry Ironside, *Looking Backward over a Third of a Century of Prophetic Fulfillment* (New York: Loizeaux Brothers, 1931), quoted in Sweeting, "From Conflict to Cooperation?" 65–66.

5. Donald Grey Barnhouse, *Revelation* (Grand Rapids: Zondervan, 1971), 335.

In the world of ordinary, nonlearned evangelicals, atavistic anti-Catholicism remains as colorful and unmistakable as ever. A representative is Jack Chick, mentioned earlier in this book. Chick, a mysterious writer or team of writers, has printed four hundred million copies of cartoon booklets (Chicklets) in seventy languages.[6] Typical is "Last Rites," where John, a hapless Catholic, is hit by a car, receives last rites, and dies. After several attempts to bargain his way into heaven, he asks of Jesus, "Don't you love the Roman Catholic Church?" A faceless Jesus replies, "How could I, John. Her false teachings are why you are going to the lake of fire."[7] In the tract "Are Roman Catholics Christians?" Chick traces the life story of Helen, a devout Catholic. After her first Communion, Chick asks, "What does Jesus think of the Roman Catholic Institution?" Answer: "He calls her the great whore." Chick speaks of the Catholic mass as making Jesus a liar[8] and the Communion wafer as the "death cookie."[9] It would be easy to dismiss Chicklets as an aberration except for the reception of these booklets. Catholic scholar Mark S. Massa notes that one Chick comic touches more people than most theologians and preachers hope to reach in a lifetime.[10]

But rejecting Catholicism is not limited to evangelicals who are paranoid or ignorant. In the heat of the debate after twenty evangelicals signed the first ECT document, R. C. Sproul, then a professor at Reformed Theological Seminary in Florida, declared, "I am convinced as were the Reformers, that justification by faith alone is essential to the gospel and that Rome clearly rejects it."[11] A few years earlier, John Green, a Catholic and an undergraduate at evangelical Wheaton College, had to wonder why his world religion professor lumped Buddhism, Islam, and Catholicism together as non-Christian faiths. (Green graduated with two degrees from Wheaton and remained a Catholic.)[12] Also at Wheaton, a faculty member who had signed ECT I received a letter from a high school friend, with quotations attached from the Council of Trent and the judgment that Catholicism "is a false gospel—a terrible gospel, a gospel if believed and followed will damn a person to hell."[13]

6. Mark S. Massa, S.J., *Anti-Catholicism in America: The Last Acceptable Prejudice* (New York: Crossroad, 2003), 100.

7. "Last Rites," www.chick.com/titlesavailable (1994).

8. "Are Roman Catholics Christians?" www.chick.com/titlesavailable (1985).

9. Massa, *Anti-Catholicism in America*, 106.

10. Ibid., 109.

11. R. C. Sproul, *Faith Alone: The Evangelical Doctrine of Justification* (Grand Rapids: Baker, 1995), 39.

12. Jeremy Webber, "Catholicism and Wheaton: A Mixed Experience," *Wheaton College Record,* December 12, 2003, 9.

13. Private letter to Mark Noll, June 20, 2001.

Mission fields remain sites where mutual rejection between Catholics and evangelicals is strongest. When in the wake of ECT I, articles in *Christianity Today* reviewed recent changes among Catholics, one letter writer complained, "Why did neither Colson nor McGrath urge us to consider Catholics as an evangelistic field desperately in need of the gospel?"[14] The region that bears special witness to this kind of mutual rejection is Latin America, although some parts of southern Europe also continue to witness harsh evangelical-Catholic antagonism. The extent to which firsthand experiences of hegemonic, mechanical Catholicism can overpower recent openings to dialogue was indicated dramatically by events at the Seventh Assembly of the World Evangelical Fellowship (WEF) at Heddson, England, in March 1980. When the general secretary of the fellowship invited two Roman Catholics (one a well-known charismatic) to the gathering as observers, consternation resulted among the Southern European representatives to the WEF. The Italian Evangelical Alliance withdrew, and the Spanish Alliance suspended its participation.[15] Meanwhile, in Latin America, despite the mutual respect initiated by Catholic and Pentecostal ecumenical dialogues, evangelical entry into Catholic territory still can lead to church-sanctioned violence. In sum, rejection of the Catholic faith as a less than Christian religion comes in many forms from many kinds of evangelicals for a variety of reasons.

Critics

However many evangelicals of however many stripes continue to regard the Catholic Church as a dangerous enemy of the gospel, many other evangelicals are now on record with a variety of more moderate criticisms. That variety can be summarized in the following categories.

First are those evangelicals who have taken careful note of recent Catholic professions about justification by faith but who just cannot believe they could be genuine. Such voices sometimes argue that so long as Trent remains a part of respected Catholic tradition, it is impossible to take seriously Catholics who profess to accept salvation by grace alone.[16] Others are not satisfied unless and until Catholics affirm the exact shape of Martin Luther's or John Calvin's definition of objective

14. Thomas F. Neagle, "Letters to the Editor," *Christianity Today*, February 6, 1995, 6.
15. *A Contemporary Evangelical Perspective on Roman Catholicism* (Wheaton: World Evangelical Fellowship, 1986), 7.
16. For example, Sproul, *Faith Alone*.

justification before God.[17] Still others say that if the Catholic Church maintains its traditional practices and teaching concerning Mary, it cannot truly affirm justification by faith.[18] Yet others worry that the recent declarations on justification represent the victory of a will to unity over a reliance on truth.

Justification by faith remains at the center of evangelical concern. While the ecumenical dialogues between Lutherans and Catholics made enormous progress on this doctrine, many evangelicals remain less than satisfied. When the first ECT document appeared in May 1994, much of the criticism from evangelicals focused on perceived fudging about this doctrine. As a partial response, an Alliance of Confessing Evangelicals published "The Cambridge Declaration" on April 20, 1996. This document, signed by roughly one hundred evangelical leaders, including several college presidents, emphasized the five *soli* of the Reformation: *sola scriptura, solus Christus, sola gratia, sola fide,* and *soli deo gloria.* Each paragraph of the statement concludes with "We reaffirm . . . We deny . . ." In these statements, the central matter of evangelical interest is obvious. For example: *"We deny* that justification rests on any merit to be found in us, or upon the grounds of an infusion of Christ's righteousness in us, or that an institution claiming to be a church that denies or condemns *sola fide* can be recognized as a legitimate church." Yet the Cambridge Declaration was considerably more than merely an anti-Catholic document. It also contained strong medicine for evangelicals, including warnings against marketing the gospel in terms of health and wealth, worship as entertainment for the self-centered, and church growth defined by sociological standards instead of the biblical gospel.[19]

Another flurry of reactions came in December 1997 after the publication of ECT II ("The Gift of Salvation"). Although this document emphasized that salvation is by grace alone through faith alone (yet with its terminology nuanced to fit both Catholic and evangelical understandings of these terms), certain evangelical leaders felt that, to preserve evangelical unity, a separate counterstatement was required. The result was "The Gospel of Jesus Christ: An Evangelical Celebration" framed by a fifteen-member drafting committee, published in March 1999, and signed by 114 notable evangelicals.[20] Yet this document,

17. For example, Michael Horton, "What's All the Fuss About? The State of the Justification Debate," *Modern Reformation,* March/April 2002, 17–21.

18. For example, S. Lewis Johnson Jr., "Mary, the Saints, and Sacredotalism," in *Roman Catholicism: Evangelical Protestants Analyze What Divides and Unites Us,* ed. John Armstrong, 119–40 (Chicago: Moody, 1994).

19. This document is available at a number of websites, including www.reformed .org/documents/cambridge.html.

20. Available in *Pro Ecclesia* 9, no. 2 (Spring 2000): 133–44.

which criticized the ECT process, was not without its own critics. On one side, members of the Alliance of Confessing Evangelicals refused to sign it because to do so "may be interpreted as a tacit endorsement of *Evangelicals and Catholics Together.*"[21] On the other side, Roger E. Olson of Truett Theological Seminary at Baylor University criticized the document for making a forensic view of salvation essential to the gospel itself, therefore pushing Anabaptists (not to mention Catholics) beyond the boundaries of orthodoxy.[22] The evangelical Congregational-ist Gabriel Fackre cautioned that "accent on the penal and personal so dominates the text that other classical Christian teachings are muted or missing."[23] Similar criticism appeared in letters to the editor of *Chris-tianity Today,* including one signed jointly by Cornelius Plantinga Jr., John G. Stackhouse Jr., and Nicholas Wolterstorff, who objected that this new evangelical statement "focuses so much on justification and so little on sanctification." These scholars also expressed surprise at "the affirmation that 'saving faith includes mental assent to the content of the gospel.' We wonder how God saves infants and mentally retarded people."[24] Such controversy might sound like inconsequential infighting within the evangelical debating club, but it was important as indicating the altered theological situation brought about by the engagement of evangelicals with the Catholic Church.

Some evangelical criticism stimulated by these discussions was not gentle. R. C. Sproul, for example, dealt more harshly with his evangelical colleagues who had joined Catholics in ways he considered inappropriate than with the Catholic Church itself. Beginning with the premise that the historic evangelical and official Catholic doctrines of justification were fundamentally irreconcilable, he assumed that "no matter what the authors' intentions ECT involves a tacit betrayal of the gospel."[25] He concluded that "the light of the Reformation is waning," and the "evangelical house totters on the brink of collapse."[26] Sproul implied that evangelicals who supported Catholic-evangelical initiatives such as ECT might fall under Paul's censure of the false teachers who were troubling the Galatian church and perverting the gospel.[27] Likewise, John MacArthur Jr. cautioned fellow evangelicals that moral solidarity

21. "News," *Moody,* September/October 1999, 37.

22. Roger E. Olson, "Evangelical Essentials? Reservations and Reminders," *Christian Century,* August 24–September 1, 1999, 817.

23. Gabriel Fackre, "Ecumenical Admonitions," *Christian Century,* August 24–September 1, 1999, 818.

24. Letters to the Editor, "An Evangelical Consensus?" *Christianity Today,* October 4, 1999, 15.

25. Sproul, *Faith Alone,* 44.

26. Ibid., 48, 183.

27. Ibid., 187–88.

pursued by ECT I, though legitimate and in some ways salutary, could easily undermine essential Christian teaching.[28]

In the colorful controversy among evangelicals following the publication of ECT I, letters to *Christianity Today* reflected considerable theological wariness, often directed toward the evangelical signers. For example, "Social activism . . . is not worth putting aside . . . the gospel of Jesus Christ, which includes salvation by grace alone, through faith alone, as revealed through Scriptures alone by the Holy Spirit. My hat is off to Mr. Colson for his zeal for unity, social activism, and spreading the gospel. However, to minimize the fact that evangelicals and official Rome preach two different gospels, which are mutually exclusive, is to deny reality."[29] Or, again, "I was appalled at Packer's condescending attitude toward those who don't buy his Catholic love affair. . . . He puts aside Scripture in favor of his agenda."[30]

In response, J. I. Packer outlined the six major criticisms that he perceived among evangelicals worried about evangelical-Catholic rapprochement: (1) Catholic brotherhood with evangelicals is a mirage, (2) Catholics think that the Holy Spirit interprets Scripture through decisions of the church, (3) Catholics do not believe in salvation by faith *alone,* (4) Catholics see conversion as both initial turning and also a lifelong process, (5) many individual Catholic churches lack adequate biblical teaching to guide spiritual maturity, and (6) signers of ECT are illegitimately seeking organic unity with the church of Rome.[31] Packer felt that these fears could be allayed. Yet his list nonetheless summarized points of major theological concern among evangelicals who remained skeptical about engagement with Catholics.

Yet as recently underscored by Gerald Bray, the Anglican professor of divinity at Beeson Divinity School, even evangelicals who remain firm critics of the Catholic system of belief and the Catholic Church are certain that individual Catholics may be saved "in spite of the system." In Bray's words, "They look at Catholics (as at everyone else) as individuals, and make up their minds accordingly. Of course, they will usually try to persuade converted Catholics to leave the Catholic Church and join an Evangelical congregation somewhere, but this is so that they can be properly fed spiritually, and not (usually) because they are just bigoted

28. John MacArthur Jr., "A Personal Word," in *Protestants and Catholics: Do They Now Agree?* ed. John Ankerberg and John Weldon (Eugene, OR: Harvest House, 1995), 11.

29. "Letters to the Editor," *Christianity Today,* January 9, 1995, 6.

30. "Letters to the Editor," *Christianity Today,* February 6, 1995, 6.

31. J. I. Packer, "Crosscurrents among Evangelicals," in *Evangelicals and Catholics Together: Toward a Common Mission,* ed. Charles Colson and Richard John Neuhaus (Dallas: Word, 1995), 154–56.

Protestants. They would say exactly the same thing to a Methodist, a Presbyterian, or a Baptist who was attending the wrong church."[32]

Partners

Many evangelicals, though aware of continuing theological differences, are ready, as a response to Christ's prayer for unity among his people, to partner with Catholics on many fronts. These fronts include social-political cobelligerency, the affirmation of "mere Christianity," a common enjoyment of historic roots, the sharing of mission and ministry, and agreement on spiritual formation.

Cobelligerency

ECT I rested substantially on a desire for social-political cobelligerency. About half of the eight-thousand-word document was a general call to unity among those who bear the name of Christ. Of the remainder, gospel witness received thirteen hundred words (and most of the subsequent criticism). Civic participation got nearly twenty-four hundred words.[33] This emphasis was not surprising since ECT initiators Charles Colson and Richard John Neuhaus remain well known for their leadership in America's culture wars. Cobelligerency is a term popularized among evangelicals by Francis Schaeffer and frequently used by J. I. Packer to speak of Christians linked with one another against forces of evil in contemporary society.[34] In a similar view, Timothy George, Southern Baptist theologian at Beeson Divinity School, has spoken of an "ecumenism of the trenches."[35] Even Carl F. H. Henry, who would not sign ECT I because of doctrinal reservations, nonetheless supported the effort by evangelicals and Catholics to combat moral problems together.[36]

Advocacy for pro-life causes is probably the theme that most unites evangelicals and Catholics. David Neff, executive editor of *Christianity Today*, has written, "Today, classic theological liberalism is no longer

32. Gerald Bray, "Evangelicals, Salvation, and Church History," in *Catholics and Evangelicals: Do They Share a Common Future?* ed. Thomas P. Rausch (Downers Grove, IL: InterVarsity, 2000), 92–93.

33. Baxter, "Toward a Decorous Rhetoric of Public Theology," 32.

34. Brother Jeffrey Gros, F.S.C., review of *Roman Catholics and Evangelicals: Agreements and Differences*, by Norman Geisler and Ralph MacKenzie, *One in Christ* 32, no. 1 (1996): 90–93.

35. Timothy George, "Toward an Evangelical Ecclesiology," in *Catholics and Evangelicals*, 142.

36. Carl F. H. Henry, "The Vagrancy of the American Spirit," *Faculty Dialogue: Journal of the Institute for Christian Leadership* 22 (Fall 1994): 7–8.

the church's main threat. As we enter a post-Christian world, one driven by consumer culture and the entertainment industry, we face more basic challenges, such as the radical devaluation of human life. In this context, we find ourselves standing with Catholic and Orthodox believers on key social issues."[37] While pro-life is often shorthand for a stand against abortion, thoughtful pro-life Christians (both evangelical and Catholic) also advocate care for the aging, medical care for the poor, adequate housing for all, and compassionate standards for immigration. Sometimes pro-life is extended to advocacy for peace, although Catholic ecumenical scholar Jeffrey Gros has noted that evangelicals tend to be less enthusiastic than Catholics about these broader expressions of pro-life.[38] Keith A. Fournier, executive director of the American Center for Law and Justice (affiliated with Pat Robertson), has argued that "Protestants and Catholics [need] to cooperate in their fight against the culture of death. . . . We Christians, regardless of our different confessions and traditions, desperately need to become allies to push back the darkness with the light of the Evangel and the empowerment of His Spirit."[39] Pat Robertson has made a similar point: "I know that people of faith were under attack as never before by common enemies so virulent that it was essential that we lay aside certain concerns over legitimate theological differences to join together and support things upon which we all agree, such as the sanctity of human life."[40] Of these evangelical affirmations of social-cultural cobelligerency, Catholic Jeffrey Gros asks provocatively, "Should it not be Jesus Christ that draws his disciples together, and not just a common enemy?"[41]

Mere Christianity

In defending participation in ECT I, J. I. Packer enumerated his substantial disagreements with Catholic theology but then outlined a basic

37. David Neff, "A Call to Evangelical Unity," *Christianity Today*, June 14, 1999, 49.

38. Gros, review of *Roman Catholics and Evangelicals*, 92. For an evangelical response to Catholics' larger view of social concerns, see Kenneth S. Kantzer, "Pastoral Letters and the Realities of Life," *Christianity Today*, March 1, 1985, 12–13. Kantzer respected and supported the Catholic bishops' "Pastoral Letter on Catholic Social Teaching and Economy," November 1984. He agreed with Catholic desires to combat poverty, arms buildup, and materialism. He did, however, point to original sin as the root cause of these evils and suggested that government intervention may not be the way to solve them.

39. Keith A. Fournier with William D. Watkins, *A House United? Evangelicals and Catholics Together* (Colorado Springs: NavPress, 1994), 14.

40. Ibid., 7.

41. Jeffrey Gros, F.S.C., "Evangelical Relations: A Differentiated Catholic Perspective," *Ecumenical Trends* (January 2000): 2, referring to the quotation from Pat Robertson in Fournier, *House United?* 7.

Christian faith that evangelicals and Catholics can hold in common—but which various liberal theologies reject:

> The drafters of ECT declare that they accept Jesus Christ as Lord and Savior, affirm the Apostles' Creed, "are justified by grace through faith because of Christ," understand the Christian life from first to last as personal conversion to Jesus Christ and communion with him, know that they must "teach and live in obedience to the divinely inspired Scriptures, which are the infallible Word of God," and on this basis are "brothers and sisters in Christ." . . . Do we recognize that good evangelical Protestants and good Roman Catholics—good, I mean, in terms of their own church's stated ideal of spiritual life—are Christians together? We ought to recognize this, for it is true.[42]

Packer's sense that many evangelicals and Catholics share what C. S. Lewis famously called "mere Christianity" has become much more common over the last forty years. San Diego Christian Forum, based in Mount Soledad Presbyterian Church, provides one example of such an evangelical-Catholic affirmation. This church offers conferences on subjects vital to Christian thinkers that feature both evangelical and Catholic speakers. The vision statement of this church-sponsored forum reads in part, "While the *form* of the message of the conferences is irenic and inclusive, the *content* is Orthodox Christianity—what C. S. Lewis termed 'Mere Christianity.'"[43]

"Mere Christianity" becomes personal when an evangelical and a Catholic join in marriage. For Elizabeth and Karl Wirth, this kind of marriage represented a positive ecumenical statement but also brought a number of problems. Accepting each others' "mere Christianity" did not diminish the salience of unresolved questions:

> Is the Protestant formula of *sola scriptura* a proper guide to church doctrine? Has God consistently led the Catholic Church through his Holy Spirit, or are the Magisterium and papal infallibility serious heresies? How is a person saved? Are we saved in the present tense at all? Is the order of Christian worship fixed—centered on a feast on the real body and blood of Christ, or centered on the proclamation of the Word? . . . Can a group of friends just start a church, or is the church only to be led by those ordained by bishops in communion with the pope?[44]

42. J. I. Packer, "Why I Signed It," *Christianity Today*, December 12, 1994, 35.
43. Ralph E. MacKenzie, "Roman Catholics and Evangelicals: Evangelizing the Culture" (paper presented at Theology Conference, Wheaton College, April 2002), 15.
44. Elizabeth and Karl Wirth, "Two Churches, One Family," *Re:Generation Quarterly*, August 1, 2002, 9.

Answers to such questions remained elusive for this couple, but the experience of a Catholic-evangelical marriage did highlight the need each tradition has for the other: "Not much in the Catholic culture helps a believer to progress beyond an eighth-grade understanding of the faith. . . . For their part, Protestants need Catholics to help them avoid becoming shallow and rootless. The Catholic Church brings two thousand years of theological reflection on every aspect of faith and culture." Despite such breakthroughs in understanding, the Wirths still grieve that when their son gets older they will need to explain "why Mommy goes to Communion and Daddy doesn't."[45]

Shared Historic Roots

"Why should Christians today care about what the church fathers . . . had to say?" asked *Christian History* magazine of evangelical theologian Christopher Hall. His reply: "'The Holy Spirit has a history.' The church does not thrive in the first century, fail in the second, then revive in the sixteenth. The Spirit never deserts the church."[46] This sense of continuity in the church and of the work of God across the centuries has encouraged many evangelicals to seek out the historic roots of Christian faith.

For many, that search leads to the Catholic Church or at least to the Catholic Church before the Reformation. It can even encourage gratitude to the Protestant Reformers for leading the way. David Steinmetz of Duke Divinity School elaborates: "The Reformation is [in part] about the early fathers, whom the Protestants wanted to claim."[47] In his 1536 preface to the *Institutes of the Christian Religion,* John Calvin tried to demonstrate to the Catholic king of France that his teachings were in complete harmony with the fathers. Steinmetz continues, "Calvin and [Philip] Melanchthon both believed it was a strong argument against a given theological position if you couldn't find authorization for it in the Fathers. All the Reformers loved Augustine (Luther, remember, was an Augustinian friar)."[48] As Steinmetz and other scholars of early Protestantism have explained, Reformers such as Calvin used early church fathers such as John Chrysostom because they appreciated these early figures as models and because they wanted to be connected to their spiritual ancestors. Since the Reformers too regarded innovation as heresy, in Steinmetz's phrase, "The Reformation was not an argument

45. Ibid., 11.
46. "The Habits of Highly Effective Bible Readers: A Conversation with Christopher A. Hall," *Christian History* 80 (2003): 9.
47. David Steinmetz, "Why the Reformers Read the Fathers," *Christian History* 80 (2003): 10.
48. Ibid.

about everything, but about just some things. It was not, for example about the Trinity or the two natures of Christ. . . . If we ask where these accepted doctrines came from—they came from the Fathers' reflections on the Bible."[49]

Some evangelicals with a theological bent imitate their Reformation forbearers by tracing theological precepts through a thousand years of medieval monasticism, back through five hundred years of the patristic period, eventually finding solid foundation in the New Testament, and then even deeper roots in ancient Judaism (as portrayed in Rom. 9–11). Protestant, Catholic, Jew: Christians enjoy a shared history with intertwining roots.

Richard Foster, a Quaker who attends an Evangelical Presbyterian Church, has been an important promoter of these deep, pre-Reformation Christian roots. His books—*Devotional Classics*[50] and *Spiritual Classics*[51]—each provide fifty-two readings drawn from the entire range of Christian history and from a variety of Christian faith traditions. Nearly half of the readings in each volume come from Catholic writers, with about half of these Catholic writings prior to the Reformation. The accompanying Scripture readings, prayers, and suggestions for practice offer spiritual nurture to evangelicals and Catholics alike.

InterVarsity Press's Ancient Christian Commentary series, which we mentioned before, is another evangelically sponsored venture that both feeds and develops evangelical interest in historic roots.[52] This commentary, twenty-nine volumes when completed, presents what seventy Christian teachers of the first six hundred years had to say about each text of the Bible. The resulting commentaries allow today's readers to see Scripture through the various lenses of early (all pre-Protestant) teachers who studied these texts.

Another example of appreciation for pre-Protestant grounding is evangelical attachment to *The Imitation of Christ*, which was written a century before the start of the Reformation. Thomas à Kempis, a devout monk in the Brotherhood of Common Life situated in what is now the Netherlands, may have been the book's copyist, its compiler, its editor, or (most likely) its author. Almost from the beginning of the Reformation, this guide to Christlike living has crossed the boundaries between

---

49. Ibid.

50. Richard J. Foster and James Bryan Smith, eds., *Devotional Classics: Selected Readings for Individuals and Groups* (New York: HarperCollins, 1990).

51. Richard J. Foster and Emilie Griffin, eds., *Spiritual Classics: Selected Readings for Individuals and Groups on the Twelve Spiritual Disciplines* (New York: HarperCollins, 2000).

52. Thomas Oden and Christopher A. Hall, eds., Ancient Christian Commentary series (Downers Grove, IL: InterVarsity, 1998–).

Protestant and Catholic. It is available today in more than one hundred languages and has been read by more than one billion people. It has been called "the second-best selling religious book of all time"—second only to the Bible.[53] Despite the obvious monastic setting of the book, evangelicals freely bring its spiritual challenges into their own time and space. That phenomenon, when joined to a growing interest in other pre-Protestant Christian literature, only strengthens the sense of a shared spiritual heritage.

Ministry and Mission

Local ministries that bring Catholics and evangelicals together now dot the globe and illustrate the potential of evangelical-Catholic partnership. A small sample illustrates these possibilities. John Armstrong, a Baptist from Carol Stream, Illinois, heads up Reformation and Revival Ministries. This organization sponsors conferences and publishes a periodical, *Reformation and Revival Journal.* Its speakers and writers come from both sides of the Reformation divide.[54] Nearby in Chicago, John Green, a Catholic, works as founder and executive director of Emmaus Ministries, which cares for sexually exploited men. Emmaus Ministries is supported by foundations, churches, and individuals representing a broad spectrum of both evangelicals and Catholics.[55] Logos Ministry in Southern California and Arizona reaches six thousand people each week in intensive two-hour sessions of Bible study. Catholic Bill Creasy, who teaches the Bible as literature at UCLA, heads up this ministry, but he attributes the work's vision to evangelical Bible teacher J. Vernon McGee. A spin-off of Logos Ministry is Life Teen, founded by Monsignor Dale Fushek. This evangelism program has gone nationwide in eight hundred Catholic parishes throughout the United States, Canada, and eleven other countries. In Phoenix, Life Teen's success among Catholic youth has drawn evangelical churches into the mix. Evangelicals there created their own systems of youth ministry based on the Catholic Life Teen model.[56]

Older evangelical ministries have also caught a similar vision for sharing their efforts with Catholics, as illustrated in chapter 1 concerning Campus Crusade for Christ's cooperation with the Light and Life Movement in Poland. In Florence, Italy, another Campus Crusade team was asked by a priest to assist parish staff in guiding a system of women's

---

53. Carolyn Nystrom, *Thomas à Kempis: Imitating Jesus* (Downers Grove, IL: InterVarsity, 2002), 12.
54. MacKenzie, "Roman Catholics and Evangelicals," 10–11.
55. Ibid., 10.
56. Ibid., 11–12.

and youth Bible studies, which eventually touched hundreds of families in that city. Another Italian Catholic ministry, Alpha-Omega, borrowed concepts from Campus Crusade's "Four Spiritual Laws" and created a similar document to use for Catholic evangelization.[57] Youth with a Mission (YWAM) has created shared ministry with Catholic-evangelical staff in Malta, Ghana, Uganda, Austria, the Philippines, and elsewhere.[58]

Similarly, Young Life, an evangelical youth ministry headquartered in Colorado Springs, has been working on partnered relationships with Catholic youth ministries for some time. In 1991, Dan Ponsetto, a Catholic campus minister from Boston College, created a manual for Young Life workers aimed at helping them guide Catholic teens in their Young Life groups. It stressed particularly the different concepts of conversion at work and instructed Young Life workers in recognizing that Catholics view conversion as a lifelong process: "It is confusing or even insulting to talk to a young Catholic about becoming a Christian when he or she has been involved in years of weekly worship, religious education, retreats, and has made a conscious decision to receive the sacrament of confirmation."[59] Not all Young Life groups function in this way, but in some areas Catholics and Young Life staff partner well in bringing the gospel of Jesus to teens.

The large evangelical relief agency World Vision once had a rocky relationship with the Catholic Church, marked by charges of proselytizing and countercharges of libel. In the early 1990s, World Vision began to change direction by looking for ways to work with local Catholic churches in needy areas. World Vision's work in the Philippines, for example, is guided by the World Vision Development Foundation, whose vice president in the year 2000 was Deogracias Iniguez, the Catholic bishop of Iba (Zambeles).[60]

InterVarsity Christian Fellowship, an evangelical campus ministry, co-sponsors an annual conference on theology. In 2002, that conference, held at Wheaton College, paired evangelical and Catholic scholars addressing related subjects. Cardinal Francis George, archbishop of Chicago, was among the speakers. Even though sponsors and hosts were solidly evangelical, Catholic Thomas Rausch could write, "Most impressive was the good will of all those present: speakers, participants and hosts. . . . At the end of the conference, the participants gathered for a 'Closing Worship.' They joined in prayer and response without any

57. Thomas P. Rausch, "Catholic-Evangelical Relations: Signs of Progress," in *Catholics and Evangelicals*, 42, referring to Kalevi Lethinen, "Evidences of New Life in Europe: Problems Associated with European Missions" (unpublished Campus Crusade staff report).

58. Rausch, "Catholic-Evangelical Relations," 43.

59. Ibid., 44.

60. Ibid., 45–47.

awkwardness or hesitation in a service that from a Catholic perspective seemed a combination of elements from the Liturgy of Hours and the Mass's Liturgy of the Word. It was good to pray together. We should do it more often."[61]

When mission and ministry unite, it is not always with evangelical predominance. David E. Bjork, the evangelical missionary to France mentioned in chapter 1, writes of such an experience. He and his family arrived in Normandy in 1979 with the challenge to plant an evangelical church that could become self-governing, self-supporting, and self-propagating. Bjork began in typical evangelical fashion by inviting new acquaintances to study the Bible with him—which Marc and Henri did. Then his new Bible students invited him to visit their church. Bjork was startled to find more than six hundred Catholics worshiping "in the presence of God's Spirit." Puzzled, he agreed to meet with the local priest. Over a period of more than three years, he came to recognize "Father Norbert as my brother in Christ." The next question became obvious: "Is it really necessary for me to establish a 'new church' in France?" David Bjork then made the difficult decision to merge his ministry into the local Catholic church.[62]

Bjork's example, an evangelical finding a cooperative ministry with Roman Catholics, is still not the norm. But it has become so common in so many places as to demand deliberation, not on whether it should take place but on the protocols to govern such activity as it occurs.

Spiritual Formation

Some evangelicals who read Catholic writers discover spiritual disciplines unfamiliar to their own evangelical heritage, including the disciplines of silence, contemplation, and deep devotion to Christ. For many in the fast-paced world of evangelicalism, these spiritual disciplines have offered a welcome respite. Evangelical groups now practice ancient *lectio divina*, a meditative prayerful way of reading Scripture and listening for God's revelation through it.[63] Evangelical retreat speaker Jan Johnson is among those who have created a Protestantized version of this Catholic tradition.[64] Christopher Hall invites evangelicals to practice *Praying with*

61. Thomas P. Rausch, "Another Step Forward," *America*, July 15–22, 2002, 9.

62. David E. Bjork, "When Obedience Leads Us into the Unknown," in *Catholics and Evangelicals*, 149–70.

63. *Lectio divina* began with early monasticism prior to the sixth century. It became part of the Rule of St. Benedict, a guidebook for Benedictine monks, an order founded by Benedict of Nursia (480–547).

64. Jan Johnson, *Listening to God: Using Scripture as a Path to God's Presence* (Colorado Springs: NavPress, 1998).

the Church Fathers, even if they must use the ancient sources with a measure of selectivity.[65] Other evangelicals avail themselves of the opportunities presented by softening relationships between evangelicals and Catholics to take retreats in monasteries for spiritual direction and refreshment. The growing prominence of evangelical spiritual directors also fosters closer connections with Catholics, since many of these directors receive their training from Catholics who draw on centuries of experience in these disciplines.[66]

Converts

Some evangelicals make the next big step. They go "home to Rome." Then, as so often with converts, some become zealous advocates of the church they once opposed. This chapter concludes by examining what they feel they have gained—and lost.

Thomas Howard was born into an evangelical family filled with pastors and missionaries, including his sister, the noted author Elizabeth Elliot. Howard was a professor of English at Gordon College when he converted to Catholicism on Holy Saturday in 1985; two days later he resigned his faculty position. It had been a twenty-year journey, begun during undergraduate days at Wheaton College, where he grew to love liturgical worship. Interviewed by *Christianity Today* shortly after converting to Catholicism, Howard said that for him the key was "the question of unity between Christ and his church." This concern led him to a revised picture of authority, which he saw as residing within the Catholic Church, a position that grew from his study of ancient Christianity. In his words, "It's clear historically why and how and when the doctrine of the papacy developed early on."[67]

Howard was convinced that becoming a Catholic did not make him less an evangelical. Indeed, he has called himself an evangelical Catholic. But he did sense personal gains and losses resulting from his conversion. On the positive side, he gained a sense of mystery of the church, he was able to dip into deeper reaches of Christian spirituality, and he was able to reclaim the Eucharist for what he saw as its real worth. Yet even as Howard expressed relief at finally being rid of what he called

65. David Neff, "Don't Read the Bible 'Alone,'" interview with Christopher Hall, *Christianity Today,* November 2003, 58.

66. For a new periodical organized mostly by Protestants that features insight into the spiritual disciplines, see *Conversations: A Forum for Authentic Transformation,* published biannually by Life Springs Resources in Atlanta.

67. John D. Woodbridge, "Why Did Thomas Howard Become a Roman Catholic?" *Christianity Today,* May 17, 1985, 48, 58.

"the desperate, barren, parched nature of evangelical worship," he also admitted, with some longing, that he missed the companionship of a "biblically literate laity."[68]

Dennis Martin, associate professor of historical theology at Loyola University in Chicago, began as a Mennonite with a historical conscience. During high school, he was stirred by Frederick W. Faber's hymn "Faith of Our Fathers." Even then, "I was looking for recognizable and tangible historical ancestors in the faith with whom I could identify."[69] Only later did he discover that the lyrics "Faith of our fathers, living still, in spite of dungeon, fire, and sword" did not refer to Reformation-era Anabaptists persecuted for their beliefs on baptism, or Protestants persecuted by Catholics. The key was discovering a verse of the hymn consistently omitted by Protestants: "Faith of our fathers, Mary's prayers / Shall win our country back to thee; / And through the truth that comes from God, / England shall then indeed be free."[70] When Martin realized that Frederick Faber was a nineteenth-century Catholic who wrote the hymn to memorialize Catholics persecuted by Protestants, it was a portent of things to come.

Martin's studies of church history led him to medieval monasticism and the history of liturgy, which both strengthened and challenged him: "I simply could not see my way clear to massage the patristic and medieval evidence into a Free Church Model."[71] Meanwhile, he began to experience frustration with Mennonite church government by consensus. He had to ask if this democratic form of church polity led to truth or merely to popularity. He also began to question how far beyond the Mennonite borders the "True Church" extended. And so to Rome.

Nine years into his life as a Catholic, Martin could write with a sense of certainty, "Catholicism . . . [possesses] codified liturgy, sacraments, priesthood, doctrine and law, permitting adult converts faithfully adhering to these structures to know that they belong."[72] He appreciates "sacramental confession" as "a very effective path to spiritual growth, a truly fruitful way to confront one's sins and overcome them."[73] And he values his part in the Catholic Church with "its stubborn insistence on an identifiable True Church."[74] Yet Martin also is aware of losses, as he says wistfully, "I miss the four-part a cappella congregational sing-

---

68. Ibid., 50.
69. Dennis Martin, "Retrospect and Apologia," *Mennonite Quarterly Review* 78 (April 2003): 168.
70. Ibid., 169.
71. Ibid., 180.
72. Ibid., 177.
73. Ibid., 188.
74. Ibid., 194.

ing immensely, but one may doubt how well that will be preserved in coming generations."[75]

Peter Kreeft, professor of philosophy at Boston College, began his spiritual sojourn as a Dutch Reformed Calvinist. After graduating from a Christian Reformed high school and from Calvin College, Kreeft became a Roman Catholic while a graduate student at Yale. It was primarily "history" that drew Kreeft to Rome: "I developed a strong intellectual and aesthetic love for things medieval: Gregorian chant, Gothic architecture, Thomistic philosophy, illuminated manuscripts." But this love was not merely a matter of taste: "I discovered in the early Church such Catholic elements as the centrality of the Eucharist, the Real Presence, prayers to saints, devotion to Mary, an insistence on visible unity, and apostolic succession. Furthermore, the Church Fathers just 'smelled' more Catholic than Protestant." Kreeft's study of history led him to a revised view of how Scripture and church relate to each other: "I was impressed by the argument that 'the Church wrote the Bible': Christianity was preached by the Church before the New Testament was written—that is simply a historical fact. It is also a fact that the apostles wrote the New Testament and the Church canonized it, decided which books were divinely inspired." With church and history combined, Kreeft came to the conclusion that "Christ founded the Catholic Church; that there is historical continuity." About the point of decision he writes, "I seemed to sense my heroes Augustine and Aquinas and thousands of other saints and sages calling out to me from the great ark, 'Come aboard! We are really here. We still live. Join us. Here is the Body of Christ.'"[76]

What does Kreeft feel he lost and gained? He gained an appreciation for the richness of God's mystery. Having come to think of Protestant theology as overly infected with Descartes's scientific view of reason, Kreeft learned to appreciate "wisdom rather than mere logical consistency, insight rather than mere calculation." He also learned to worship God through all of his senses, not merely the mouth and ears of Protestantism. Perhaps most important, he found himself swimming within the two-thousand-year stream of historical Christianity. But Kreeft also speaks of losses. He inherited from his evangelical roots a serious concern for truth that he finds sadly missing among many Catholics. For example, although he finds Catholic theology quite clear on the subject of justification by grace through faith, "well over 90% of the students I have polled . . . expect to go to Heaven because they tried, or did their best, or had compassionate feelings to everyone, or were sincere.

75. Ibid., 188.
76. Peter Kreeft, "Hauled Aboard the Ark," www.peterkreeft.com/topics/hauled-aboard .htm (accessed February 27, 2004).

They hardly ever mention Jesus." And he misses music. He remembers evangelical worship with "beautiful hymns, for which I would gladly exchange the new, flat, unmusical, wimpy 'liturgical responses' no one sings in our masses." Kreeft envisions a time when all of these losses will be redeemed. "I think in Heaven, Protestants will teach Catholics to sing and Catholics will teach Protestants to dance and sculpt."[77]

Scott and Kimberly Hahn moved along slightly different paths. Scott, assistant professor of theology and Scripture at Franciscan University of Steubenville, is also founder and director of the Institute of Applied Biblical Studies and editor of the *Bulletin of Applied Biblical Studies*. In the past twenty years, he has given more than six hundred talks, many of them available through a widely used system of tape distribution. Meanwhile, Kimberly, who holds a master's degree in theology from Gordon-Conwell, cares for their six children—and also fills frequent speaking engagements. They tell their tandem stories in an autobiographical book titled *Rome Sweet Home*.[78]

Scott began his life in a nominal Presbyterian home, was steered away from delinquency by a Young Life worker, and then was deeply and thoroughly converted to Jesus Christ. After graduating from Grove City College, Scott, now married to Kimberly, attended Gordon-Conwell Seminary, from which he graduated in 1982.[79] He then began his career as pastor of a Presbyterian church, taught at a local Presbyterian seminary, and kept up a voracious reading program. Hahn maintains that it was Scripture itself, particularly as it speaks of God's covenant, that led him to the Catholic Church: "I wanted to see people fired up about the Old Testament and its relationship to the New—the Old flowing into the New. . . . As I dug deeper in my study, a disturbing pattern began to emerge: the novel ideas I thought I had discovered had actually been anticipated by the early Church Fathers."[80] Hahn's intense study of Scripture also led him to think about Scripture itself: "I began to see how important liturgy was for the covenant, especially in Hebrews."[81] On Scripture and authority: "I kept pushing [on *sola scriptura*]. 'Isn't this ironic? We insist that Christians can believe only what the Bible teaches. But the Bible doesn't teach that *it* is our *only* authority.'"[82] Then he was led to other doctrines such as the Eucharist: "Why would it have offended the Jews so much if Jesus was only talking about faith and a

77. Ibid.
78. Scott and Kimberly Hahn, *Rome Sweet Home: Our Journey to Catholicism* (San Francisco: Ignatius Press, 1993).
79. Hahn later earned a Ph.D. in systematic theology from Marquette University.
80. Hahn, *Rome Sweet Home*, 44.
81. Ibid., 43.
82. Ibid., 52.

symbolic sacrifice of his flesh and blood?"[83] To the pain of his parents, his professors, his former church, and his wife, Scott Hahn converted to Catholicism at the Easter Vigil of 1986.[84]

Kimberly Hahn's journey began earlier and progressed longer but ended the same way. She was raised in a sturdy evangelical family, early on made a personal decision for Christ, worked with Scott at Grove City in his Young Life ministry, and married him shortly after graduation.[85] At Gordon-Conwell, she supported pro-life causes while studying theology. This combination of interests led her to wonder if abortion and contraception were in some way connected. In typical evangelical fashion, she headed to Scripture to find out. Her conclusion: "Fertility, in Scripture, was presented as something to be prized and celebrated rather than as a disease to be avoided at all costs."[86] Later she would conclude that in this small but important area of her life she was already becoming Catholic. Sacraments provided another tug. Much later, as she reluctantly stood by as their daughter Hannah was baptized into the Catholic Church, Kimberly said, "I was not prepared for the beauty of the baptismal liturgy. It was everything I would have prayed for my daughter."[87] At Easter of 1990, Kimberly also entered the Catholic Church.

What do the Hahns feel they gained and lost? Scott is convinced that Scripture teaches the essentials of Catholic theology and that the early Christian fathers rightly created the foundation of true Christian faith. Kimberly has come to value Mary. She accepts the Catholic belief that when Jesus gave his mother to John, the act prefigured his giving of her to each beloved disciple: "Instead of seeing Mary as a tremendous obstacle to me, I was beginning to see her as a precious gift from the Lord—one who loved me, cared for me and prayed for me with a mother's heart."[88]

But like most who cross the chasm of the Reformation, the Hahns experience loss as well as gain. Kimberly misses the sense of community in evangelical churches: "When we would go to Mass, people would come in and leave their coats on, looking like they were ready to bolt as soon as they received the Host. (I would never go to dinner at someone's house and leave my coat on!) For an evangelical Protestant used to fellowship and friendly conversation after the service, it was a shock to discover that most people did not intend to stay and greet one another."[89] Similarly, Scott writes:

83. Ibid., 139. See also John 6:42–69.
84. Ibid., 72.
85. Ibid., 8–9.
86. Ibid., 35.
87. Ibid., 117.
88. Ibid., 156.
89. Ibid., 141–42.

When evangelical Protestants convert to the Catholic Church, they often enter into a kind of "ecclesiastical culture shock." They leave robust congregational singing, practical biblical preaching, a conservative pro-family political voice in the pulpit and a vital sense of community, with various prayer meetings, fellowships, and Bible studies to choose from each week. In contrast, the average Catholic parish usually finds itself lacking in these areas. While these converts typically feel that they have "come home" by becoming Catholics, they do not always *feel* "at home" in their new parish families.[90]

Much of Scott Hahn's ministry now works to encourage Catholics to experience a spiritual discipleship of the sort he experienced as a young evangelical. At other times he is wooing evangelicals to join him in coming to Rome.

Not all evangelicals who convert to Rome do so after intensive study. The conversion of popular singer John Michael Talbot came after disillusioning experiences with both rock 'n' roll music and Protestant fundamentalist religion. In the midst of crises, Talbot was greatly assisted by Father Martin of Alverna, a Franciscan retreat center. Under Father Martin's tutelage, Talbot became a Roman Catholic and then went on to perform music that appeals to great numbers of modern American Christians of all sorts. Talbot's appeal has been neatly captured by Scot McKnight, an evangelical theologian who published an important article on evangelicals who became Catholics:

I once attended one of his concerts, at a small monastery in Wisconsin. John Michael walked in with a background vocalist, took a seat on a stool, tuned his guitar quickly, closed his eyes, sang his songs for 1 hour and 45 minutes, stood up and said, "May the peace of the Lord be with you!" The more liturgically trained, and we were not among them, knew what to say next. He then exited the front. I have never been in a more worshipful setting.[91]

McKnight, whose study was mentioned in chapter 3, interviewed thirty evangelicals who became Roman Catholic and then analyzed reasons for their conversions. Four principle causes emerged, *certainty, history, unity,* and *authority,* all of which have been intimated in the personal accounts already examined. McKnight's description of reasons for converting to Catholicism is important in itself, but it also offers to contemporary evangelicals a clearer picture of their own strengths and weaknesses.

90. Ibid., 165.
91. Scot McKnight, "From Wheaton to Rome: Why Evangelicals Become Roman Catholic," *Journal of the Evangelical Theological Society* 45 (September 2002): 455–56.

Among McKnight's subjects, an unmet desire for *certainty* was an important spur to conversion. Kristine Franklin, an evangelical missionary to illiterate people, mused, "I had to be absolutely sure, before God, that what I was telling them was, in fact, the Christian Faith, free from error. It had to be one hundred percent Truth. The problem was, using my 'Bible alone' principle, I had no way to be absolutely sure."[92] Another evangelical, Bob Sungenis, fretted, "We were in and out of five different Presbyterian churches within the next five years, each move being due to disagreements on the pastor's interpretation of the Bible."[93] For evangelicals operating under such pressures, certitude from a higher source offers welcome relief.

Considerations of *history* have also drawn many evangelicals toward Rome. Neophyte evangelical students of church history are almost always startled to find that Christians of the early centuries were Catholic. As they study, they create spiritual friendships with Ignatius, Justin Martyr, Irenaeus, Tertullian, Hippolytus, Augustine, and wonder what and who else they have missed. Catholic convert Marcus Grodi commented, "The more I read church history and Scripture the less I could comfortably remain Protestant."[94] If these students also sampled liturgical worship with its ancient hymns and creeds, they sensed a long-missed rootedness with early believers who sang and said the same words. In McKnight's phrase, "It is no trivial matter that evangelicals have quartered Church history and excluded the first three-quarters."[95] To these evangelicals, the antidote to historical shortsightedness is the Catholic Church.

The ideal of *unity* is also a force drawing evangelicals to Rome, especially since it exploits favored evangelical images for the church: communion of saints, body of Christ, community of believers. Evangelicals can wince at Peter Cram's description of Protestantism as "one long, continuous line of protesters protesting against their fellow protesters, generating thousands of denominations, para-churches, and 'free churches,' which are simply one-church denominations."[96] Longing for an end to these endless divisions, disillusioned evangelicals such as Cram seek out the Catholic Church, where they can enter the mass in Hong Kong or Nairobi, São Paulo or Vancouver, and find roughly the same liturgy, the same Scripture passages, the same sacraments, and the same beliefs.

A principle of *authority* can also create restful security for evangelicals weary of constantly reinventing the theological wheel. Even though

92. Ibid., 462.
93. Ibid., 461–63.
94. Ibid., 464.
95. Ibid., 463–65.
96. Ibid., 466–68.

evangelicals enjoy many strong traditions for interpreting Scripture, the responsibility for interpreting and responding remains individual. As McKnight states the problem, "This democratization of Scriptural interpretation, leading inevitably to the authority of the individual conscience, is intolerable for some evangelicals, because everyone gets to believe what he or she wants."[97] Catholic convert David Lowry expressed the relief many converts feel. "Why this greater joy? Because I do not have to be the judge in judgment of the Catholic Church, of the Scriptures, or even of myself. It's not my job."[98]

Most other evangelicals who also long with similar intensity for certainty, history, unity, and authority do not become Catholics. For them, the objections to Rome remain weightier than what Catholicism offers. Yet to observe why some evangelicals become Roman Catholics is certainly to gain a better sense of contemporary Catholic-evangelical terrain and of weaknesses in evangelicalism that require attention.

Taking Stock

Evangelicals respond to Catholics in many ways ranging from outright rejection to conversion. Most evangelicals who enter into greater contact with Catholics, however, practice various forms of partnership pointing toward mutual acceptance. The dramatic religious and cultural shifts of the past forty years have increased the sense of a shared Christian faith—shared but not identical. Differences remain and deserve to be faced. But where those differences do not preclude joined efforts, more and more evangelicals and Catholics are joining to serve God together with as much creativity as God-given skills and divinely appointed limitations allow. The needy of the world care little whether the Christian before them is evangelical or Catholic but much whether they might encounter the love of Christ and the truth of the gospel that can redeem the soul.

Meanwhile, evangelicals who remain highly critical of Catholic theology and practice have much to teach members of both traditions. Their persistence in criticism points to genuine weaknesses within Catholicism as well as to outdated prejudices. Both bodies can also become self-corrective as they listen to stories of conversion. This chapter treated only evangelical to Catholic conversions. Were it a different book, it would be important to hear from the many who convert from Catholicism to various branches of Protestantism. Heeding the reasons why

97. Ibid., 468–70.
98. Ibid., 469.

people find Christ or see Christ more clearly in one tradition instead of the other involves questions of great importance. But this shared love of Christ also prepares for eternity, where, at least in the hopes expressed by Peter Kreeft, evangelicals will teach Catholics to sing and Catholics will teach evangelicals to sculpt and to dance—all in praise of God.

8

AN AMERICAN ASSESSMENT

This chapter represents an exercise in prudential reasoning. It is an effort to sort out the current situation by analyzing the position of evangelicals and Catholics with respect to main themes in American history. In the next chapter, we feature biblical and theological reasoning, but here the emphasis is historical and political. As such, this chapter benefits from an extraordinary flourishing of historical writing that over the last few decades has greatly illuminated both the place of evangelical Christianity in shaping the early character of American public life and the place of Roman Catholicism as an uneasy participant in that same public life.[1] The chief consideration, alluded to briefly in chapter 3, is the tangled development of America's main political tradition over against the evolving expressions of both evangelicalism and Catholicism. Even a crude sketch of that political history clarifies a great deal about recent religious developments. Any consideration of "public Christianity" at the current moment must also take into account the widely publicized sex scandals in the Catholic Church and important structural realities such as the tremendous pluralism that now exists within both Catholicism and evangelicalism. The latter does not receive the glare of publicity that has been devoted to the former, but it is also critical. The contemporary

1. This chapter puts to use that solid historical literature in impressionistic and introductory fashion, but readers who wish to engage it more substantially can find many of the relevant studies listed in the further reading section.

relationship between Catholics and evangelicals concerns much more than a political story, but it is also never less.

Shifting Affinities: Evangelicals, Catholics, and Political Liberalism

The political story that has made a significant contribution to the contemporary reengagement of American Catholics and evangelicals is unusually complicated. Yet though this story is complex, it can be summarized succinctly: From about the end of the eighteenth century until roughly the middle of the twentieth century, most American evangelicals were mostly at home with most expressions of American political liberalism. In that same period, Catholics in America expressed considerable ambiguity with respect to American political liberalism, which explains why so many non-Catholic Americans once looked upon Catholicism as a civil as well as a religious threat. Since the mid-twentieth century, a series of decisive alterations has occurred: American political liberalism has evolved in a more clearly secular direction, American Catholics have come to accept some aspects of the liberal tradition about which they had earlier been ambiguous, and American evangelicals have begun to modify their once wholehearted embrace of political liberalism. The result today is a political landscape in which evangelicals and Catholics, because they are following the contrasting trajectories of their own traditions, have ended up in positions much closer to each other—and from which it is much easier to understand each other—than could have been imagined in 1800 or 1900 or even 1950.

Learning from Tocqueville

A remarkable insight into these political realities is provided by Alexis de Tocqueville's *Democracy in America,* which he published in two parts (1835, 1840) after having made an extensive journey throughout North America from May 1831 to February 1832. The religion that Americans practiced was a main theme of Tocqueville's work, especially as he contrasted largely Protestant adherence in North America with the establishmentarian Catholicism he knew from his native France. (At the time of Tocqueville's visit, the number of Catholics was increasing rapidly in the United States, but over 90 percent of all religious adherents were still Protestant of one sort or another; the percentage of Catholics in France was even higher.)

Tocqueville indicated early in the book's introduction why religion was so important for his analysis of America. He did so by commenting on the alliance in France between traditional religious convictions and conservative political beliefs: "Religion has for the time being become enmeshed with the powers that democracy is bent on destroying." As he reflected on the movement toward liberalization in France that had only shortly before he embarked for America led to violence in the streets, Tocqueville said that in his part of the Old World "religious men do battle against liberty, and friends of liberty attack religion."[2]

The contrast Tocqueville found in the New World could not have been more striking. As he interpreted American history, Tocqueville saw a strong elective affinity between the type of Protestants who had first settled the continent and principles of liberty that were developed in opposition to Roman Catholicism:

> The greater part of English America was populated by men who, having broken away from the authority of the pope, never submitted to any supreme religious authority again. They therefore brought to the New World a Christianity that can best be described as democratic and republican: this singularly favored the establishment of a republic and democracy in temporal affairs. From the beginning, politics and religion were in harmony, and they have remained so ever since.[3]

In a word, "Americans so completely confound Christianity with liberty that it is almost impossible to induce them to think of one without the other." That identification in America was "a vital article of faith."[4]

The kind of liberty Tocqueville was talking about was the principle element in American "political liberalism." This liberalism, in the sense meant during earlier periods of American history, designated systems of political organization that stressed the liberty of individuals in a state of nature, their rights in society, and their freedoms over against coercive authority. As Tocqueville used the word *republican*, he meant government organized in such a way as to limit inherited or aristocratic power. Put positively, republican principles looked to the practice of virtue by substantial elements of the entire population that would lead to the enjoyment of freedom and the flourishing of society. Republicans invariably held that vice (usually defined as luxury, indolence, and corruption among the elite) promoted the corruption of government, led to tyranny, and ruined the social fabric.[5]

2. Alexis de Tocqueville, *Democracy in America*, trans. Arthur Goldhammer (New York: Library of America, 2004), 12–13.

3. Ibid., 332.

4. Ibid., 338.

5. For these and other terms that Tocqueville helped popularize, see Mark A. Noll, "Glossary," in *America's God, from Jonathan Edwards to Abraham Lincoln* (New York: Oxford University Press, 2002), 563–68.

Tocqueville's essential point was that the Protestant faiths that flourished in America enjoyed a natural affinity with democratic and republican government. They had been born in protest against the heavy hand of state-church aristocracies (both Protestant and Catholic), and they had developed even stronger affinities for self-definition, self-organization, and self-guided activity during the transition from colonial dependence on Britain to independent self-government. By contrast, at least in his day, the Catholicism that maintained an immense presence in France and some other European countries was aligned with aristocratic and monarchical government. European Catholic leaders were becoming more and more worried about the wanton exercise of popular power even as modern liberal democrats challenged more and more of the church's ancient prerogatives. Following the logic of Tocqueville's description, it was all but inevitable that many Americans would look upon Roman Catholicism as a challenge to republican politics as well as to Protestant religion.

Democracy in America actually makes a more complicated argument than this because Tocqueville held that Catholicism, as defined by its own internal character, was in reality the religion "most favorable to equality of conditions." Tocqueville tried to make this case by pointing out that in Catholicism all worshipers are religiously equal before the priest and that Catholic dogma and practice are exactly the same for all Catholic adherents. Yet Tocqueville seriously undercut his own argument when he conceded that Catholicism promotes "equality of conditions" only if "priests are excluded from government."[6] But in Europe, Catholic priests, bishops, and the pope had long taken an active part in governmental affairs and were lobbying hard, even as Tocqueville wrote his book about America, to stay involved in government. In fact, when on his North American journey Tocqueville traveled to Quebec, he found the French Catholics of that province deficient in education, reluctant to participate in politics, and passive about social activity. According to Tocqueville, the Catholic Church was responsible for these deficiencies.[7]

The Image of Protestant Liberty versus Catholic Tyranny

In general, Tocqueville's account of a natural affinity between American Protestants and republican democracy resonated with much greater force than his counterintuitive claim about Catholics being disposed to "equality of conditions." Already by the 1830s, Americans had experi-

6. Tocqueville, *Democracy in America*, 332–33.
7. Olivier Zunz, "Chronology," in ibid., 886.

enced several episodes that they could only regard as Protestant liberty escaping the clutches of Catholic tyranny. So it had been in 1688–1689 when politically active colonists eagerly hailed the Protestant William of Orange as England's new king who was rescuing the nation (and its colonies) from the malevolent plots of James II, the Catholic monarch whom William ousted.

Then in a series of colonial wars with France, the equation became set in stone. To stand firm with Britain against its French foe was also to defend Protestantism and freedom against Catholicism and despotism. So it was in King George's War of the mid-1740s and also the French and Indian (or Seven Years') War that began in 1754. The equation was expressed widely in the colonies, for example, from Samuel Davies of Virginia in 1755, "I would rather fly to the utmost end of the earth, than submit to French tyranny and Popish superstition. . . . Shall slavery here clank her chain, or tyranny rage with lawless fury?"[8] It was all but the same with Nathanael Taylor of Connecticut in 1762 as he told a group of English and American troops what would have happened if French Catholicism had prevailed in the war: "Nothing but intolerable Tyranny. . . . Not only our civil Liberties taken away, and our private Property seized; but we ourselves obliged to yield an implicit Faith and blind Obedience to the Dictates of spiritual Tyrants."[9] In the context of such assertions, it is clear that George Whitefield's outrageous statement about Catholicism quoted in chapter 2 was not just religious bigotry but at least a partial product of a specific historical milieu.

During the American Revolution, patriots maintained these principles but came to see Britain not as a friend of liberty but its foe. Britain's recognition of the Catholic Church in French-speaking Canada (the Quebec Act of 1774) only proved to patriots that the mother country had sold her heritage of freedom cheaply. After the war, conservative revolutionaries worried about the pace of reform and the unprecedented lengths to which many ordinary people wanted to take the grand and universal principles stated in the Declaration of Independence. The Constitution of 1789 slowed the democratic rush a little but left fully intact the American commitment to republicanism as well as the American suspicion of Catholicism as antidemocratic.

Even in the 1830s, just as Tocqueville was completing the trip that gave him the experience analyzed in his book, Americans thought they could see proof for their interpretation of Catholicism as the enemy

8. Samuel Davies, "On the Defeat of General Braddock, Going to Forte-De-Quesne" (July 20, 1755), in *Sermons on Important Subjects*, 4th ed. (New York: J & J Harper, 1828), 3:169–71.

9. Nathanael Taylor, *Praise Due to God for All the Dispensations of His Wise and Holy Providence* (New Haven: J. Parker, 1762), 17–18.

of liberty. In 1832, Pope Gregory XVI, who had been elected as pontiff only the year before, issued the encyclical *Mirari Vos* on liberty of conscience.[10] Gregory's pontificate had already been disturbed by foreign invasion; he had also come to the papal throne at a time when growing numbers of Europeans were promoting skepticism, free thinking, and a disregard for Christian tradition, even as they pushed for liberal political reform.

In response, Gregory stood firm for "the unity which is built upon the See of Peter"—that is, on the hereditary authority of the papacy. The parts of Gregory's encyclical that eventually created a negative impression for the American Protestants who were paying attention concerned political order. The church was never to be "subject to civil authority." Moreover, in the pope's view, it was indifference to the things of God more than anything else that fueled the modern lust for liberty. In a passage that attacked licentiousness and the exaltation of individual conscience over all else, Gregory gave voice to opinions that liberty-loving Americans were sure to take the wrong way:

> This shameful font of indifferentism gives rise to that absurd and erroneous proposition which claims that *liberty of conscience* must be maintained for everyone. It spreads ruin in sacred and civil affairs, though some repeat over and over again with the greatest impudence that some advantage accrues to religion from it. . . . Experience shows, even from the earliest times, that cities renowned for wealth, dominion, and glory perished as a result of this single evil, namely immoderate freedom of opinion, license of free speech, and desire for novelty.

Nor did Gregory help the reputation of Catholicism in America when, forty years after the implementation of the First Amendment to the United States Constitution had ruled out an establishment of religion by the federal government, he denied that things would improve "from the plans of those who desire vehemently to separate the Church from the state, and to break the mutual accord between temporal authority and the priesthood."

For Americans worried about the threat of Catholicism to civil liberty, things got only worse when Gregory was succeeded in 1846 by Pius IX. Although Pius was known as a political liberal during his rise through the church hierarchy, his viewpoint shifted dramatically as a result of the European revolution of 1848. After the Papal Estates were taken over by revolutionary forces and Pius had to rely on a French

---

10. Gregory XVI, *Mirari Vos*, in *The Papal Encyclicals*, vol. 1, 1740–1878, ed. Claudia Carlen, IHM (New York: Consortium, 1981), 235–41 (the following quotations are from pars. 7, 9, 14, 20).

army to regain his lands, the pope turned militantly conservative. This conservatism was manifest religiously in his promotion of devotion to the Virgin Mary, which culminated in 1854 with his definition of the immaculate conception of Mary. To Pius IX, heightened Marian devotion was meant to win back common people to Catholic tradition and to woo them from infatuation with liberal politics. His conservativism was also shown as he guided the First Vatican Council (1869–70) in making a formal declaration of papal infallibility.

Politically, conservatism became the leitmotif of Pius IX's pontificate, nowhere more obviously than in his "Syllabus of Errors" from 1864. Reactions to this document, including reactions from some faithful Catholics, were even more negative than reactions to the pope's proclamation about Mary. In a series of propositions, the "Syllabus of Errors" detailed what it labeled the mistaken notions of the modern age. The errors included quite a few that seemed like positive achievements to most Americans. For example, the pope held that it was an error to think that "the whole governance of public schools wherein the youth of any Christian state is educated . . . may and should be given to the civil power." Likewise, it was an error to think that "the Church should be separated from the state, and the state from the Church." It was also erroneous to hold that "in this our age it is no longer expedient that the Catholic religion should be treated as the only religion of the state, all other worships whatsoever being excluded." (In other words, Catholicism should be authorized as the only religion of the state.) Finally, as a summation, the pope declared that it was an error to believe that "the Roman pontiff can and ought to reconcile and harmonize himself with progress, with liberalism, and with modern civilization."[11]

Change at Rome began to be manifested when in 1878 Pius IX was succeeded by Leo XIII, the modern pope who in the century before John Paul II most effectively articulated ancient Christian truths for modern world audiences.[12] Yet however cautiously Leo stated his positions, there was no denying that he was a Catholic traditionalist on questions of civil order as well as of doctrine. So it was that in a carefully argued encyclical from 1885, *Immortale Dei*, Leo tried to distinguish between civil governments that fulfilled their God-given responsibilities and those that did not. Leo asserted that the form of government was not the critical issue but rather what the government, however constituted, actually did. Yet even as he allowed for the kind of democracies found in

11. Pius IX, "Syllabus of Errors," in *Readings in Church History*, vol. 3, *The Modern Era, 1789 to the Present*, ed. Colman J. Barry, O.S.B. (Westminster, MD: Newman, 1965), 70–74 (quotations from pars. 45, 55, 77, 80).

12. For an appreciation, see Mark A. Noll, "A Century of Social Teaching: The Legacy of Leo XIII and Abraham Kuyper," *Markets and Morality* 5 (2002): 137–56.

the United States, he nonetheless spoke out sharply against governments defined as "nothing more or less as the will of the people."[13]

Along with strong statements about the Catholic Church as the full manifestation of God's will on earth, Leo made assertions about the civil order that could only raise, at least for many Americans, the specter of overweening church power. Thus, he rejected the notion that "all questions of religion are to be referred to private judgment; that every one is free to follow whatever religion he prefers, or none at all if he disapprove of all." He questioned the wisdom of "the sovereignty of the people" as being only "a doctrine exceedingly well calculated to flatter and to inflame many passions, but which lacks all reasonable proof, and all power of insuring public safety and preserving order." And he seemed to endorse church-sponsored censorship by saying that "the liberty of thinking, and of publishing, whatsoever each one likes, without any hindrance, is not in itself an advantage over which society can wisely rejoice."[14]

Americans nervous about Catholicism as a civil threat bridled at this line of papal pronouncements, which, as opposed to Tocqueville's contention, seemed to suggest the dangerous political ambition of the church. When combined with the residual anti-Catholicism of their British heritage and the steady flow of reports from places in the world (such as Latin America) where the church worked hand in glove with oppressive regimes, American Protestants had, at least to their own satisfaction, all the reasons required for mobilizing against Catholic power in the United States. Whether that mobilizing meant preaching antipapal sermons, attacking churches and convents, or warning the public away from Catholic candidates for public office, Protestants thought they were justified in their anti-Catholic actions.

So it was that in the 1850s, the Know Nothings enjoyed considerable success in electing members of Congress and state legislatures with a strong anti-Catholic platform. And images from the church came to serve as markers of despotism. Thus, when the Baptist polemicist J. R. Graves took off after the Methodists, the worst thing he could think to say about their church was that it deserved to be called "the Popery of Protestantism."[15] When the Supreme Court in 1857 effectively struck down the antislave laws of northern states, abolitionists pointed out how natural it was for Chief Justice Roger Taney, himself the highest ranking Catholic in all of nineteenth-century American government, to

13. Leo XIII, *Immortale Dei*, in *The Papal Encyclicals*, vol. 2, 1878–1903, ed. Claudia Carlen, IHM (New York: Consortium, 1981), 107, par. 24.

14. Ibid., 108–11 (quotations are from pars. 26, 31, 32).

15. J. R. Graves, *The Great Iron Wheel: Or Republicanism Backwards and Christianity Reversed* (Nashville: Graves & Marks, 1855), 169.

push the Court to defend slavery.[16] (The fact that Taney had long before freed his own slaves was barely noticed at the time.)

Catholics Protest the Charge of Tyranny

Catholics protested against this tide of political suspicion, sometimes with great vigor. In 1826, for instance, the bishop of South Carolina, John England, was invited to speak before the Congress of the United States. In his address, which provided a rare opportunity for a Catholic, England responded directly to the charge that Catholics could not be good citizens because they "profess to owe obedience to a foreign authority," the pope. England's reply was forthright: "We recognise no such authority. I would not allow to the Pope, or to any bishop of our church, outside this Union, the smallest interference with the humblest vote at our most insignificant balloting box. . . . You must, from the view which I have taken, see the plain distinction between spiritual authority and a right to interfere in the regulation of human government or civil concerns."[17]

Less than two decades later, Orestes Brownson, an energetic man of letters who had only recently become a Catholic, tried to reverse the charge that Catholics were antidemocratic. On the contrary, according to Brownson, as the title of his essay put it, "Catholicity Necessary to Sustain Popular Liberty." In Brownson's view, democracies could flourish only when the people were virtuous; Protestant churches in a democracy were only and always functions of the will of the people; because people tended as easily to vice as to virtue, Protestant churches offered no security for virtue; and therefore Catholicism was desperately required to make a government like that of the United States work:

> The Roman Catholic religion, then, is necessary to sustain popular liberty, because popular liberty can be sustained only by a religion free from popular control above the people, speaking from above and able to command them—and such a religion is the Roman Catholic. . . . It was made not by the people, but for them; is administered not by the people, but for them; is accountable not to the people, but to God.[18]

16. John T. McGreevy, *Catholicism and American Freedom: A History* (New York: Norton, 2003), 49, 59.

17. "John England Addresses Congress, 1826," in *Creative Fidelity: American Catholic Intellectual Traditions*, ed. R. Scott Appleby, Patricia Byrne, and William L. Portier (Maryknoll, NY: Orbis, 2004), 142–43.

18. Orestes A. Brownson, "Catholicity Necessary to Sustain Popular Liberty" (1845), in *Readings in Church History*, 3:151.

Later, in 1905, another bishop, John Ireland, reiterated the assertion that American Catholics embraced as fully as could possibly be imagined the political principles of the United States government:

> You ask: What is the attitude of the Catholic Church toward a republican form of government? . . . It is . . . Catholic doctrine that in America loyalty to the Republic is a divine precept, and that resistance to law is a sin crying out to heaven for vengeance. To the Republic in America the Church accords the honor and respect due to the representative of divine authority in temporal affairs, and her prayer for the Republic is that it may secure to the people what its professors permit them to expect—the largest possible share of civil liberty.[19]

When in 1927 the Catholic governor of New York, Alfred E. Smith, began to be considered as a presidential candidate, Protestant alarm exploded. In a plaintive reply to a learned attack on Catholicism by an Episcopalian who cited numerous church documents demonstrating (to his satisfaction) that Catholicism contradicted American democracy, Smith responded with a personal credo:

> I believe in the worship of God according to the faith and practice of the Roman Catholic Church. I recognize no power in the institution of my Church to interfere with the operations of the Constitution of the United States or the enforcement of the law of the land. I believe in absolute freedom of conscience for all men and in equality of all churches, all sects, and all beliefs before the law as a matter of right and not of favor. I believe in the absolute separation of Church and State.[20]

Informally, when Smith was queried about his views on Pope Leo XIII's encyclical *Immortale Dei,* he indicated the farcical character of the debate by asking, "Will somebody please tell me what in hell an encyclical is?"[21]

But still the drumbeat of suspicion went on, and among many types of American Protestants. Deep into the twentieth century, the Ku Klux Klan recruited members as much for its stance against Catholics as against African Americans. As shown above, leading evangelicals as late as 1960 could not imagine how a Catholic president could preserve the nation's heritage of freedom. A decade before the 1960 election, mainstream Protestants and other American elites made two books by Paul Blanshard into national best-sellers. These volumes—*American*

---

19. "John Ireland on the Church as the Mother of Liberty and the United States as a Providential Nation, 1905," in *Creative Fidelity,* 148.

20. Quoted in James Hennesey, S.J., *American Catholics: A History of the Roman Catholic Community in the United States* (New York: Oxford University Press, 1981), 252.

21. Ibid.

Freedom and Catholic Power and *Communism, Democracy, and Catholic Power*—repeated charges that had been heard in America for three hundred years about the Catholic Church's character as "antidemocratic . . . intolerant . . . separatist . . . un-American."[22]

Accounting for Political Antagonism

Why were such charges so enduring? Three reasons can be given. First, many Protestants had so securely linked their own view of American ideals to religion as practiced by Protestants in America that they could not imagine any valid Christian expression that did not wholeheartedly embrace these ideals.

Second, the inherited, intuitive practices of Catholicism reflected values that did not necessarily or always parallel the values of liberal democracy. Catholics tended to see the individual against the backdrop of an inherited community instead of the community as a function of individuals. They preferred structural authority to personalized authority, and they thought of Christian identity as something given to adherents by the church rather than something acquired by individuals themselves. As many Catholics through the years pointed out, their values did not exactly contradict the principles of democratic liberalism, but neither did they support them without reservation.

The third reason for the enduring suspicion that Catholicism contradicted main aspects of American democracy is that, often enough, highly visible Catholics publicly stated as much. In the 1840s, for example, Bishop John Hughes of New York, who had defended Catholic churches against Protestant mobs by arming parishioners to stand guard, spoke out unambiguously about what he saw as American problems. To Hughes, Americans were dangerously mad about acquiring wealth, which resulted from the excessive individualism of American political and social principles, which were a direct manifestation of Protestantism. As historian Patrick Carey summarizes Hughes's position, these American difficulties were "the inevitable result of the Protestant doctrine of justification by faith alone."[23]

In 1870, the same Orestes Brownson who had earlier claimed that American democracy needed Roman Catholicism to survive, changed his tune. Now Brownson was disillusioned with how American democratic and republican principles seemed to be exaggerating individual-

22. For expert discussion, see McGreevy, *Catholicism and American Freedom*, 166–69.

23. Patrick W. Carey, ed., *American Catholic Religious Thought* (New York: Paulist Press, 1987), 40.

ity and personal freedom into monstrosities that threatened to destroy Christianity itself:

> I defend the republican form of government for our country, because it is the legal and only practicable form, but I no longer hope anything from it. Catholicity is theoretically compatible with democracy . . . , but practically, there is, in my judgment, no compatibility between them. According to Catholicity all power comes from above and descends from high to low; according to democracy all power is infernal, is from below, and ascends from low to high. This is democracy in its practical sense, as politicians and the people do and will understand it. Catholicity and it are as mutually antagonistic as the spirit and the flesh, the Church and the World, Christ and Satan.[24]

With occasional Catholic voices such as those of Hughes and Brownson added to a situation in which the hereditary instincts of Catholicism never entirely matched the hereditary instincts of Protestantism in its American forms, civil tension remained inevitable. So it was with Samuel Davies, Nathanael Taylor, and George Whitefield during the French and Indian War, so it was with Paul Blanshard and leading evangelicals in the years after World War II, and so it seemed destined to be forever. But, in fact, this Catholic-evangelical tension did not last forever. In the last half century, the political ground has shifted, and it has shifted decisively.

Change since the Mid-twentieth Century

What changed, first, was Catholicism itself. As we have observed several times in earlier chapters, the Second Vatican Council opened a new day for Catholic interactions with modern culture. On political matters, in particular, the American Jesuit John Courtney Murray, with others who felt that universal principles of natural law could be construed as defending democracy, carried the day at the council. The resulting declaration on religious liberty, *Dignitatis Humanae*, represented a momentous breakthrough. This declaration began by reiterating traditional teaching: "We believe that [the] one true religion continues to exist in the Catholic and Apostolic Church." But then it did not draw the political conclusions from this basic premise that earlier councils and popes had drawn. Rather, it asserted in clearest terms that the church stood for the exercise of freedom:

24. Quoted in Hennesey, *American Catholics*, 197.

The Vatican Council declares that the human person has a right to religious freedom. Freedom of this kind means that all men should be immune from coercion on the part of individuals, social groups and every human power so that, within due limits, nobody is forced to act against his convictions in religious matters in private or in public, alone or in association with others. The Council further declares that the right to religious freedom is based on the very dignity of the human person as known through the revealed word of God and by reason itself. This right of the human person to religious freedom must be given such recognition in the constitutional order of society as will make it a civil right.[25]

Whatever once had been the case, Vatican II moved Catholicism as a whole in the direction of political liberalism. Much in Catholic tradition that had cut against American democratic ideals was gone.

A second major change of recent decades was a continued extension of personal freedom in American law and legislation that went far beyond what Protestants had once embraced as a political expression of their religious faith. There is a certain irony here. Protestants in an earlier America had championed nonsectarian liberty as a way of keeping Catholics, for example, from reading the Douay-Rheims translation of the Bible in publicly funded schools. Rather, it was the King James Version (considered by Protestants a nonsectarian text) that public school children should read. But over the course of the twentieth century, American society expanded, changed, and pluralized. Fewer and fewer local jurisdictions defined liberty for all in terms of generic Protestant practices. When the federal government expanded its authority, first for some economic matters in the depression and World War II and then for most areas of life in succeeding decades, the equation between inherited Protestant practices and American freedom broke down. Soon governments came to prohibit any reading of Scripture in the public schools that Protestants had done so much to establish.

The third change lay in evangelical reactions to this new situation. Most Protestants came to accept the use of federal power to end government-ordained racial segregation, but most evangelicals could not accept the expansion of personal rights to include abortion on demand, the practical end of censorship of books, movies, and cable TV, and the sanctioning of homosexual relationships. If this is where American freedom led, many evangelicals concluded, they did not want to follow. And so it came about that as Catholics moved to accept some principles long practiced in American political liberalism, evangelicals shrank back from embracing these principles as fully as they once had. Many

25. Austin P. Flannery, ed., *Documents of Vatican II* (Grand Rapids: Eerdmans, 1975), 799–800.

evangelicals, in fact, now find sentiments expressed by Pope Leo XIII in *Immortale Dei*, which caused such consternation among Protestant lovers of freedom when it was first issued in 1884, similar to their own views. It would take only the replacement of "Catholic" with "Christian" in the following assertion to make the pope's words into a cry around which many evangelicals at the start of the twenty-first century would gladly rally: "Let this be understood by all, that the integrity of Catholic faith cannot be reconciled with opinions verging on naturalism or rationalism, the essence of which is utterly to do away with Christian institutions and to install in society the supremacy of man to the exclusion of God."[26]

Changes in Catholicism, changes among evangelicals, and changes in American society define the larger religious-political story of recent decades. That story is indispensable for understanding the breakthroughs that have occurred in relationships between evangelicals and Catholics.

Sex Scandals

But what of current events? What, in particular, of the sex scandals that have recently racked the Catholic Church in the United States and a few other countries? Adequate response to all that is involved in these scandals would take another book, but for our purposes, two broad points can be made.

First, when considering the sex scandals of recent American Christian history, it is important to realize that there have been at least three scandals rather than just one. First was the cave-in by Protestants, including most evangelicals, on divorce. That cave-in began in the 1930s and 1940s and was complete by the 1970s. Where once Protestant churches had stood foursquare against divorce, except in rare and extreme cases, almost all now accept it as an unquestioned part of contemporary life. Good pastoral reasons certainly exist for gentle treatment of divorced individuals and special solicitude for their children. But no principled theological excuse can exonerate the Protestant churches for failing to work hard at promoting high ideals for marriage, high standards for marriage partners, and high expectations for the care of children. Evangelicals bemoan the mores of sex and family that have prevailed in modern America, and with good reason. But evangelicals must also be honest in recording their own contribution to this sorry situation.

The second scandal was the failure of the Catholic Church concerning birth control. How this failure is interpreted depends on views taken

26. Leo XIII, *Immortale Dei*, 117, par. 47.

concerning Pope Paul VI's 1968 encyclical *Humanae Vitae,* which continued the Catholic prohibition against all forms of birth control except
the rhythm method. If one believes, as most evangelicals do, that birth
control can be practiced conscientiously in Christian marriage, then the
scandal lies with the pope. Prohibiting a practice on the basis of shaky
natural-law reasoning so as not to have to alter received church tradition
looks like the exercise of unwarranted human power that Protestants
have complained about in the papacy for centuries. The huge problem
that resulted in the Catholic Church—where most lay Catholics blithely
disregard official church teaching while bishops stand by placidly in
complicit acquiescence—is, in this reading, a disaster that the pope
brought upon the church himself.

But if the situation is read differently—if one concludes that either
Humanae Vitae was correct or that fidelity to the pope's declaration was
more important than opinions concerning the correctness of the encyclical—then the scandal resides with the bishops. By not daring to resist the
strong forces of American individualism applied to the sphere of sex and
family, the bishops rendered themselves suspect as upholders of church
tradition. Defending *Humanae Vitae* with vigor would have badly hurt
the bishops' credibility. Not defending it did even more damage.

Yet a third interpretation of *Humanae Vitae* places the scandal squarely
with the American laity. If lay Catholics had become so comfortable with
common American practices of birth control that they could simply
shrug off a conclusive (though not necessarily infallible) declaration
of the pope, then something was perhaps amiss with lay Catholicism.
American Catholics were, in this interpretation, choosing American-style
freedom over Catholicism.

The problems of *Humanae Vitae* are singularly Catholic problems.
They arise from conflicting loyalties to individualistic habits acquired
in America and Catholic habits nurtured through the centuries. Protestants, who have Americanized to an even greater degree than Catholics
and who have largely given up on the ideal of the church as a practicing
worldwide community, may nonetheless glimpse what is at stake for
American Catholics with this issue. Protestant weaknesses have protected Protestants from the damage this scandal, however interpreted,
has inflicted on the Catholic Church.

The third sex scandal involves the priestly abuse of adolescents and
children. That scandal, which involved incidents stretching back to the
1960s and 1970s, broke with a fury in the early twenty-first century.[27]
The scandal concerned what had happened and also how what happened

27. For a record of the scandal as it unfolded, see Investigative Staff of the Boston
Globe, *Betrayal: The Crisis in the Catholic Church* (Boston: Little, Brown, 2003).

was covered up by the bishops. Consideration of this sex scandal leads to the second major point that we as evangelicals want to make for the purpose of this book: Almost everything that evangelical Christians would want to say about these scandals has been said, and said well, by Catholics themselves.

In the first instance, the scandal shows how self-serving, complacent, and insensitive the American bishops as a body had become. Although not true for all, many bishops were functioning not as the shepherds of wounded sheep but as managers of an endangered portfolio. They were concerned more with their own power than with empowering the laity. Yet this criticism has been made by Catholics of all sorts, whether liberal, moderate, or conservative.[28]

In a particularly shrewd observation, the Catholic journalist Peter Steinfels pinpoints the bishops' main problem—for the sex scandal and much else—as not following the guidance of the Second Vatican Council. Among the council's key decisions was its resolve to define the Catholic laity as "the people of God." Among its clearest mandates was an injunction to put Catholic laity to work more creatively. But despite this straightforward exhortation, the American bishops, according to Steinfels, hoarded power for themselves, discouraged appropriate lay leadership, and stifled the very help they most urgently needed.[29] An evangelical interpretation of Steinfels's critique would see Vatican II beginning to implement "the priesthood of all believers," almost in Protestant fashion, only to be sandbagged by the bishops' stultifying resistance to change.

Moderate and conservative Catholics have also made the sort of spiritual diagnosis that evangelicals would want to make.[30] Here the basic problem is sin—for those who carried out the abuse and those who covered it up. For sin, the first antidote is repentance, faith in the redeeming work of Christ, and trust in the power of the Holy Spirit to accomplish the holiness that Christians so often evoke but so rarely seek with their whole hearts. This remedy has been presented by many Catholics in many forms. Only by treating human sin and divine forgiveness as such is there any lasting hope for either victims or perpetrators.

28. For an unusually sharp statement of these themes, see the addresses of Scott Appleby and Margaret Steinfels before the United States Catholic Conference of Bishops in Dallas, June 13, 2002.

29. Peter Steinfels, *A People Adrift: The Crisis of the Roman Catholic Church in America* (New York: Simon & Schuster, 2003), 253–55, 340, and many other illuminating passages.

30. For passionately reasoned examples, see both the 2004 report of the Church's National Review Board and the commentary on that report in Richard John Neuhaus, "The Catholic Reform," *First Things*, May 2004, 59–65; and June/July 2004, 64–69.

Moderate and conservative Catholics have also decried the dalliance with homosexuality as an acceptable active lifestyle that the church tolerated from the 1960s into the 1980s. Almost all evangelicals would echo this same judgment. Such Catholic voices usually go on to say the vitally necessary things that most evangelicals also want to say about the need to treat homosexually inclined persons with as much grace and tolerance as Christian believers owe to all other people.

About the only thing that evangelicals might add to Catholic commentary on the Catholic sex scandal would concern mandatory clerical celibacy. But even on this matter, evangelicals would want to advance slowly. We evangelicals believe that Scripture clearly sanctions married pastors, but we are also aware of being uncomfortable around the injunctions from the apostle Paul about it being better for Christians to remain as he was (unmarried) than to marry (1 Cor. 7:8, 25–29) or Jesus' approval of those who "have renounced marriage because of the kingdom of heaven" (Matt. 19:12). Moreover, evangelicals who take seriously how frequently sexual sins have infected the lives of evangelical ministers might pause in their condemnation of Catholicism. Historically considered, celibate monks, nuns, and priests kept the Christian faith alive, almost all by themselves, for more than one thousand years (roughly 500 to 1500). Since the Reformation, alert Protestants have also realized that the great gains in having a married clergy (for example, providing models for the Christian household and for fellowship in works of the gospel) have been balanced by real difficulties (for example, the hindering of missionary, social, and other kinds of Christian work by domestic responsibilities). The fact that single women, voluntarily celibate, have played a disproportionately large role in Protestant missionary work as well as in the actual ministry of many local congregations should suggest a degree of caution in criticizing Catholic clerical celibacy.

The contemporary sex scandals in the Catholic Church have damaged many individuals irreparably, even as they brought disgrace to the cause of Christ. But as evangelicals, we see in these scandals no cause for self-satisfied gloating but much to ponder about parallel disorders in our own house.

Pluralism Within and Without

A last word on the contemporary situation for Catholics and evangelicals is required concerning the wide diversity now found in both traditions. The time is long past when responsible analysts could speak of either Catholics or evangelicals as a homogenous unit. An awareness of pluralism has been a truism in the discussion of American Protestants since the end of the nineteenth century, but only in recent decades have historians taken seriously the near impossibility of lumping together (as only a partial list) Protestant mainliners, fundamentalists, liberals, Lutheran "evangelical catholics," Lutheran Americanists, Pentecostals, Disciples of Christ, Plymouth Brethren, and a thousand and one other variations.

The larger Protestant reality is true also of evangelicals. With no formal structure uniting those who share evangelical faith, with evangelicals strewn across multitudes of denominations, with no institutional voice presuming to speak for or to all evangelical Protestants, with deep theological, ecclesiastical, and social differences dividing evangelicals from one another, it is presumptuous ever to speak casually about a common evangelical attitude toward Catholics or anything else. In particular, fissures among evangelicals loom largest because of race. Despite professions of spiritual unity in Christ, the racial divide still erects nearly insurmountable obstacles between white evangelicals and black evangelicals who, though they share much in beliefs and moral practices, are kept far apart by social and political affinities.[31] In addition, throughout the contemporary world, the relative wealth of Western evangelicals serves to isolate them increasingly from the relative poverty of evangelicals in the two-thirds world.[32] From the Protestant side, therefore, it is necessary to talk with extreme care about the often diverse elements that fit under the term *evangelical*.

The same reality is equally true on the other side as well. Despite persisting tendencies, especially among non-Catholics, to speak of a unified Catholic Church, such efforts are nearly as indefensible as applying generalities to Protestants. Catholics do retain a structural unity symbolized by the pope and the church's hierarchy, but it would be wise for Protestants to let Catholics say what that structure means. Speaking as a Catholic theologian, Richard McBrien once described the current scene as one in which "there are sometimes sharper divisions *within* the Roman Catholic Church than there are between certain Catholics and certain Protestants."[33] Sociologist Andrew Greeley (who is also a Catholic priest) has made the same point: "Every generalization about

31. See Michael O. Emerson and Christian Smith, *Divided by Faith: Evangelical Religion and the Problem of Race in America* (New York: Oxford University Press, 2000); and Curtiss Paul DeYoung et al., *United by Faith: The Multiracial Congregation as an Answer to the Problem of Race* (New York: Oxford University Press, 2003).

32. This is the situation described, for example, in Paul Freston, *Evangelicals and Politics in Asia, Africa, and Latin America* (New York: Cambridge University Press, 2001).

33. Richard P. McBrien, "Roman Catholicism: *E Pluribus Unum*," in *Religion and America: Spirituality in a Secular Age*, ed. Mary Douglas and Steven M. Tipton (Boston: Beacon, 1983), 181.

values that begins with the word 'Catholic' is likely to be misleading, if not erroneous, precisely because the generalization will mask substantial differences in values that exist among the Catholic subpopulations."[34] Given the religious pluralism *within* Christian families, there is much more opportunity now than even fifty years ago to find meaningful fellowship across, as well as significant strife within, traditional evangelical and Catholic communities.

At least two results flow from this new situation. First, dialogue between evangelicals and Catholics has created not only more opportunities for mutual encouragement but also more opportunities for heightened tensions among Protestants and among Roman Catholics. To look at matters from just one side, different strands within the evangelical stream find significant differences in those aspects of Catholicism to which they are attracted. Pentecostal evangelicals, for example, may appreciate Catholic openness to the subjective working of the Spirit but continue to dislike formal Catholic hierarchy; confessional Reformed evangelicals may appreciate Catholic objectivity about the sacraments but dislike Catholic ways of explaining how faith should be active in love; the new wave of academic evangelical philosophers may appreciate the tough-minded tradition of Catholic philosophical reflection but shy away from the way that such philosophy has been used to define expressly Catholic dogma; Anabaptist evangelicals may appreciate the dedication of the Catholic monastic tradition but worry about the application of Catholic just-war teaching to modern international conflict; Baptist evangelicals may appreciate the strong Catholic defense of life but reject out of hand the centralizing theology of the Catholic hierarchy; and Arminian evangelicals may appreciate the space that Catholics preserve for the exercise of free will but express reservations about the primacy of the papacy. The opening of Catholic-evangelical dialogue, in short, will almost certainly intensify Protestant debates among themselves.

Taking Stock

Evangelicals who study Roman Catholicism today must take seriously questions of religious faith and practice that have created tensions between the two communions since the days of the Reformation. Our conviction that these are still the most important questions means that we turn to such issues in the final chapter of the book. At the same time, however, it is also appropriate for believers in the United States

34. Andrew M. Greeley, *The American Catholic: A Social Portrait* (New York: Basic Books, 1977), 252.

to reflect on how their own national history has played a role in relationships between evangelicals and Catholics. We hope to have shown in this chapter that civil politics have always loomed large in Catholic-evangelical encounter and that, while political realities exacerbated the tension between evangelicals and Catholics in the first century and a half of United States history, during the last half century, political realities have eased the way to a more propitious relationship. Other contemporary realities, such as the well-publicized sex scandals or the fact of intra-traditional pluralism, complicate that relationship but only make careful theological analysis more, rather than less, necessary.

9

IS THE REFORMATION OVER?

This last chapter tries to take the measure of modern Catholicism, evaluated from the perspective of evangelical history and theology. It is an impressionistic and rhetorical assessment, at least in part because analysis of contemporary Catholicism at a depth appropriate to the importance of the subject would require a lifetime of extensive research and careful casuistry. What a provisional treatment can do is consider areas of agreement and disagreement, suggest a broader perspective for how the contemporary situation might be interpreted, and then return to the question of our title: Is the Reformation over?

Short decades ago, the degree of mutual respect and cooperation that evangelical Protestants of a certain kind and Roman Catholics of a certain kind now enjoy was unimaginable. Of course, not all evangelicals and not all Catholics either desire or have experienced such a breakthrough to more positive relationships. Evangelicals open to closer cooperation with Catholics have usually had positive contact with individual Catholics who, for one reason or another, leave a strong impression of devotion to Jesus. In addition, such evangelicals have often been pushed to think carefully about theological boundaries, where they come from and what they mean. Evangelicals willing to explore cooperation with Catholics may have a strong commitment to some variety of Protestantism, often rooted in the Reformation, but they also usually display a willingness to let contemporary experience influence how that religious heritage should be understood, applied, and articulated.

Catholics open to closer cooperation with evangelicals have likewise usually had positive personal connections with evangelicals whose faith they respect. Such Catholics tend to be located in the moderate or moderate-conservative wings of the church and to be encouraged by statements from Vatican II about the presence of the Holy Spirit in other Christian movements. They often worry as much about the advance of godless secularism in the world as evangelicals do about the advance of theological modernism among Protestant churches, and they regard the small wing of Catholic conservatism that rejects Vatican II as unrepresentative of true Catholicism.

Most important for creating the possibility of cooperation between evangelicals and Catholics is an openness to experience and a willingness to rethink boundaries. The experience is of individuals, movements, projects, reforms, insights, writings, or pious practices coming from the other tribe that, even if such experiences do not make complete sense in light of their own tribe's inherited traditions, nonetheless bear the unmistakable stamp of Jesus Christ. The boundary reconsideration involves letting such experiences play a role in defining what Christianity is and indicating how Christian faith should be lived out in the world. The assertions that follow about evangelicalism and Catholicism today pertain to representatives of these traditions whose cooperation in many particulars of faith and witness has already been well established.

Questions of Belief

Among evangelicals and Catholics who are open to cooperation there now exists a broad and deep foundation of agreement on the central teachings of Christianity. Such evangelicals and Catholics affirm together the Trinity, the sinfulness of humanity, the saving love of God extended to sinners in the person and work of Jesus Christ, the redeeming power of the Holy Spirit to change men and women into servants of God, and the wholesome integrity of God's law. Whatever differences may still exist between such Catholics and evangelicals with respect to the foundations of Christianity are infinitesimal when compared to differences between traditional Christianity as described above and modernist Christianity of all sorts. Differences on basic Christian convictions between Catholics and evangelicals fade away as if to nothing when compared to secular affirmations about the nature of humanity and the world.

The growing recognition of how deep and firm such common doctrinal affirmations are represents a great historical reversal. Although agreement on foundational Christian teachings has always been present, at least to some degree, since the origins of Protestantism in the sixteenth century, only in recent decades have the depth and significance of these common doctrinal affirmations been visible. This alteration of perspective should indicate to anyone of a historical cast of mind that we still live in the age of miracles.

More specifically, such Catholics and evangelicals trust equally in the full inspiration and final authority of the Bible. On Scripture, they stand together against modernistic proposals from within the churches that would treat Scripture as only a product of human consciousness; together they stand against the non-Christian world in affirming that the Bible communicates normative revelation from God.

Notwithstanding a common affirmation of the inspiration and authority of Scripture, however, major differences do continue to separate Catholics and evangelicals on how to interpret the Bible. Catholics rely in principle more on the voice of tradition and the formal teaching magisterium of the church; evangelicals rely in principle more on the personal appropriation of Scripture and (in practice) on particular traditions of interpretation defined by local leaders, regional networks, and individual institutions. Because of these hermeneutical differences, evangelicals continue to regard some Catholic practices and dogmas as unscriptural (however much they look to Catholics like dogmas and practices legitimately rooted in Scripture). Conversely, the evangelical rejection of some Catholic dogmas and practices as unscriptural looks to Catholics not like trust in the Bible but like caving in to the skepticism, individualism, and functional antisupernaturalism of the secular Enlightenment.

For example, rejection of the Catholic mass—as a sacrifice featuring bread and wine transformed into the body and blood of Christ—is to many evangelicals a simple matter of trusting the Bible (e.g., "The Spirit gives life; the flesh counts for nothing. The words I [Jesus] have spoken to you are spirit and they are life" [John 6:63]). The rejection is also a doctrinal imperative required by the once-for-all saving efficacy of Christ's death on the cross. By contrast, to most Catholics, rejection of the mass is the rejection of a practice anchored in Scripture (e.g., "I tell you the truth, unless you eat the flesh of the Son of Man and drink his blood, you have no life in you" [John 6:53]), developed through the centuries as a certain means of divine grace, and set aside only by those for whom modern notions of rationality mean more than the mysteries of a merciful providence.

For many Catholics and evangelicals, however, it has become important to insist that continuing differences in how best to interpret Scripture arise not from significant differences about the character of divine revelation in the Bible as such but from different customs, habits, or principles associated with understanding and putting to use a divinely authoritative Bible.

It is the same for justification by faith, about which many Catholics and evangelicals now believe approximately the same thing. To put this expanding area of agreement in more precise terms, it is more precise to say that many Catholics and evangelicals now affirm that a God-honoring, Scripture-based, and orthodox theology of justification by faith is found where the following two propositions are believed separately and together: (1) Salvation is an absolutely free gift from God. (2) There is no Christian salvation that is not manifest in good works.

Precisely how these two propositions are to be understood as individual Christian doctrines and then held together in faithful Christian practice does produce disagreement. But as we have noted, this disagreement is found as much within evangelicalism and within Catholicism as between Catholics and evangelicals. As earlier chapters have indicated, official Catholic teaching, especially as articulated in the *Catechism* and "The Joint Declaration on the Doctrine of Justification," now seems to fall somewhere between John Wesley's Arminianism and the Augustinian positions maintained by Martin Luther and John Calvin. All of these depictions of salvation by grace through faith are closer to one another than to other positions commonly held by some evangelicals—whether forms of Arminianism that, like the revival theology of Charles Finney, give priority in salvation to the exertions of the human will; some forms of Anabaptist soteriology that define salvation more as imitating Christ than as having the righteousness of Christ imputed to the sinner; or other sectarian Protestant doctrines in which the agency of the unredeemed sinner occupies a more central place in salvation than found in official Catholic teaching; as well as Lutheran and Calvinistic Augustinianism and Arminian Wesleyanism.

Thus, on the substance of what is actually taught about God's saving work in the world, if not always on the exact terminology used to describe that saving work, many evangelicals and Catholics believe something close to the same thing. If it is true, as once was repeated frequently by Protestants conscious of their anchorage in Martin Luther or John Calvin that *iustificatio articulus stantis vel cadentis ecclesiae* (justification is the article on which the church stands or falls), then the Reformation is over.[1]

To be sure, on questions about justification, a difference is still important between Catholics and evangelicals concerning the merciful

---

1. For a helpful discussion from a contemporary Lutheran perspective, see Carl E. Braaten, *Justification: The Article by Which the Church Stands or Falls* (Minneapolis: Fortress, 1990).

means through which God provides his grace for the justification of sinners. But again, more and more Catholics and evangelicals express the opinion that differences over the means of grace need not overwhelm common affirmations concerning the basic character of God's justifying grace. Of those continuing differences, many concern the issue of how justification is imparted and received, and on that and related issues the church comes front and center.

The Church as the Crux of Catholic-Evangelical Disagreement

The most serious disagreements continue to exist between Catholics and evangelicals over questions of the church. Controversy over the papacy, the Virgin Mary, the sacraments, the mandatory celibacy of priests, and other matters can all be debated on their individual merits. But in each case, persistent evangelical-Catholic disagreement also grows from a different conception of how God fashions the body of Christ in the world, what he has called that body to be for believers, and how he has empowered it to carry on the work of building his kingdom.

The Papacy and the Magisterium

The papacy remains an issue of conflict in large part because evangelical interpretations of Scripture and history lead to a rejection of stated Catholic teaching. Evangelicals do not find a basis in Scripture for what Catholics affirm about the pope: "The Roman Pontiff, by reason of his office as Vicar of Christ, and as pastor of the entire Church has full, supreme, and universal power over the whole Church, a power which he can always exercise unhindered."[2] Nor do evangelicals necessarily believe what Catholics say about the church hierarchy, that it is "dedicated to promoting the interests of their brethren, so that all who belong to the People of God . . . may attain to salvation."[3] Evangelicals, in contrast, think they see too many instances in which the hierarchy has been dedicated to promoting the interests of itself so that all who wield church office may attain more power for themselves.

Evangelical interpretations of Scripture hold that the promise of Christ to Peter in Matthew 16:18 ("You are Peter, and on this rock I will build my church, and the gates of Hades will not overcome it") relates more to the gospel confession Peter had just made in Matthew 16:16 ("You are

2. United States Catholic Conference, *Catechism of the Catholic Church* (New York: Doubleday, 1994), 254, par. 882.
3. Ibid., 252, par. 874.

the Christ, the Son of the living God"), and that all believers are called to make as well, than to a formal office passed down from Peter, as the vicar of Christ, to his successor bishops. Evangelicals also believe that the binding and loosing, which is also spoken of in Matthew 16:19 ("I will give you the keys of the kingdom of heaven; whatever you bind on earth will be bound in heaven, and whatever you loose on earth will be loosed in heaven") refers to the power of the gospel at work through all believers rather than to the power of the gospel as channeled through the church's ecclesiastical hierarchy.

Evangelical objections to the papal office and to the exercise of papal power run deep, as seen in the early days of the Reformation when Martin Luther called the papacy "Anti-Christ" because through abuse of church office it kept people from Christ.[4] Yet as with Luther, who professed a willingness to accept a reformed papacy that honored Christ, the most basic evangelical issue is not the papacy per se but the belief that the church is first spiritual (all who believe in Christ from whatever ecclesiastical communion) and only secondarily a human institution. From this angle, modern Catholics have no difficulty in agreeing that popes and bishops make mistakes, and some are willing to concede that these mistakes have sometimes been grievous. But the essential Catholic claim remains that the church established by Christ on earth to carry out his work is tangible not virtual, objective not subjective, unified not fragmented, universal (= catholic) not local, visible not imaginary. Once that Catholic commitment is in place, institutions such as the papacy and the teaching magisterium become as natural as they are indispensable. Evangelicals, however, wonder if this high view of church borders on idolatry, placing in the church a power reserved for God alone.

The Blessed Virgin Mary

In a similar manner, Mary remains an issue of conflict because evangelicals are opposed to giving any human the titles, honor, or centrality in salvation that belong to Jesus Christ alone as the unique human-divine Redeemer. This issue, however, is probably one in which evangelical and Catholic practices differ more than evangelical and Catholic dogmas, since evangelical beliefs about the Bible compel an honored place for this one who, in the angel's words, was "favored" (Luke 1:28), and Catholic dogmas about salvation insist that Mary is only first among the redeemed.

4. Martin Luther, *On the Papacy at Rome* (1520), in *Luther's Works*, vol. 39, ed. Eric W. Gritsch (Philadelphia: Fortress, 1970), 49–194.

Yet the potential for ongoing discord arises whenever Catholics let the *language* of Marian devotional practice, which always sounds excessive to evangelicals anyway, become official doctrine. When that happens, as with the 1950 papal pronouncement concerning the bodily assumption of Mary, the worst fears of evangelicals are confirmed. In this first (and only) exercise of papal infallibility as defined by the First Vatican Council of 1870, Pope Pius XII made not only a powerful statement about Mary but an even stronger one about the papal office:

> By the authority of our Lord Jesus Christ, of the Blessed Apostles Peter and Paul, and by our own authority, we pronounce, declare, and define it to be a divinely revealed dogma: that the Immaculate Mother of God, the ever Virgin Mary, having completed the course of her earthly life, was assumed body and soul into heavenly glory.
>
> Hence if anyone, which God forbid, should dare willfully to deny or to call into doubt that we have defined, let him know that he has fallen away completely from the divine and Catholic faith. . . .
>
> It is forbidden to any man to change this, our declaration, pronouncement, and definition or, by rash attempt, to oppose and counter it. If any man should presume to make such an attempt, let him know that he will incur the wrath of Almighty God and of the Blessed Apostles Peter and Paul.[5]

As this encyclical indicates, differences over Mary are also functions of differences over the church. It is not just that Marian devotion is authorized by Catholic teaching and deeply ingrained in church practice and therefore woven into the very fabric of Catholic life. It is also that, in her special role as mother of the Son of God, Mary expresses for Catholics the corporate character of humanity in general and, even more, the corporate character of the church. Devotion to Mary, which to evangelicals looks like compromising Christ as sole mediator between God and humanity, is for Catholics a corporate means of participating in the grace that God gave to the world, literally, through her. Marian practice is essentially ecclesial practice.

The Sacraments

Differences between Catholics and evangelicals over the sacraments are serious, but, as we have seen, evangelicals themselves are divided on what the sacraments are and how they should be used. With respect to what the sacraments are, the fundamental differences do not yield a

---

5. Pope Pius XII, *Munificentissimus Deus* (Defining the Dogma of the Assumption), "Papal Encyclicals Online," www.papalencyclicals.net/Pius12/P12MUNIF.htm (accessed May 14, 2004).

strictly Catholic-Protestant divide. Rather, there are two separations. The most basic difference lies between Protestants who view the sacraments as events when Christians remember what God has done for them and then give him praise through that remembrance, and Catholics (along with some Protestants) who view the sacraments as events when God on his own initiative does something of saving significance to and for his people. Oversimplified, the difference is between baptism (of adults) viewed as a step of obedience versus baptism (of infants) viewed as an expression of God's grace to the child and a gift of initiation into the church. Likewise, the difference is between the Lord's Supper considered as a memorial of Christ's death versus the Eucharist as the "real presence" of Christ with his people.

On the next level, however, even evangelicals who both baptize babies and look upon the Lord's Supper as genuinely offering in some sense the "real presence" of Christ do not advocate a Catholic position. The divide at this level comes from a difference of doctrine about how God on his own initiative carries out his sacramental work of saving significance. Both can agree that this sacramental work takes place when the church's properly designated ministers pronounce the gospel words of promise that are connected with the sacramental signs. Catholics typically stress more the properly designated ministers, Protestants the gospel words of promise.

Again, however, there is a key difference between all Catholics and all Protestants, and the key to that difference is the church. In an evangelical economy of salvation, God's sacramental gifts come to individual Christians via the church. In the Catholic economy of salvation, God creates and sustains the church in order to offer through it his sacramental gifts. For Catholics, the church and its officers are essential as the institutional prerequisites for the sacraments in a way that they are not for evangelicals.

Mandatory Clerical Celibacy

Evangelicals consider it an easy matter to dispense with mandatory celibacy for priests and members of religious orders. All it takes is a proof text, in this case 1 Timothy 4:1, 3: "The Spirit clearly says that in later times some will abandon the faith and follow deceitful spirits and things taught by demons. . . . They forbid people to marry and order them to abstain from certain foods, which God created to be received with thanksgiving by those who believe and who know the truth." (Also relevant is 1 Tim. 3:5.)

For Catholics, by contrast, "celibacy is a sign of this new life [dedicated to the Lord and to the affairs of the Lord] to the service of which the Church's minister is consecrated."[6] In its wisdom and for its own purposes, the church has decided that priests and members of most religious orders should be celibate. The fact that Catholicism provides for married priests in its Eastern rite (or Uniate) churches and also sometimes allows married Protestant ministers who convert to function as married Catholic priests suggests the deeper issues at stake. For Catholics, clerical celibacy is not, as evangelicals like to regard it, a question to be decided simply on its own merits, on the basis of relevant biblical teaching. It is, rather, a question of Catholic procedure mandated by the church for the purpose of carrying out what it considers its essential tasks as the active presence of God in the world. Therefore, priests are celibate because the church says so. No other reason is needed. Once again, a contested difference between Catholics and evangelicals boils down to a contested understanding of the church.

Contrasting Perspectives

In sum, the central difference that continues to separate evangelicals and Catholics is not Scripture, justification by faith, the pope, Mary, the sacraments, or clerical celibacy—though the central difference is reflected in differences on these matters—but the nature of the church. For Catholics, the visible, properly constituted, and hierarchically governed church is the principal God-ordained agent for the work of apostolic ministry. For evangelicals, the church is the body of Christ made up of all those who have responded to the apostolic proclamation of the God-given offer of the forgiveness of sins in Jesus Christ.

The position of the church in major formulations of doctrine underscores the divide that remains. It was therefore characteristic of evangelicalism that the Lausanne Covenant of 1974, which is the most widely embraced evangelical statement of faith from the twentieth century, did not feature the church as a central theme. Instead, after opening paragraphs on "The Purpose of God," "The Authority and Power of the Bible," and "The Uniqueness and Universality of Christ," the covenant eventually in its sixth paragraph took up the subject under the title "Evangelism and the Church." Granted, Lausanne was aimed at providing a wide variety of evangelicals with a basis for sharing the gospel rather than at developing a doctrinal creed for an institutional Christian church. But to speak for a broad range of evangelicals, it was necessary to remain vague about the church as such: "In the church's mission of sacrificial service evangelism is primary. World evangelization requires the whole

6. *Catechism of the Catholic Church*, 440, par. 1579.

church to take the whole Gospel to the whole world. The church is at the very center of God's cosmic purpose and is his appointed means of spreading the Gospel." Even these general statements required immediate qualification: "The church is the community of God's people rather than an institution, and must not be identified with any particular culture, social or political system, or human ideology." The covenant went on to acknowledge weaknesses in evangelical ecclesiology: "We confess that our testimony has sometimes been marred by sinful individualism and needless duplication." Yet the antidote was better function rather than the proper form: "We pledge ourselves to seek a deeper unity in truth, worship, holiness, and mission."[7]

By contrast, the Catholic *Catechism* begins with words from Pope John Paul II that place the hereditary structure and the institution of the church in the forefront of defining and propagating its doctrine:

> John Paul, Bishop
> Servant of the Servants of God
> For Everlasting Memory
>
> To my Venerable Brothers the Cardinals, Patriarchs, Archbishops, Bishops, Priests, Deacons, and to all the People of God.
>
> Guarding the Deposit of Faith is the Mission which the Lord Entrusted to His Church, and which she fulfills in every age.[8]

The essential difference reflected in how the church appears, almost haphazardly, in the Lausanne Covenant and how it appears, with un-mistakable centrality, in the Catholic *Catechism* can be summarized suc-cinctly. For Catholics, the church constitutes believers; for evangelicals, believers constitute the church. For Catholics, individual believers are a function of the church; for evangelicals, the church is a function of individual believers.

This divide is deep because it is a question of different (and deeply ingrained) practice as much as or more than it is a question of conflict-ing doctrines. In the best book ever published by an American Catholic on evangelical Christianity, William Shea phrases the essential issue like this: "Are we to imagine that salvation is a gift to individuals who then go on to decide to form a church, or does God's grace constitute a community of lost souls (say, Twelve of them!) by membership in which

7. John Stott, ed., *The Lausanne Covenant* (Minneapolis: World Wide Publications, 1975), 30.
8. *Catechism of the Catholic Church*, 1.

the souls are no longer lost? This is the heart of the issue: is it an entire people or individual persons that God saves?"[9]

From contrasting practices (and views) of the church then come the typical complaints made by evangelicals about Catholics and vice versa. Evangelicals cannot understand how in good conscience a genuinely Christian church could have long engaged (and in limited areas of the world can still engage) in coerced constraint of large populations in an effort to exert hegemonic control over entire local societies. Only by confusing the prerogatives of God and the prerogatives of humanity could this situation have survived so long. Evangelicals, further, cannot understand how the Catholic Church can be genuinely Christian if it tolerates so casually the substitution of church adherence for Christian practice—this is the problem of nominal belief and nominal practice that evangelicals and even converts to Catholicism see whenever they look at Catholicism as a whole. To be sure, Catholic leaders do address this problem, but to evangelicals it seems as if they do not mean it. How can the church tolerate a definition of Christianity that looks more to one-time baptism and an ethnic-type of identification as a definition of what constitutes a Christian and tolerate what looks like a nearly complete indifference to the vast numbers of Catholics who do not seem to be concerned about practicing any kind of Christianity at all?

Catholics respond to such questions with a full list of their own. When they observe the bloomin', buzzin' confusion that is evangelical Christianity, their bewilderment can be just as great as when evangelicals look at Catholic fixations on the corporate character of the church. Their questions might go like this: As Catholics we cannot imagine that genuine Christianity could be as torn apart as evangelical Protestantism, and for such a never-ending list of sinfully schismatic reasons: personality disputes, ego trips, preferences in music, preferences in sermon length, preferences in politics, economic class, race, denominational pride, eccentric interpretations of a limited part of the Bible, very eccentric interpretations of a limited part of the Bible, and so on.

Or again, as Catholics we cannot understand how evangelicals can claim to be Christian and limit their faith to what goes on in their heads—to words, preaching, testimonies, books, more words—with no real attention given to the ligaments of Christian community: no real sacraments, no real sense that Christ died for bodies as well as for heads, no real appreciation for what comes to us through the physical senses. Does it not indicate the thinness of evangelicalism that most of the good Christian literature, almost all of the good Christian painting,

9. William M. Shea, *The Lion and the Lamb: Evangelicals and Catholics in America* (New York: Oxford University Press, 2004), 286–87.

and a substantial part of really serious Christian scholarship are done by Catholics?

Visceral cross-denominational reactions are noteworthy, not because they highlight differences in particular doctrines or particular practices but because they are rooted in alternative conceptions of what it means to be Christian. The Anglican sociologist David Martin once described these alternatives more analytically than polemically: "Evangelicalism is clear about our equal need of redemption but poor in its provision for artistic and sensitive souls. Catholicism may be less democratic but it is decidedly superior in its provision for the varieties of the human spirit."[10] These alternative conceptions of what it means to be Christian are rooted in what it means for a body of humans to make up the Christian church.

Why Do These Fundamental Differences Exist?

At this point it would be natural to ask what Catholics and evangelicals who want to expand areas of fruitful cooperation should do. But that question is premature if we do not first ask why such fundamental differences exist and how they should be interpreted.

Historically, major evangelical-Catholic differences were treated as issues of Christian fidelity. Evangelicals held that Catholics were wrong, usually sinfully so. Catholics responded in kind. More recently, as in the ecumenical dialogues, the ECT initiatives, and many other cooperative ventures, judgments about the other group's errors have not vanished, but they have been relativized by new affirmations concerning what can be believed and done together, despite remaining shortcomings on the other side. Just how to evaluate those remaining shortcomings—willful sins? sins of ignorance? mere mistakes?—is not clear.

An alternative explanation is possible from both within and outside the churches. The more cynically minded might suggest that a postmodern explanation provides the best account for continuing Catholic-evangelical difference. Since in postmodern analysis convictions about others are always a function of power over others (or power desired over others), we might expect Catholic-evangelical differences to continue as long as those who hold the contrasting convictions stand to lose power by giving them up. A drastic reform of the papacy and the Catholic hierarchy along lines demanded by Protestants since the days of Martin Luther would require a self-abnegating relinquishing of authority on a scale

10. David Martin, *Christian Language and Its Mutations* (Burlington, VT: Ashgate, 2002), 198.

never before witnessed in human history. Similarly, for the leaders of evangelical denominations, congregations, parachurch agencies, and organizations to cede their own authority and come under the jurisdiction of even a dramatically reformed papacy would require an exercise of self-denial almost as gargantuan (and unthinkable). High-minded Catholics and evangelicals should probably take offense at reducing principled disagreements to the mere exercise of power. Yet Catholics and evangelicals examining themselves with Christian realism may recognize that such crassly postmodern analysis contains a germ of truth.

A third approach to interpreting the continuing differences between Catholics and evangelicals might recognize them as (for now at least) incommensurable, but for reasons having more to do with historical circumstances than with sinful error, mistakes, or the exercise of power. This view benefits from how a few Christian thinkers have brought reasoning from special and general revelation to bear on the nature of intra-Christian difference.[11] The overarching purpose is to find a way of viewing Catholic-evangelical disagreement positively, as a result of God's providential oversight, as well as negatively, as a result of God's permission of human failing.

In this interpretation, the beginning point is to recognize that there exist at least four quite distinct types of Christianity, each one reflecting a positive development (or incarnation) of Christian faith and practice singularly well adopted to a particular set of historical circumstances. This interpretation represents a historical or missiological rather than a strictly doctrinal approach to the questions of what Christianity is in its essence and how one strand of Christianity might evaluate another strand of Christianity with insight as well as judgment. Underlying this interpretation is the conviction that, though God and his revelation in Christ are one, Christianity may become (in Paul's phrase) "all things to all people" (1 Cor. 9:22).

11. For this interpretation, prompting has come from David Tracy's account of alternative Christian "imaginations" in *The Analogical Imagination: Christian Theology and the Culture of Pluralism* (New York: Crossroad, 1981), 405–21; Louis Bouyer's analysis of the role of philosophy in Reformation theologies, *The Spirit and Form of Protestantism* (Westminster, MD: Newman, 1956); David Martin's understanding of religious-political parallels in *A General Theory of Secularization* (New York: Harper & Row, 1978); and David N. Livingstone's description of how geography influences all forms of intellectual effort in *Putting Science in Its Place: Geographies of Scientific Knowledge* (Chicago: University of Chicago Press, 2003). The vocabulary of "translation," "language," and "incarnations" that follows depends heavily on Lamin Sanneh, *Translating the Message: The Missionary Impact on Catholics* (Maryknoll, NY: Orbis, 1989); Andrew F. Walls, *The Missionary Movement in Christian History* (Maryknoll, NY: Orbis, 2002); and Lamin Sanneh, *Whose Religion Is Christianity? The Gospel beyond the West* (Grand Rapids: Eerdmans, 2003).

Because the four main expressions of Christian faith arose to fit the particular circumstances of particular places and particular eras in the history of Christianity, it is appropriate to present them in order of appearance.[12]

First is Eastern Orthodoxy, constituted in an enduring form in the third to fifth centuries and given shape by its adaptation to the Hellenism of the Mediterranean world. Orthodoxy may be considered a result of translating the Hebrew and Aramaic thought forms of Scripture into Hellenistic Greek.

Then comes Western Roman Catholicism, constituted first by Augustine's theology (fifth century) and Benedict's monasticism (sixth century) and then receiving definitive form in the ninth to thirteenth centuries with the renewal of monasticism, the institutional reforms of Pope Innocent III, the inspiration of Francis of Assisi, and the theology of Thomas Aquinas. Roman Catholicism took its distinctive shape by providing the religion for European forms of state-church Christendom. It may be considered a result of the translation of Hellenistic Greek Christianity into Latin.

Third arises evangelical Protestantism, constituted in two stages—the sixteenth-century reform of the Catholic Church and the eighteenth-century revivals of Protestantism. This expression took its distinctive shape by adopting Western Catholic Christianity to a new Europe marked by nationalism, the discovery of the individual, and, eventually, the Enlightenment. It may be considered a result of the translation of Latin Christianity into the vernacular languages of Europe.

Fourth comes Pentecostalism, constituted in many places around the world during the course of the twentieth century as an adaptation of historic forms of Christianity or the spontaneous combination of missionary Christianity and local religious traditions. Pentecostalism has taken a distinctive shape in the adaptation of Christianity to the free-flow of goods, services, cultural products, and peoples characteristic of the globalizing world economy. It may be considered a result of the translation of European and North American Christianity into the indigenous tongues of the two-thirds world.

In this picture, the emergence of Orthodoxy represents the successful planting, against all odds, of a deeply thought-through Christianity in the Roman-Byzantine Mediterranean world. In turn, the character of Orthodoxy was fixed by the depth of biblical reflection, represented best by Athanasius (296–373) and the Cappadocian fathers (Basil of

---

12. For a brief treatment of the historical figures and events mentioned in the next few paragraphs, see Mark A. Noll, *Turning Points: Decisive Moments in the History of Christianity*, 2nd ed. (Grand Rapids: Baker, 2000).

Caesarea, 330–79; Gregory of Nazianzus, 329–89; Gregory of Nyssa, 330–95), on what it meant for the human being Jesus Christ to express God's fullest revelatory disclosure of himself to humanity (the Nicene-Constantinopolitan Creed, 325/381) and what it then consequently meant for Jesus Christ to be in his one integrated person both fully human and fully divine (the Council of Chalcedon, 451). Today, the survival of Orthodoxy represents a continuing Christian tradition in which the blinding metaphysical reality of God taking flesh, in the words of the Nicene Creed, "for us and for our salvation," continues to supply spiritual lifeblood to a wide range of churches.

Second, fully formed Roman Catholicism represents the successful planting, against all odds, of a strongly communal Christianity in the tribal regions of Europe. In turn, the character of Catholicism was fixed by the depth of practical Christian action that was required to humanize and unify the warring tribes of Northern Europe (Charlemagne), to renew the inner resources of practical Christian living in an age of great barbarism (tenth-century monastic renewal), to express the lordship of Christ over the mind (Thomas Aquinas), and to demonstrate the love of Christ to the whole of the world that he had created (St. Francis). Today, the survival of Catholicism represents a continuing Christian tradition in which the tangible ideal of a God-ordained and God-sustained community continues to quicken a wide range of Christian teaching, social construction, intellectual labor, and pious fervor.

Third, the emergence of Protestantism represents the successful emergence, against all odds, of vigorous Christianity in an early modern Europe driven by the rise of nationalism, with both nationalism and Christianity intellectually energized as well as intellectually imperiled by the Enlightenment. In turn, the character of Protestantism was fixed by the existential power of biblical preaching, represented best by Martin Luther, John Calvin, John Wesley, and Jonathan Edwards, on what it meant for God to draw human beings as individuals to himself in the love of Jesus Christ and to inspire these individuals to godly service by a vision of the power and beauty of God's love in Jesus Christ. Today, the survival of evangelical Protestantism represents a continuing Christian tradition in which the life-transforming implications of what it meant for Christ to live, die, and reign *pro me* (for me) continue to supply great spiritual comfort to individuals and remarkable encouragement to Christian service.

Fourth, the emergence of Pentecostalism represents the successful planting, against all odds, of a life-transforming Christianity in the rootless (but also selectively empowering) globalization of the modern political and commercial economy. In turn, the character of Pentecostalism is being fixed by all-or-nothing efforts at experiencing the direct power of the Holy Spirit in response to the direst of human circumstances. These efforts are represented best by locally initiated Christian movements emerging from the social chaos of Africa's recent history of colonization and decolonization, the mayhem of the Chinese cultural revolution, and the vast sprawls of urban poverty in Latin America and elsewhere in the world. Today, the spread of Pentecostalism represents a new Christian tradition in which the living possibility of union and communion with God through the Holy Spirit is bringing light to many of the direst situations in the world.

Within each of these four main expressions of Christianity can be found what C. S. Lewis might have called "mere Christians" who believe substantially similar things about the inspiration and authority of Scripture, the Trinity, the centrality of the work of Christ for human salvation, and the power of the Holy Spirit as the motive force for holy living in the world.[13] Yet at the same time, each tradition expresses these realities with a characteristic accent:

- The Orthodox emphasize the mystical mysteries of God.
- Catholics stress the power of God to build his city.
- Evangelicals stress the transformation of individuals and through individuals the shaping of civil society.
- Pentecostals stress direct empowerment from the Holy Spirit.

Christian Traditions as Languages

The closest analogy to a Christian world divided into these instantiations of Christian faith might be the general condition of humanity divided into the world's various languages. In such terms, these major expressions of Christian faith may be likened to language families.

- Each stands closest to the "language" from which it emerged: Catholicism emerged from Orthodoxy, Protestantism emerged from Catholicism, Pentecostalism emerged from Protestantism.
- Each represents a family of languages rather than a single tongue: Thus, Russian Orthodoxy in Moscow is quite different in many ways from Syrian Orthodoxy in South India or Antiochean Orthodoxy in Chicago, yet these different Orthodox churches share much more

13. For an assessment of what has become a much-cited phrase, see Mark A. Noll, "C. S. Lewis's 'Mere Christianity' (The Book and the Ideal) at the Start of the Twenty-First Century," *Seven* 19 (2002): 31–44.

in common with one another than with Catholic, evangelical, or Pentecostal churches in their own regions.

- Each language family, however distinct, has also enjoyed at least some contact with representatives of other language families. The result can be much borrowing of vocabulary, some crossover of syntax, and a great deal of awareness of how the other languages work.

- In some cases, individuals become multilingual and can function in more than one language family (usually evangelical-Pentecostal). For most people, however, the first language truly learned and appropriated remains the mother tongue. While it is possible to pick up different degrees of reading, understanding, and even speaking ability in other tongues, that is more easily done with languages closer to one's own than with those farther away.

- Most people can never learn another language as well as they know their mother tongue, and even those who shift entirely to speaking a new language (i.e., who convert) usually retain inflections, vocabulary, and accents of the mother tongue.

But, of course, it is also necessary to qualify this analogy. The varieties of Christian tradition have undergone change over time. They are porous in receiving influences from other religious and cultural factors. They do not remain fixed in their conditions of origin. And they adjust to new locations where they come to exist. Each tradition also borrows from its current surrounding culture and era. For example, today's permutations of these four Christian traditions are influenced (depending on location) by postmodernism, affluence, poverty, power, or oppression. In addition, there are genuine hybrids—for example, some Anglicans have functioned as both Protestants and Catholics; Uniate churches are made up of Orthodox and Catholic elements; charismatic movements can comprehend Catholics, Protestants, and Pentecostals. Yet the major Christian traditions do clearly bear the stamp of their originating circumstances, and once established, major Christian traditions do replicate themselves even as they pass through new circumstances. Like languages, the Christian traditions are handed down unselfconsciously from generation to generation as complete systems of belief and practice.

If reasoning about the major Christian traditions as languages does reflect reality, it explains a good deal about Catholic-evangelical relations. Recent breakthroughs, especially since the Second Vatican Council, represent the migration of languages moving closer to each other but by no means an end to systematic linguistic difference. It is obvious that Roman Catholics and evangelical Protestants still represent differ-ent ways of approaching, internalizing, articulating, and expressing the Christian faith. The overlap is much more obvious than it ever was, but there are still two systems at work.

Viewed in this light, much else becomes clear about Catholic-evan-gelical exchange. For example, it is only marginally useful for evangeli-cals to quote Bible verses at Roman Catholics, for whom authoritative interpretations of Scripture are deeply ingrained that deny the force of the texts as used by evangelicals. Or again, it is only marginally useful for Catholics to describe the ineluctable bonds between Scripture and tradition to evangelicals, who value Scripture for its ability to challenge tradition. When Catholics practice devotion to Mary as an avenue to worshiping God, they will remain confused by evangelical concerns about idolatry. Meanwhile, Catholics will find evangelical churches stark and devoid of visual aids to worship and wonder at the void. Likewise, an evangelical's urgent request inviting a Catholic to pray the sinner's prayer and "invite Jesus into your heart so that you can be saved" will startle a Catholic who was baptized into salvation, confirmed by per-sonal testimony of faith, and regularly receives the body and blood of Christ in the Eucharist.

What can we make of a world of multiple tongues? Continuing differ-ences between Catholics and evangelicals should be regarded as both a problem and a gift. They constitute a problem because serious Christ-fol-lowers of one sort simply cannot understand why serious Christ-followers of another sort believe and act as they do. They represent a gift because, by the mercies of God, more and more Christ-followers of one sort are coming to recognize the sanctity, holiness, and telltale manifestations of the Holy Spirit among serious Christ-followers of other sorts. The gift in this realization is to see that God has always been bigger than our own group's grasp of God, that he has been manifesting himself at times, in places, and through venues where others have not expected him to be present at all.

Terms used by missiologists to describe the ability of Christianity to be planted and replanted in new cultures grasp the reality of partly compat-ible and partly incompatible Christian systems. Continuing differences among different families, or languages, of serious Christ-followers testify to the capacity of the once-incarnate Son of God to come alive repeat-edly and continuously in human cultures differentiated greatly from one another. What we see today may be described as an incarnation of Christ in Catholic form and an incarnation of Christ in evangelical form. Since there is only one Christ, these incarnations are pulled toward each other. Since they constitute different cultures, different traditions, and different languages, the incarnations retain the differences characteristic of cultures, traditions, and languages.

From many parts of Scripture, it is clear that differences in language will continue in heaven, though (presumably) with mutual comprehension. Perhaps a variety of emphases on how much Scripture, tradition, and the church prepared the way for uninterrupted fellowship with God will also continue through eternity.

Where Are We Now?

Christian believers must take seriously the prayer of Jesus in John 17: "My prayer is not for them alone. I pray also for those who will believe in me through their message, that all of them may be one, Father, just as you are in me and I am in you. May they also be in us so that the world may believe that you have sent me" (vv. 20–21). Because of this prayer and the many other scriptural injunctions to Christian unity, believers must never rest with a relativistic acceptance of Christian fragmentation. While the goodness of God has enabled different forms of Christianity to emerge and flourish in adaptation to different times and cultures, this is the same God who revealed himself once for all humanity in Jesus Christ and who calls all believers to fellowship in this one Redeemer, Lord, light, and master of all. In the current reality of a fragmented body of Christ, believers should thank God for openings leading to engagement, dialogue, and cooperation.

But to make such openings substantial instead of superficial, Catholics and evangelicals need to go deeper into the trusted resources of their own traditions—self-critically but also confidently and persuasively—in order to internalize the ideals that constitute the traditions. At the same time, however, they must listen to critiques from fellow believers, especially since critiques now often come with appreciation for what is being critiqued. Critics from within one's own tradition and critics from the other tradition will be most effective when they focus on the overall shape and structure of the tradition as a whole. The best sort of criticism is the kind sampled in chapter 7, especially where critics treat the other tradition with love or converts remember the good they have left behind.

The current situation in the United States poses unusual opportunities as well as unusual perils for evangelical-Catholic engagement. From the evangelical angle, a realistic assessment of engagement with Roman Catholics must begin with a realistic assessment of evangelicalism. That assessment leads to some curious conclusions. The formalism, the anthropocentric worship, the power mongering, and the egotism—which Protestants saw so clearly in Roman Catholicism for many centuries—now flourish on every hand within Protestant evangelicalism.[14] Although evangelicals sometimes live up to their own highest standards for living out the gospel, much in evangelicalism is in need of reformation. From the other angle, evangelicals examining Roman Catholics will find surprises. An exaltation of divine grace, a concern for disciplined holiness, an expression of service to the poor in the name of Jesus, and an ability to apply the depths of Scripture to the complicated ethical questions of modern existence—which Protestantism came into existence to recover—now exist in one form or another throughout Roman Catholicism.

Evangelicals who cherish the Reformation heritage face especially poignant issues in the modern climate. We are the ones who think we hold most tenaciously to the Reformers' teachings about the radical sinfulness and irremediable finitude of human existence. But with fresh eyes to see, we can now observe these human failings as readily in the churches descended from the Reformation as in Catholicism. We are also able to see traits approved by historic Protestantism in the most luminous expressions of modern Catholicism: the ethical *gravitas* of Pope Leo XIII and Pope John Paul II; the moving depictions of grace in the writings of G. K. Chesterton, J. R. R. Tolkien, Evelyn Waugh, and Malcolm Muggeridge; or the "good works" of a different kind from Mother Teresa, Henri Nouwen, and the L'Arche community founded by Jean Vanier.[15] However much such observations might disconcert evangelical descendants of the Reformation, we can take heart from the Reformers' teachings about the incredible fecundity of divine grace and so perhaps turn toward Roman Catholics with as much charitable expectancy as fearful dread.

Contemporary pluralism may also enhance the ability to make discriminations. If relatively important theological differences still divide Catholics and evangelicals, nonetheless, the contemporary world needs to hear more about what Catholics and evangelicals share in common than about their legitimate disagreements. J. I. Packer has spotlighted this issue well by pointing to "the currently urgent task of upholding

14. For example, see David F. Wells, *No Place for Truth: Or Whatever Happened to Evangelical Theology* (Grand Rapids: Eerdmans, 1993); idem, *Losing Our Virtue: Why the Church Must Recover Its Moral Visions* (Grand Rapids: Eerdmans, 1998); and Michael Scott Horton, *Made in America: The Shaping of Modern American Evangelicalism* (Grand Rapids: Baker, 1991).

15. L'Arche communities exist for the support of people with intellectual handicaps; the last years of Henri Nouwen's life were spent as a member of a L'Arche community. See Jean Vanier, *Becoming Human* (Toronto: Anansi Press and the Canadian Broadcasting Corp., 1998).

faith in the Trinity, the Incarnation, the inerrancy of Scripture, and the primacy of the evangelistic and pastoral imperative according to Scripture, against the secularist, relativist, and antinomian onslaught to which these things are being subjected in our time both without and within the churches." As Packer concludes, with many others who have also striven for perspective on the modern condition,

> the cobelligerence of Catholics and Protestants fighting together for the basics of the creed is nowadays more important [than discussion of individual doctrines], if only because until the cancerous spread of theological pluralism on both sides of the Reformation divide is stopped, any talk of our having achieved unity of faith will be so irrelevant to the real situation as to be both comic and pathetic.[16]

Theologically considered, the recent engagement of evangelicals and Catholics testifies to a significant confluence of opposites. Catholics, whose ecclesiology is so high that the church as an institution is integral to its understanding of the gospel, and evangelicals, whose ecclesiology is so low that the church is often forgotten in their proclamation of the gospel, have been backing toward each other in a world where the gospel itself has become a costly commodity. In this awkward dance, many Catholics and evangelicals have bumped into each other, back to back. What should they do when they turn and try to ponder what to make of these others who seem so obviously to be honoring the gospel but in such strange terms, with such strange practices, and in such strange conjunction with other Christian realities?

As these explorations proceed, Catholics find among evangelicals, besides a lot of dross, the joyful personal experience of justification by God's free grace and the beauties of activistic personal piety. Evangelicals find among Catholics, besides a lot of dross, a functioning concept of church, a powerful Christian sense of the material world, and a long tradition of balanced political theology.

These explorations do not result in what Samuel Johnson once declaimed with characteristic finality, "For my part, Sir, I think all Christians, whether Papists or Protestants, agree in the essential articles, and that their differences are trivial, and rather political than religious."[17] The differences, of course, are not trivial; they are deeply rooted in history, culture, and habits. Yet the actual situation that currently exists is

16. J. I. Packer, foreword to George Carey, *A Tale of Two Churches: Can Protestants and Catholics Get Together?* (Downers Grove, IL: InterVarsity, 1985), ii.

17. James Boswell, *Life of Johnson*, ed. John Wilson Croker (London: John Murray, 1866), 138 (June 23, 1763).

closer to what Johnson described than to the extreme antagonism that prevailed almost everywhere less than four decades ago.

In a situation where it is all too easy to lapse into romanticized, partial, excitable, irresponsible, or self-serving evaluations, summary judgments must be properly qualified. It is important to assert, for instance, that the Roman Catholic Church continues to tolerate a great quantity of syncretism, lifeless formalism, hegemonic Constantinianism, and dangerous capitulation to sub-Christian varieties of both modernism (power) and postmodernism. But it is also important to note that the world of evangelical Christianity is beset with great quantities of practical Pelagianism, lifeless informality, narrowly sectarian Gnosticism, and dangerous capitulation to sub-Christian varieties of both modernism (epistemology and apologetics) and postmodernism.

Within the Catholic Church, furious internal battles are now taking place that engage a range of theological opinions and religious practices that are nearly as incompatible as those found among the various strands of Protestantism as a whole. At least to non-Catholics looking on from the outside, it is not certain that forces clearly aligned with classical "mere Christianity" will win all of those battles. Moreover, despite the great changes within the Catholic Church over the last forty years that have allowed for a much clearer enunciation of historic trinitarian orthodoxy, the Roman Catholic Church is not moving toward a full embrace of classically evangelical doctrine and practice.

But a similar situation also exists among evangelicals. Evangelicalism is torn by debates over how much contemporary cultures can be accommodated in authentic gospel witness. It is riven by old theological controversies and new battles as well, such as how much cooperation is possible with Roman Catholics. It is threatened with therapy substituting for the gospel and entertainment posing as worship. It is divided into multitudes of individual empires, some communicating Christ with estimable creativity, others the mere projection of ego, and many mixed in origin and character. Nonevangelicals looking in from the outside would be justified in worrying about the fate of evangelical Christianity. Moreover, despite many genuine signs of gospel life, evangelicals as a whole are not returning to embrace the forms of classical Reformation faith and practice.

The political functions of religion must also be considered in any general assessment. In some areas of the world where Catholics have historically exercised civil as well as religious hegemony, *aggiornamento* has been realized only partially, if at all. The peaceful cooperation that Pope John XXIII foresaw with Protestants and other "men of good will" is still sadly absent in some parts of Latin America and other regions as well. Although the church's focus on spiritual matters has sharpened over the last century, the Catholic weakness for letting power politics rule at the expense of reliance on the Holy Spirit seems all too obvious to observers inside and outside the church.

Critics of evangelical political mobilization can probably find just as many things to criticize. In the great rush by American evangelicals to right-wing Republican Party partisanship, it is obvious that evangelicals have at least sometimes acted with the innocence of serpents and the wisdom of doves.

What, in these circumstances, can be concluded? With all proper qualifications having been made, it is important for evangelicals who desire a realistic assessment of the Roman Catholic Church to imitate Nathanael in the first chapter of John's Gospel. Nathanael, when he was told by a faithful disciple to "come and see" who Jesus was and what he was doing, went and saw. When, therefore, we evangelicals look at the situation as it has actually come to exist in the Roman Catholic Church—when, that is, we study the papal encyclicals of the last quarter century, read the ecumenical dialogues on justification by faith and on many other historically contentious topics, ponder the new Catholic *Catechism,* reflect on the use made by Catholics of Alpha and the *Jesus* film, and consider the openness at many levels of the Catholic Church to a Bible-centered and Christ-focused religion that looks strangely like evangelical Christianity—then we are in a position to consider whether the Reformation is over.

Unfortunately, historians can only look backward, and therefore it falls to practitioners by their actions to show if the Reformation is really over. Yet asking whether the Reformation is over may not even be the most pertinent question. It may be more to the point to ask other questions: Is God truly going to draw people from every tribe and tongue and people and nation—and major Christian tradition—to worship together the Lamb who was slain? Can he really make of them—all these tongues and peoples and traditions—a single kingdom united in the body of his Son Jesus Christ? Should believers in an all-powerful, all-merciful God doubt that such signs and wonders might still take place?

Not so very long ago Catholics and evangelicals looked upon each other as orcs and elfs and were as repelled by orc-speech and elf-speech as it was possible to be. Today, it is more like ents and hobbits, not yet speaking the same language and certainly misunderstanding much that the other says but nonetheless communicating quite well and actually learning from the apparent idiosyncrasies of the other tongue. Might God do even more? Look around. Listen. It is happening right before our eyes and ears. *Soli Deo gloria.*

FURTHER READING

C hristian believers, whether Catholic or evangelical, have every
 good reason to write with faith, hope, and charity about their
own understanding of Christianity and the understanding of Christianity maintained by others. The injunctions of the apostle Paul in 1 Corinthians 13 deserve to be taken seriously for bibliographical purposes
as well as for every other purpose. In the oceans of published material
available on the subjects treated in this book, readers should seek out
solid, thoughtful theological expositions (faith), realistic assessments
of the past and future (hope), and, above all, books that put gospel
standards to work in self-criticism as well as in criticizing the views of
others (love). We have tried to write this book under this mandate and
are pleased to say that many of the most helpful works on Catholic-
evangelical concerns now do so as well.

This note on further reading is divided thematically. We draw attention
to works that we found especially helpful for our purposes, but readers must remember that the number of publications on the pertinent
subjects is vast beyond measure.

Catholicism: Official Documents

It is always desirable, when trying to grasp the character of a different
branch of the Christian faith, to study officially approved literature. Life
on the ground may look different from life explained from the top, but
without that view from on high, it is impossible to sort out what is found
on the ground. For understanding contemporary Roman Catholicism,
there is no substitute for beginning with official Catholic documents. To

that end, the *Catechism of the Catholic Church* (New York: Doubleday, 1994) is probably the best place to begin for the reasons spelled out in chapter 5. Behind the *Catechism*, however, lies the momentous work of the Second Vatican Council, whose official records are available in Austin P. Flannery, ed., *Documents of Vatican II* (Grand Rapids: Eerdmans, 1975). Also critical for documentary solid grounding are Claudia Carlen, IHM, ed., *The Papal Encyclicals, 1740–1981*, 5 vols. (New York: McGrath/Consortium, 1981); and the encyclicals of Pope John Paul II. A selection of the latter has been made available in *John Paul II: The Encyclicals in Everyday Language* (Maryknoll, NY: Orbis, 1996); almost all of the pope's encyclicals, along with other official documents, have been published in English translation as individual pamphlets by Pauline Books and Media (www.pauline.org). The pope's *Crossing the Threshold of Hope* (New York: Knopf, 1995) is an outstanding introduction to his thought. Although it is not an "official" biography, the study of John Paul II's life by George Weigel was undertaken with access to Vatican sources and represents a solid introduction. See George Weigel, *Witness to Hope: The Biography of Pope John Paul II* (New York: HarperCollins, 1999).

Especially important for points of Catholic-Protestant comparison are the official dialogues that have been taking place since the 1960s and that are the subject of chapter 4. They are available, along with much helpful editorial material and records of Catholic dialogues with non-Protestants, in Harding Meyer and Lucas Vischer, eds., *Growth in Agreement: Reports and Agreed Statements of Ecumenical Conversation on a World Level* (New York: Paulist Press, 1984; Geneva: World Council of Churches, 1984); and Jeffrey Gros, Harding Meyer, and William G. Rusch, eds., *Growth in Agreement II: Reports and Agreed Statements of Ecumenical Conversations on a World Level, 1982–1998* (Grand Rapids: Eerdmans, 2000; Geneva: World Council of Churches, 2000).

Catholicism: Documents and Reference

For the study of Catholicism in America, there are a number of outstanding histories, some of which are mentioned below. Outstanding collections of documents include private writings but also statements from episcopal synods and other official bodies. See, as among the best, John Tracy Ellis, ed., *Documents of American Catholic History*, 2nd ed. (Milwaukee: Bruce, 1962); Patrick W. Carey, ed., *American Catholic Religious Thought* (New York: Paulist Press, 1987); and a nine-volume series from Orbis edited by Christopher J. Kauffman that includes R. Scott Appleby, Patricia Byrne, and William L. Portier, eds., *Creative Fidelity:*

American Catholic Intellectual Traditions (2004); and Timothy Matovina and Gerald E. Poyo, eds., *Presente! U.S. Latino Catholics from Colonial Origins to the Present* (2000). For documents covering all of Catholic history, consult Colman J. Barry, O.S.B., ed., *Readings in Church History*, 3 vols. (Westminster, MD: Newman, 1965).

For help with the Catholic big picture, two reference works are essential: *The Catholic Encyclopedia*, 15 vols. (New York: Robert Appleton, 1907–12), with later supplements; and *New Catholic Encyclopedia*, 15 vols. (New York: McGraw-Hill, 1967), also with later supplements. Both of these encyclopedias are filled with authoritative articles. They are also of great help in tracking changes occasioned by the Second Vatican Council, especially when comparing the tone and content of articles on the same topics. The *New Catholic Encyclopedia* has recently appeared in a completely new second edition (Detroit: Thomson/Gale, 2003), where shifts of emphasis again make for fascinating reading. Orientation to the statistical picture for Catholics in the United States and elsewhere is provided in Bryan T. Froehle and Mary L. Gautier, *Catholicism USA: A Portrait of the Catholic Church in the United States* (Maryknoll, NY: Orbis, 2000); and idem, *Global Catholicism: Portrait of a World Church* (Maryknoll, NY: Orbis, 2003).

Evangelicals and Catholics Together

The initiative titled Evangelicals and Catholics Together (ECT), the most serious public effort in recent American history aimed at strengthening engagement between Catholics and evangelicals, has been widely noticed. Again, as with the official teaching of the Catholic Church, the place to begin wrestling with this unofficial effort is the public documentary record:

- ECT I: "The Christian Mission in the Third Millennium," *First Things* (May 1994): 15–21 (also published with commentary in Charles Colson and Richard John Neuhaus, eds., *Evangelicals and Catholics Together: Toward a Common Mission* [Dallas: Word, 1995]).
- ECT II: "The Gift of Salvation," *Christianity Today,* December 8, 1997, 35–37.
- ECT III: "Your Word Is Truth," in *Your Word Is Truth*, ed. Charles Colson and Richard John Neuhaus, 1–8 (Grand Rapids: Eerdmans, 2002).
- ECT IV: "The Communion of Saints," *First Things* (March 2003): 26–33.

Broad, objective commentary on the ECT process is found in Jennifer V. Suvada, "A Study of the Evangelical Protestant Reception of the Document *Evangelicals and Catholics Together*, from Its Release in March 1994 through December 1996, Including a Case Study of the Southern Baptist Convention" (M.A. thesis, Trinity Evangelical Divinity School, 1997); and Nathan Andrew Baxter, "Toward a Decorous Rhetoric of Public Theology: Evangelicals and Catholics Together—Betrayal, Alliance, or Good Beginning" (Ph.D. diss., Indiana University, 1999).

Commentary that is generally negative on the initiative appears in John Armstrong, ed., *Roman Catholicism: Evangelical Protestants Analyze What Divides and Unites Us* (Chicago: Moody, 1994); John Ankerberg and John Weldon, eds., *Protestants and Catholics: Do They Now Agree?* (Eugene, OR: Harvest House, 1995); R. C. Sproul, *Faith Alone: The Evangelical Doctrine of Justification* (Grand Rapids: Baker, 1995); and Michael S. Horton, "What's All the Fuss About? The State of the Justification Debate," *Modern Reformation*, March/April 2002, 17–21.

Opinions of evangelicals who support the initiative can be sampled in J. I. Packer, "Why I Signed It," *Christianity Today*, December 12, 1994, 34–37; Timothy George, "Catholics and Evangelicals in the Trenches," *Christianity Today*, May 16, 1994, 16; Timothy George, "Evangelicals and Catholics Together: A New Initiative. 'The Gift of Salvation': An Evangelical Assessment," *Christianity Today*, December 8, 1997, 34–35; and in the books issued with ECT I and ECT III noted above.

Evangelical Assessments of Catholicism

An especially solid and fair reading of modern Catholic theology, which takes into account developments since the Second Vatican Council, is Norman L. Geisler and Ralph E. MacKenzie, *Roman Catholics and Evangelicals: Agreements and Differences* (Grand Rapids: Baker, 1995). Probably the most extensive general effort at a balanced historical report on the developments of recent decades is Donald W. Sweeting, "From Conflict to Cooperation? Changing American Evangelical Attitudes towards Roman Catholics: 1960–1998" (Ph.D. diss., Trinity Evangelical Divinity School, 1998). Among the best pre-Vatican II Protestant efforts to assess Catholicism with charity and yet with doctrinal integrity is Jaroslav Pelikan, *The Riddle of Roman Catholicism* (New York: Abingdon, 1959). A book that took the measure of Catholicism at about the same time and with careful attention to official Catholic statements, though with less charity, is Loraine Boettner, *Roman Catholicism* (Philadelphia: Presbyterian & Reformed, 1962).

Works that document an earlier Protestant willingness to make posi-tive use of some aspects of Catholicism include John Barker, *Strange Contrarieties: Pascal in England during the Age of Reason* (Montreal: McGill-Queen's University Press, 1975); and Patricia A. Ward, "Madame Guyon and Experiential Theology in America," *Church History* 67 (Sep-tember 1998): 484–98. A particularly interesting instance of Protestant charity to Catholicism is John Wesley, *A Letter to a Roman Catholic* (1749), in *The Works of John Wesley,* 14 vols., ed. Thomas Jackson (London: Wesleyan Conference Office, 1872), 10:80–86. This document has been published separately—with interesting commentary reflecting Catholic changes since Vatican II and the modern ecumenical situation—by Odd Hagen (president of the World Methodist Council), Augustin Cardinal Bea (president of the Vatican Secretariat for Christian Unity), and Mi-chael Hurley, S.J., as *John Wesley's Letter to a Roman Catholic* (Nashville: Abingdon, 1968).

It was rare for evangelicals to pay serious attention to the Second Vatican Council, but a welcome exception to that rule was provided by David F. Wells, *Revolution in Rome* (Downers Grove, IL: InterVarsity, 1972).

What might be called phase 1 of more open relations between Prot-estants (including evangelicals) and Catholics after the Second Vatican Council can be usefully sampled in a number of books: T. F. Torrance, *Theology in Reconciliation: Essays toward Evangelical-Catholic Unity in East and West* (Grand Rapids: Eerdmans, 1976); James Atkinson, *Mar-tin Luther: Prophet to the Catholic Church* (Grand Rapids: Eerdmans, 1983); Mark Edwards and George H. Tavard, *Luther: A Reformer for the Churches* (New York: Paulist Press, 1983); and George Carey, *A Tale of Two Churches: Can Protestants and Catholics Get Together?* (Downers Grove, IL: InterVarsity, 1985).

Phase 2, dating from the mid-1990s, has seen a growing number of works that bring Catholics and evangelicals into face-to-face dialogue. Such timely and often important works include Keith A. Fournier with William D. Watkins, *A House United? Evangelicals and Catholics Together* (Colorado Springs: NavPress, 1994); Felipe Fernández-Armesto and Derek Wilson, *Reformations: A Radical Interpretation of Christianity and the World, 1500–2000* (New York: Scribner, 1996); Thomas P. Rausch, ed., *Catholics and Evangelicals: Do They Share a Common Future?* (Downers Grove, IL: InterVarsity, 2000); Elizabeth and Karl Wirth, "Two Churches, One Family," *Re:Generation Quarterly* (August 1, 2002): 9–12; and Dwight Longenecker and David Gustafson, *Mary: A Catholic-Evangelical Dialogue* (Grand Rapids: Brazos, 2003).

This second phase has also been well served by serious theological analyses that sometimes include consideration of ECT but often go much farther afield as well. Such works include Alister A. McGrath, "The New Catholic Catechism," *Christianity Today,* December 12, 1994, 28–33; J. Daryl Charles, "Evangelicals and Catholics Together: One Year Later," *Pro Ecclesia* 5 (Winter 1996): 73–90; J. Daryl Charles, "Assessing Recent Pronouncements on Justification: Evidence from 'The Gift of Salvation' and the Catholic *Catechism,*" *Pro Ecclesia* 8 (Fall 1999): 459–74; Douglas A. Sweeney, "Taming the Reformation: What the Lutheran-Catholic Justification Declaration Really Accomplished—And What It Did Not," *Christianity Today,* January 10, 2000, 63–65; Stephen J. Duffy, "Southern Baptist and Roman Catholic Soteriologies," *Pro Ecclesia* 9 (Fall 2000): 434–59; A. N. S. Lane, *Justification by Faith in Catholic and Protestant Dialogue: An Evangelical Assessment* (London: T & T Clark, 2002); and Mark Husbands and Daniel J. Treier, eds., *Justification: What's at Stake in the Current Debates* (Downers Grove: InterVarsity, 2004).

A special subgenre of evangelical writing on Catholicism comes from evangelicals who have converted to Rome and from commentary by others on those conversions. Examples, many of them poignant about both what is gained and what is left behind, include Thomas Howard, *Evangelical Is Not Enough: Worship of God in Liturgy and Sacrament* (San Francisco: Ignatius, 1984); John Woodbridge et al., "Why Did Thomas Howard Become a Roman Catholic?" *Christianity Today,* May 17, 1985, 46–62; Scott and Kimberly Hahn, *Rome Sweet Home: Our Journey to Catholicism* (San Francisco: Ignatius Press, 1993); Scot McKnight, "From Wheaton to Rome: Why Evangelicals Become Roman Catholic," *Journal of the Evangelical Theological Society* 45 (September 2002): 451–72; Dennis Martin, "Retrospect and Apologia," *Mennonite Quarterly Review* 77 (April 2003): 167–96; Ivan Kauffman, "On Being Mennonite Catholic," *Mennonite Quarterly Review* 77 (April 2003): 235–56; and Peter Kreeft, "Hauled Aboard the Ark," www.peterkreeft.com/topics/hauled-aboard.htm (accessed February 27, 2004).

Another special category featuring incisive Protestant assessment of Catholicism that should be of special interest to many evangelicals is the set of Catholic-Lutheran dialogues that led in 1999 to "The Joint Declaration on the Doctrine of Justification." The results of those dialogues can be pursued in several reports found in the two volumes titled *Growth in Agreement* mentioned above: "The Gospel and the Church" (1972), "The Eucharist" (1978), "The Ministry in the Church" (1981), *Confessio Augustana* (1980), "Ways to Community" (1980), "Martin Luther—Witness to Jesus Christ" (1983), and "Facing Unity: Models, Forms, and Phrases of Catholic-Lutheran Fellowship" (1984). The Lutheran-Catholic dialogues in the United States were published by Augsburg Press as *The Status of the Nicene Creed as Dogma of the Church* (1965), *One Baptism for the Remission of Sins* (1965), *The Eucharist as Sacrifice* (1967), *Eucharist and Ministry* (1970), *Papal Primacy and the Universal Church* (1974), *Teaching Authority and Infallibility in the Church* (1980), *Justification by Faith* (1985), and *The One Mediator, the Saints, and Mary* (1992).

Catholic Assessments of Evangelicalism

Serious Catholic assessments of evangelicalism were a long time in coming, but both quality and quantity have been increasing rapidly. An early attempt, remarkably charitable for its era, was Louis Bouyer, *The Spirit and Forms of Protestantism*, trans. A. V. Littledale (Westminster, MD: Newman, 1956). Useful history is found in Jay P. Dolan, "Catholic Attitudes toward Protestants," in *Uncivil Religion: Interreligious Hostility in America*, ed. Robert N. Bellah and Frederick E. Greenspahn, 72–85 (New York: Crossroad, 1987); while a sign of things to come could be seen in Albert Boudreau, *The Born-Again Catholic* (Locust Valley, NY: Living Flame Press, 1980). But now the most comprehensive study is William M. Shea, *The Lion and the Lamb: Evangelicals and Catholics in America* (New York: Oxford University Press, 2004), which combines rare historical insight and provocative theological wisdom in equal measure. A longtime promoter of Catholic-evangelical engagement is Brother Jeffrey Gros, F.S.C., whose book reviews and articles have helpfully treated many special aspects of the subject. His opinions can be sampled in "Evangelical Relations: A Differentiated Catholic Perspective, *Ecumenical Trends* 29 (January, 2000): 1–9; "A Journey of Faith: Reformed and Catholic," *Reformed Review* 52 (Spring 1999): 235–53; and "Toward a Dialogue of Conversion: The Pentecostal, Evangelical, and Conciliar Movements," *Pneuma* 17 (Fall 1995): 189–201.

Evidence of more vigorous, perceptive, and sometimes painfully accurate assessments of evangelicals by Catholics has recently been multiplying. Examples include Thomas Rausch, "The Los Angeles Catholic/Evangelical Dialogue," *Ecumenical Trends* 26 (1997): 93–95; Carl E. Olson, *Will Catholics Be "Left Behind"? A Catholic Critique of the Rapture and Today's Prophecy Preachers* (San Francisco: Ignatius, 2003); and James Turner, "The Evangelical Intellectual Revival," in *Language, Religion, Knowledge: Past and Present* (Notre Dame: University of Notre Dame Press, 2003).

An unusual (and remarkable) gauge of how much interchange has come to exist between Catholic and evangelical worship is documented in Felicia Piscitelli, "Protestant Hymnody in Contemporary Roman Catholic Worship" and "Appendix III: Hymns in Roman Catholic Hymnals," in *Wonderful Words of Life: Hymns in American Protestant History and Theology*, ed. Richard J. Mouw and Mark A. Noll, 150–63, 269–72 (Grand Rapids: Eerdmans, 2004).

Roman Catholics in America

The story of Catholicism in America has been receiving first-rate historical treatment from a number of scholars for more than a quarter century. Among the best of the books are Philip Gleason, *Keeping the Faith: American Catholicism Past and Present* (Notre Dame: University of Notre Dame Press, 1987); idem, *Contending with Modernity: Catholic Higher Education in the Twentieth Century* (New York: Oxford, 1995); idem, ed., *Contemporary Catholicism in the United States* (Notre Dame: University of Notre Dame Press, 1969); James Hennesey, S.J., *American Catholics: A History of the Roman Catholic Community in the United States* (New York: Oxford, 1981); Jay P. Dolan, *The American Catholic Experience* (Garden City, NY: Doubleday, 1985); idem, *In Search of an American Catholicism: A History of Religion and Culture in Tension* (New York: Oxford, 2002); John T. McGreevy, *Parish Boundaries: The Catholic Encounter with Race in the Twentieth Century* (Chicago: University of Chicago Press, 1996); and idem, *Catholicism and American Freedom: A History* (New York: Norton, 2003).

These notable works are joined by many others, often on more narrowly defined topics and often just as illuminating. They include Gerald P. Fogarty, S.J., "The Quest for a Catholic Vernacular Bible in America," in *The Bible in America*, ed. Nathan O. Hatch and Mark A. Noll, 163–80 (New York: Oxford, 1982); R. Scott Appleby, *"Church and Age Unite!" The Modernist Impulse in American Catholicism* (Notre Dame: University of Notre Dame Press, 1992); Jenny Franchot, *Roads to Rome: The Antebellum Protestant Encounter with Catholicism* (Berkeley: University of California Press, 1994); R. Scott Appleby and Mary Jo Weaver, eds., *Being Right: Conservative Catholics in America* (Bloomington: Indiana University Press, 1995); Patrick W. Carey, *The Roman Catholics in America* (Westport, CT: Praeger, 1996); David J. O'Brien, *Public Catholicism*, 2nd ed. (Maryknoll, NY: Orbis, 1996); Charles B. Hanson, *Necessary Virtue: The Pragmatic Origins of Religious Liberty in New England* (Charlottesville: University Press of Virginia, 1998); Richard Lougheed, *La Conversion Controversée de Charles Chiniquy: Prêtre Catholique devenu Protestant* (Quebec: La Clairière, 1999); and Michael Zöller, *Washington and Rome: Catholicism in American Culture* (Notre Dame: University of Notre Dame Press, 1999).

Perceptive commentary on Catholicism in the United States is hardly limited to historians. Sociologist and priest Andrew Greeley is a past master of such analysis. See, as examples, *The American Catholic: A Social Portrait* (New York: Basic Books, 1977); *The Catholic Imagination* (Berkeley: University of California Press, 2000); and *The Catholic Revolution: New Wine, Old Wineskins, and the Second Vatican Council* (Berkeley: University of California Press, 2004). As an indication of much other valuable literature by sociologists, see Dean R. Hoge et al., *Converts, Dropouts, and Returnees: A Study of Religious Change among Catholics* (Washington, D.C.: United States Catholic Conference, 1981); and Dean R. Hoge, *Young Adult Catholics: Religion in the Culture of Choice* (Notre Dame: University of Notre Dame Press, 2001).

Politics (construed broadly) is the subject of perceptive studies in a two-volume series edited by Margaret O'Brien Steinfels titled American Catholics in the Public Square: *American Catholics and Civic Engagement: A Distinctive Voice* (Lanham, MD: Sheed & Ward, 2004); and *American Catholics, American Culture: Tradition and Resistance* (Lanham, MD: Rowman & Littlefield, 2004).

Theological analysis of unusual insight was pioneered by the Jesuit scholar John Courtney Murray in *We Hold These Truths: Catholic Reflections on the American Proposition* (New York: Sheed & Ward, 1960). Murray's most important intellectual successor is Richard John Neuhaus, editor of *First Things,* where his opinions can be sampled monthly. A book written shortly before Neuhaus became a Roman Catholic provides one of the best accounts as to why evangelical Christians should take the potential contributions of Catholicism to American social health more seriously than we often have: *The Catholic Moment: The Paradox of the Church in the Post-Modern World* (San Francisco: Harper & Row, 1987).

Nearly the equal to Neuhaus in theological wisdom and more broadly attuned to the parish life of ordinary Catholics is the journalist Peter Steinfels, who in *A People Adrift: The Crisis of the Roman Catholic Church in America* (New York: Simon & Schuster, 2003), includes discussion of the recent sex scandals and much more besides. Those scandals have been documented extensively in the pages of the *Boston Globe,* whose reporters also published *Betrayal: The Crisis in the Catholic Church* (Boston: Little, Brown, 2003). Richard Neuhaus's compelling assessment of efforts to right the wrongs revealed by these scandals can be read in "The Catholic Reform," *First Things* (May 2004): 59–65; and (June/July 2004): 64–69.

American Anti-Catholicism

A special subcategory of works in American Catholic history explores the hostile treatment Catholics received for much of that history. Among such studies, two older ones are still the best: Sister Mary Augustina (Ray), B.V.M., *American Opinion of Roman Catholicism in the Eighteenth Century* (New York: Columbia University Press, 1936); and Ray Allen Billington, *The Protestant Crusade, 1800–1860* (New York: Macmillan, 1938). A full roster of other worthy examinations that have added depth to the picture include John J. Kane, *Catholic-Protestant Conflicts in America* (Chicago: Regnery, 1955); James H. Smylie, "Phases in Protestant Anti-Roman Catholic Relations in the United States: Monologue, Debate, and Dialogue," *Religion in Life* 34 (Spring 1965): 285–69; Barbara Welter, "From Maria Monk to Paul Blanshard: A Century of Protestant Anti-Catholicism," in *Uncivil Religion: Interreligious Hostility in America*, ed. Robert N. Bellah and Frederick E. Greenspahn, 43–71 (New York: Crossroad, 1987); Nancy L. Schultz, *Fire and Roses: The Burning of the Charlestown Convent, 1834* (New York: Free Press, 2000); and Thomas C. Berg, "Anti-Catholicism and Modern Church-State Relations," *Loyola University Chicago Law Journal* 33 (Fall 2001): 121–72. Two outstanding recent volumes appeared almost simultaneously with a nearly similar message that historic anti-Catholicism has the capacity to reinvent itself in the present: Philip Jenkins, *The New Anti-Catholicism: The Last Acceptable Prejudice* (New York: Oxford, 2003); and Mark S. Massa, S.J., *Anti-Catholicism in America: The Last Acceptable Prejudice* (New York: Crossroad, 2003). Helpful comparison with the story on the other side of the Atlantic is provided by John Wolffe, *The Protestant Crusade in Great Britain, 1829–1860* (Oxford: Clarendon, 1991).

The particularly large role that anti-Catholicism has played and continues to play in the history of American public education is the subject of a number of perceptive books, including Andrew M. Greeley, *An Ugly Little Secret: Anti-Catholicism in North America* (Kansas City: Sheed Andrews & McMeel, 1977); Rockne M. McCarthy, James W. Skillen, and William A. Harper, *Disestablishment a Second Time: Genuine Pluralism for American Schools* (Grand Rapids: Eerdmans, 1982); Philip Hamburger, *Separation of Church and State* (Cambridge: Harvard University Press, 2002); and many of the historical studies mentioned above.

Evangelicals in America

Literature on the synergy between Protestant and "American" values may rightly be considered a series of footnotes to Alexis de Tocqueville, *Democracy in America*, trans. Arthur Goldhammer (New York: Library of America, 2004). In the nineteenth century, an influential book that made some of Tocqueville's points for a slightly later era, but without Tocqueville's detached balance, was written by the strongly Protestant

Josiah Strong: *Our Country: Its Possible Future and Its Present Crisis* (New York: American Home Missionary Society, 1885). Among recent historical footnotes to Tocqueville that bear directly on how the arguments of this book were developed are Daniel Walker Howe, *The Political Culture of the American Whigs* (Chicago: University of Chicago Press, 1979); Harry S. Stout, *The New England Soul: Preaching and Religious Culture in Colonial New America* (New York: Oxford, 1986); Richard V. Pierard and Robert Dean Linder, *Civil Religion and the Presidency* (Grand Rapids: Academie, 1988); Nathan O. Hatch, *The Democratization of American Christianity* (New Haven: Yale University Press, 1989); Richard J. Carwardine, *Evangelicals and Politics in Antebellum America* (New Haven: Yale University Press, 1993); Allen C. Guelzo, *Abraham Lincoln: Redeemer President* (Grand Rapids: Eerdmans, 1999); George M. Marsden, *The Soul of the American University from Protestant Establishment to Established Nonbelief* (New York: Oxford, 1994); Mark A. Noll, *American Evangelical Christianity* (Oxford: Blackwell, 2001); and idem, *America's God, from Jonathan Edwards to Abraham Lincoln* (New York: Oxford, 2002).

Broader Landscapes

Coming to grips with Catholic-evangelical relationships in the United States can only benefit from broader awareness of what is happening overseas. For a general sense of developments pursued from one particular angle, see Peter Hocken, *The Spirit of Unity: How Renewal Is Breaking Down Barriers between Evangelicals and Roman Catholics* (Cambridge: Grove Books, 2001). The following is a sampling from other venues:

Southern Europe and Latin America: *A Contemporary Evangelical Perspective on Roman Catholicism* (Wheaton: World Evangelical Fellowship, 1986); and M. Daniel Carroll R., "The Evangelical-Roman Catholic Dialogue: Issues Revolving around Evangelization. An Evangelical View from Latin America," *Trinity Journal* 21 (2000): 189–207.

Poland: David Hill Scott, "Evangelicals and Catholics Really Together in Poland, 1975–1982," *Fides et Historia* 34 (Winter/Spring 2002): 89–109.

France: David E. Bjork, *Unfamiliar Paths* (Pasadena: William Carey, 1997).

Ireland: "What Is an Evangelical Catholic?" issued from Dublin in the Republic of Ireland and Rostrevor in Northern Ireland, June 1992; and "Evangelicals and Catholics in Ireland" (1998).

Nigeria: Chika-Odinaka, *Catholic and Born Again* (Lagos, Nigeria: Oracle Books, 1997).

Scotland: John Tallach, *A Plea against Extremism: The Views of Calvin, Hodge, and Others on Some Aspects of the Roman Catholic Church* (Tain, Ross-shire: Christian Focus, 1989).

The most important twentieth-century statement reflecting something close to a doctrinal consensus of world evangelicals and therefore a standard against which to measure official statements such as the Catholic *Catechism* is John Stott, ed., *The Lausanne Covenant* (Minneapolis: World Wide Publications, 1975).

The way in which the rapidly shifting character of world Christianity might affect Catholic-evangelical relations in the United States is a subtheme of important recent missiological work, much of which finds Catholic-evangelical differences less salient than issues of power, poverty, education, health care, and first-order evangelization. For some of the best of that literature, see Andrew F. Walls, *The Missionary Movement in Christian History* (Maryknoll, NY: Orbis, 1996); idem, *The Cross-Cultural Process in Christian History* (Maryknoll, NY: Orbis, 2002); Dana Robert, "Shifting Southward: Global Christianity since 1945," *International Bulletin of Missionary Research* (April 2000): 50–58; Philip Jenkins, *The Next Christendom: The Coming of Global Christianity* (New York: Oxford University Press, 2002); David Martin, *Pentecostalism: The World Their Parish* (Oxford: Blackwell, 2002); and Lamin Sanneh, *Whose Religion Is Christianity? The Gospel beyond the West* (Grand Rapids: Eerdmans, 2003).

For understanding basic tendencies deeply rooted in the historical consciousness of Catholics and evangelicals, the discussion of analogical (Catholic) and dialectical (Protestant) imaginations is provocative in David Tracy, *The Analogical Imagination: Christian Theology and the Culture of Pluralism* (New York: Crossroad, 1981). Equally helpful as a reminder about how being situated in a particular place affects how the world appears is David N. Livingstone, *Putting Science in Its Place: Geographics of Scientific Knowledge* (Chicago: University of Chicago Press, 2003); and David Martin, *A General Theory of Secularization* (New York: Harper & Row, 1978). Finally, for one effort at describing the general history of Christianity as a story in which both Catholics and evangelicals are necessary but not monopolistic, see Mark A. Noll, *Turning Points: Decisive Moments in the History of Christianity,* 2nd ed. (Grand Rapids: Baker, 2000).

After this book was completely prepared for the press, we discovered a substantial booklet by Geoffrey Wainwright that represented the published version of the 2000 Père Marquette Lecture in Theology from Marquette University. Its title is remarkably similar to our own: *Is the Reformation Over? Catholics and Protestants at the Turn of the Millennia* (Milwaukee: Marquette University Press, 2000). Reading this work so very late perhaps excuses us from the charge of simply appropriating a good title, but it also means that we were not able to make use of Wainwright's substantial insights, which have been hard-won through his longtime leadership in some of the ecumenical dialogues that, as it happens, we do discuss in our book. Especially his treatments of Scripture and tradition, Mary, the papacy, and the church would have enriched what we had to say. Yet since Wainwright's well-argued theological conclusions come close to our own in answering the question posed by our shared title, it is a pleasure to recommend his work to those who want to go deeper in exploring this important subject.

INDEX